A FEEI
AND A

Dane R. Gordon

University Press of America,® Inc.
Lanham · New York · Oxford

Copyright © 2002 by
University Press of America,® Inc.
4720 Boston Way
Lanham, Maryland 20706
UPA Acquisitions Department (301) 459-3366

12 Hid's Copse Rd.
Cumnor Hill, Oxford OX2 9JJ

Library of Congress Cataloging-in-Publication Data

Gordon, Dane R.
A feeling intellect and a thinking heart / Dane R. Gordon.
p.   cm
Includes bibliographical references and index.
1. Religion—Philosophy. I. Title.
BL51 .G686 2002
210—dc21   2002026716 CIP

ISBN 0-7618-2372-7 (paperback : alk. ppr.)

To my wife
Judith Edwards Gordon

Contents

Preface

Two Remarkable Things:

Philosophy of religion is theoretical, yet it is practical. It is objective, yet it is personal. It may threaten belief, yet philosophy is necessary at times to save it. People are attracted to philosophy, yet they are puzzled by it.

Philosophy is attractive because it deals with issues of great importance: the meaning of existence (if there is a meaning), the nature of human identity, whether or not we are free to choose what we want to do, or whether what we want to do is determined by what we have done. Philosophy is concerned with ethical norms and long-term goals. It asks questions about them. One writer defined philosophy as a persistent attempt to think things through. It is reflective but it is critical. It wants to know what reasons there are for a belief and how those reasons can be justified.

But philosophy would seem to be contrary to the nature of religion; in particular because of the importance it gives to critical thinking. Religious teaching (allegedly) comes from a divine source, so we do not have to question it as much as learn from it. We learn what is the meaning of our existence, the nature of human identity, and how we should behave. We don't have to ask critical questions because religious teaching is (allegedly) self-validating, conveyed generally through holy books, or revelation, or by the deliberations of men and women guided by God. But philosophy challenges that. Philosophy of religion, although attractive, is therefore puzzling. Its two terms appear to conflict.

The puzzlement is often tinged with apprehension. "If I study philosophy of religion won't I lose my faith?" Possibly. But faith can also be lost by neglect and by misunderstanding, by lazy thought and misinformation. At a minimum, philosophy of religion enables a person to do what is surprisingly difficult to do: think clearly about religious matters. To encourage that is the purpose of this book.

Human beings are remarkable in at least two ways. Of course they use language, they talk, write, stand upright and so on. But particularly and notably, they believe in something beyond themselves, they have religious belief, and they self-consciously don't believe.

Not to believe is remarkable because not believing assesses a structure of thought, a commitment to something with promises of various goods, and decides "no." It does this hardly ever with a full understanding of the structure, but enough for the individual to reach a decision. Not believing addresses a number of metaphysical issues regarded by many as of great importance to life, and concludes that they are not of importance to life. It is an assertion that life can be lived in terms of this life alone. Whether intentionally or not, not-believing echoes the views of one ancient writer, Epicurus, and one twentieth-century writer, Jean Paul Sartre. Both rejected the idea that humans were dependent upon or answerable to any power beyond themselves, Epicurus, aggressively, Sartre, sadly. Why sadly? Sartre was aware that in giving up God one gives up a great deal. To him it was no small matter to live life on ones own.

But belief is also remarkable, and it is irrepressible, so widespread, so persistent, so earnest one might wonder why anyone would not believe.

The current intellectual climate in Western Europe and North America, in general, "the West," is not anti-religious. Far from it, as current statistics show. But differing from earlier times religious claims are regarded, along with other claims, as open to examination. Scientific, sociological, psychological, religious claims are expected to provide not *a* reason why we should accept them but a coherent structure of mutually supporting reasons. When considered together they should make sense.

This is the endeavor of philosophy of religion, to try to make sense of claims about religion. We will begin, then, with what may be the most difficult and, for many, the most urgent namely, the being, the nature and the experience of God.

Synopsis of the Chapters

1)   "God?"
      The title of the chapter is a question because the issue of
      God's existence, his/her character and relations with people
      are questions. Here we discuss the so-called proofs of God's
      existence. The proofs do not really prove, but they serve an
      important purpose in terms of the human desire to know.

2)   "If There is a God, What is God Like?"
      This chapter discusses the traditional attributes of God as they
      are known in Western thought, but it considers also how the
      character of God is understood in African and Indian societies.

3)   "Mysticism, Religious Experience."
      Personal experience of the divine is vivid to those who have it,
      but carries little weight for others. How do we assess its
      importance, and what about religious experience induced
      artificially, by drugs for example?

4&5) "The Problem of Evil and the Problem of the Problem of
      Evil."
      The problem of evil is widely regarded as a major impediment
      to religious belief. I consider that quite wrong, and describe
      such a view as the problem of the problem of evil.

6)   "Death and After Death."
      We may be able to live life without God, but none of us can
      avoid death, what the Apostle Paul described as "the last
      enemy." A primary concern of most religions has been to
      overcome the enemy. This chapter considers various attempts
      people have made, and some of the philosophical problems
      connected with them.

7)   "Miracles."
      Belief in miracles is widespread. Some claim to have had
      experience of them. But it is not clear what is meant by

miracle. This chapter discusses several definitions. Perhaps none is correct, or perhaps they are all correct. Perhaps each of us has a private definition validated by personal experience.

8)   "Science and Religion."
        Science and religion have been regarded as antagonists, but in light of recent scientific advances that appears simplistic. Scientists as well as non-scientists are asking whether both can be understood objectively as parts of an ultimate whole.

9)   "Religion and Ethics."
        Is ethics dependent on religion (as Reinhold Niebuhr claims) or entirely independent (Peter Atkins)? Certainly life can be lived without religious beliefs. Yet there are questions. Why do so many people look to religion as the source of their moral convictions? And does the striking agreement in ethical teaching between the world's major religions have any significance?

10)   "Religion and Language."
        Without language, at least from the human side, there could be no religion. Only by means of language are we able to express what we believe. But language is finite, what it attempts to express religiously is infinite. This is the source of many practical and philosophical problems discussed in the chapter.

11)   "Religion and Education."
        The United States is ambivalent about the role of religion in education. In the country's earlier days religion was regarded as central to education. Now it is guarded against, often treated with suspicion. That is not the case elsewhere. In Muslim countries, in India, in traditional African religions, religion and education are inseparable. Even in the US, what is known as civil religion exercises a pervasive influence. One might call it a covert compromise between what people want and what Constitutional interpretations allow.

12) "Many Religions."
High-speed travel, international business and finance, and the activities of the United Nations have brought people together from different countries with different religions as never before. The Immigration and Nationality Act of 1965 led large numbers of Asiatics to settle in the United States. These developments prompt three questions discussed in this chapter.

- What is the relation of the Christian faith to other faiths?
- What is the comparative value of any of these faiths?
- How far can one relate sympathetically to a religious faith other than one's own without abandoning one's own?

13) "A Feeling Intellect and Thinking Heart."
In the opinion of this writer thought and feeling are intimately connected, particularly in the study of philosophy of religion. Western tradition has emphasized the importance of the intellect, non-western traditions have given much more attention to feeling, intuition, and subjectivity. Both emphases are necessary when attempting to understand issues related to what often cannot be dealt with rationally or even objectively. The role of intuition and feeling are at times essential. Yet without intellectual discipline religious reflection may evaporate into emotion. Hence the title of the book. To deal with the subject of philosophy and religion effectively one needs a feeling intellect, but also a thinking heart.

.

Acknowledgments

This book had its beginnings in lectures prepared for a cou5rse at the American University in Bulgaria whose President, faculty and staff showed me great hospitality and kindness.

I am indebted to Ms. Corinne Heschke for the skillful way in which she transformed my handwritten manuscript into camera-ready copy.

I wish to thank the following publishers for permission to use passages from their books:

Kees W. Bolle. *The Bhagavadgītā*, A New Translation. Berkley and Los Angeles, California, London, England, University of California Press, Copyright © 1979. Used with permission.

Robert Ernest Hume. *The Thirteen Principal Upanishads*, translated form the Sanskit, Second Edition Revised. London, Oxford University Press, 1931. Used with permission.

Thomas Merton. *The Way of Chuang Tzu*, copyright © 1965 by The Abbey of Gethsemani. Reprinted by permission of New Direction's Publishing Corporation.

Chapter 1

God?

Do We Put God In The Dock?

If we step aside from philosophy, if we take the position of the non-philosopher, isn't there something unreal about the manner in which we examine the concept "God?" We do it so dispassionately, as if God were an artifact. We assume the position of an investigator as if it were an ordinary thing to do - as if God were in the dock charged with the offence of not existing and required to prove that he is.

The Apostle Paul was overwhelmed with wonder as he reflected on God. We are cool. We look to arguments, the stuff of philosophy. But arguments? Isn't trying to prove that God exists by arguments like trying to explain why we love our wife? That seems incongruous, yet not the other. At least we can see our wife, she exists in space. She is not hypothetical. When we want to identify the status of something we don't comprehend, whom we cannot see, hear, smell, touch, taste, whom we cannot locate, yet whom nevertheless we describe and analyze, whose thoughts we determine, whose intentions we anticipate, there surely must be some reason, some argument to make sense of what we are trying to do.

We Reduce What is Too Large For Us.

Some persons feel comfortable with God. "God is my co-pilot," says the bumper sticker. We reduce what is too large for us to accommodate in our limited understanding. Winston Churchill, we say, was a failure at school. Thomas Aquinas was fat; Wagner was a bad husband; St. Teresa a schizophrenic. We may suspect that were we to embrace the immensity of God we would be reduced ourselves.

As ordinary people with so-so faith, as theologians, or philosophers, we try to encompass God in the circumference of the familiar. The apocopated vision we achieve can occupy a lifetime of speculation without our ever having to open the furnace door.

Perhaps God is not to be found in the furthest stretch of what we imagine we are, but in the smallest intensity of what we do not understand we could be.

Elijah called on God's power, and God gave it. Then Elijah lost his nerve and fled. When he found God again it was not in an earthquake or a storm but in a still small voice, as the biblical record explains. It was as if God were repudiating the exercise of his power on Mount Carmel, as if that great event were as unlike his true character as muscle strength is a true indication of the character of a human.

What did the still small voice say? The scripture reports the words of God to Elijah, but not the ringing dissonance, he must have felt.

We Must Listen Harder and More Quietly

The incident tells us we must listen harder and more quietly. Across the world people are doing that. They are doing it in Africa, in India, in China, in North America, in Latin America, among the Inuit, among the Pygmies of the Kalahari Desert. *The New York Times* prints a complete magazine section about God.[1] A writer wins a Pulitzer Prize for his book, *God: A Biography*.[2]

How deep is the interest, how enduring will it be? We have a choice, someone quipped, "Coffee, tea or He." A woman explained, "God is where my deep center is." We could turn that around "My deep center is where God is." for it may be difficult to think of a deep center without God, or something like God. We invite only our trusted friends into the intimacy of our lives. Trust is essential, yet in trusting we take a risk, and in trusting the most sensitive part of our lives we take a great risk. That is why we are interested in God. A child, at any period of history, in any place, requires certain kinds of care. Similarly, however hard wired we may be into this electronic age, the need for spiritual assurance pushes us in the direction of Elijah.

The Me Millennium

Two years after its issue on God, and close to the end of this millennium, *The New York Times* printed a magazine on 'Me', the "Me Millennium." "Ok, what about Me?" asks the headline. "We put self at the Center of the universe. Now, for better or worse we are on our own." proclaims another.[3]

"When the world was ringed by what Matthew Arnold referred to as the "Sea of Faith," and God was ensconced at its center, our asking 'What about my needs?' would be seen to be invalid. What would any one individual's need amount to when placed next to God's?"[4] Things have changed. God is no longer at the center. God has been driven out. But this has not been really to human advantage. At the end of an old millennium, at the beginning of the new "it is easier to evict God from the Big House than to find a new tenant."[5] God has been put away but hasn't gone away. The freedom of "me" which seemed such a desirable goal isn't as desirable once we have it. "We've lived with the me-centered universe long enough now to wonder if this is a good thing."[6] Where are the benefits unless we make as firm a foundation for ourselves as the discredited God, or whatever it is that "God" represents? It provided some stability, some purpose to some people.

How Many Feel This Way?

How many feel this way? Look at the shelf space given over to God in the big bookstores. Philosophy of religion, I'd say, is in business. Unlike the earlier "age of faith," as it is called, when God was everything and life otherwise nothing. God is now an option. The center may not be, but increasingly is, occupied by Me. Not always too happily. So people are looking. Should Someone Else be at the center?

Yet we hesitate, we're not sure. It's like the hesitation a divorced person has about getting remarried. Suppose it doesn't work again? Suppose I find a life centered on God is disappointing, or demands too much, or sets the sights too high, or he abandons me for a prettier, more devout believer? I want to be as sure as I can about a rerun. I want to be as sure as I can about God. For a big move like this, I check the background, I talk with friends who know the person, who may have lived with him or her, I am interested in characteristics, quirks, oddities, that could put me off. I am interested in how *real* the person is. Am I dealing with, a persona or the genuine thing? These are the questions we ask about God, and often we're reluctant to ask the already committed, the experts, and the theologians. We don't quite doubt them, but we want to be sure that whoever it is - is fair, objective, sympathetic yet critical. We may not find it in God's camp. A philosopher? That's pretty self-serving from this writer, and not all philosophers are outside God's camp. Yet the *intention* of the philosopher who examines religion is to be objective, critical, fair, whether or not a believer. It's a philosophic commitment whether or not the intention is realized.

Three Approaches to "God?"

In that spirit we can take three approaches to considering the question "God?" Expressed in rather heavy terminology they are these. First, the approach of considering attributes: what kind of God is it/he/she? Second, the approach by way of experience, finding out from those who know God, who have lived with God. Third, the approach by way of proofs, trying to determine how real God is. The first two will be the topics of separate chapters. The last, proofs, will be the topic of this.

Proofs: Empirical or a Posteriori

We might first ask what do we mean by proofs. Simplistically it is showing that something is what it is supposed to be. If I want to borrow money from a bank the loan officer will ask me for proof of my credit worthiness, credit reports, references and so on. If I apply for the job of a lifeguard the person in charge will want proof that I have been trained in life saving techniques, a certificate from a recognized school or training program. This kind of proof depends upon facts: a certificate, a credit rating to convince someone that what I say about myself is true. I am therefore making claims about myself based on factual or empirical data. An argument that I am credit worthy because of thus and such empirical data is called an *a posteriori* argument. After reviewing the argument a person decides yes or no. This is the kind of argument we use most of the time. In general it serves our purpose well. It has a defect though, namely that an empirical argument or an a posteriori argument can never be a hundred percent certain. For the most part this is theoretical. That the sun will rise in the morning is so certain we would be foolish to doubt, yet it is not impossible to imagine it would not. The Titanic was almost certainly unsinkable. It was *almost* certainly, not absolutely: and, as we know, it sank.

A Priori Proof

Another kind of argument, quite distinct from this is called a priori. An a priori argument is independent of experience. It doesn't depend on fact. A simple example is the equation 2+2=4. This argument is absolutely certain, unlike the empirical, a posteriori argument, it cannot be wrong. The reason is that the one side of the equation equals the other: 2+2 must and always will equal 4 because that is how we have set it up. Definitions follow this pattern. A woman who has had unfortunate experiences with men may say, "All men are liars." She cannot prove it factually; to do so would require testing the truthfulness of every living man. One doubts that that could be done. But as a definition, given a man, that man is a liar. Man means liar. This will hold always for every man. But like 2+2=4 it suffers from the weakness of not giving us any more information than is contained within itself. As an assertion it is more than likely empirically false, as a definition it is empirically irrelevant.

Proving That God Exists

We need to be aware of these two kinds of arguments when we consider the proofs, or the arguments for the existence of God. If earlier I wrote that there is an unreality about our attempts to examine the character and even the existence of God, that unreality is even more pronounced in our attempts to employ the proofs. The proofs don't prove. That is so well known and so quickly determined one wonders what is the point of spending time on them. Intellectually interesting, intriguing to discuss, but not any more taken as seriously as they were.

In an age when faith is dominant proofs, assumedly, (though not actually) would not be needed. Why bother to prove what one is sure of? But in an age when critical questions are asked the proofs, it is claimed, don't hold up in the convincing way we would expect from proofs.

The Teleological or Design Argument

William Paley, an Anglican clergyman, published a book in 1802 in which he presented as a proof of the existence of God the wonderful design to be found in nature. His argument was that the universe around us exhibits evidence of design. It was obviously planned; whoever planned it had an end in view, hence the term teleological, from the Greek teleios or end. The argument is this: the universe is so intricately formed and works so well, there had to be a designer. Who else but God, for only God could design a universe. Paley imagined someone finding a watch on the ground in the country and trying to argue that the pieces of the watch, hand, cogs, glass cover and so on simply came together by chance over a great period of time. Almost everyone would regard that as a ridiculous idea. If there is a watch there most be a watchmaker. Surely it follows that the universe, far more intricate than a watch, requires a universe maker.

By the late eighteenth century much had been learned about the human body, about animal and plant life and about the heavens. Early editions of Paley's book had illustrations of human anatomy, the eye, the heart, other parts of the body, of the sting of a bee, of a venus fly trap, of the rings around Saturn, and of a watch. The book was written to convince all but the most resolutely skeptical that as no *person* could have created all this, the only explanation is that it was the result of an exceptional intelligence, namely God.[7]

It was a huge success, running through several editions. Paley's enthusiastic readers quite ignored what David Hume had written more than twenty years before. Paley's argument was based upon the perfection of the world's design. Hume had challenged that. Far from being perfect the universe has so many flaws it might have been made by a novice God, or perhaps a very old God, past his prime. Why else is there evil in the world? And why suppose that God is the creator, and not a committee of Gods working from a plan, as ship builders' work from plans drawn by someone else? We know about building houses and ships, and making watches. We know nothing about building a universe. How confident can we be that the one we do know gives us a reliable model of the other which we don't?[8] Hume confounded his heresy for sober-minded believers by doing it with whimsy and good humor. He seemed to be attacking not simply the arguments, but the presumption and pomposity that lay behind them, and the naïveté of those who accepted them.

His criticisms fell on deaf ears because there seemed to be no reasonable alternative explanation to account for physical existence. It was not until fifty-seven years later that Darwin's *Origin of Species* was published and introduced the concept of evolution.[9] After Darwin it was no longer impossible to imagine how an eye could exist without an intelligent designer. It evolved over a very long period of time.

But thoughtful believers might still have reflected that the process of evolution itself was remarkable. It could be as difficult to imagine it just happening as for an eye just to appear. The jump to God as an explanatory hypothesis was by no means unwarranted. Less thoughtful believers still look upon the theory of evolution as a threat to the faith. They claim it is only a theory and cannot be relied upon, unaware of the fact that no empirical claim (such as is the conclusion of the teleological argument) can be a hundred percent certain, so, to that extent, cannot be relied upon. As I write this, there is an issue in the United States over a ruling by the Kansas State School Board to eliminate reference to evolution from school textbooks.[10] The members of this board are unaware, it would seem, that the failure of any stage of an empirical argument does not stop a further process of inquiry and experimentation. This is a reason why it is important to understand arguments for the existence of God as particular examples of arguments for any empirical claim.

Contemporary Variants of the Teleological Argument

Since the eighteenth century and early nineteenth century, that is, since Paley published his book, a great deal more has been discovered about the physical universe. This has led to a variant of the teleological argument which to some believers is more effective. Richard Swinburne, a contemporary philosopher, distinguishes between two kinds of natural order, spatial order that he describes as regularities of co-presence, and temporal order, regularities of succession. It was the first kind of order which attracted Paley, seen in the structure of an eye, the design of a leaf, the movement of the planets. But this order depends upon a second order, temporal order, regularities of succession, the fundamental laws of nature apart from which the first order would not be possible. Within the past two weeks we have been told that with little error, the universe is 12 billion years old[11] and that the distance of a galaxy has been gauged at 23.5 million light years.[12] Throughout this length of time, and across that huge distance the fundamental laws of nature are constant. Such data alone do not imply a creator God, but they support Swinburne's contention that while an argument based upon the one order is vulnerable to Humean type criticism the other order is not so obviously vulnerable. According to Swinburne,

> ...the orderliness of nature is a matter of the vast uniformity in the powers and liabilities of bodies throughout endless time and space...Science cannot explain why...bodies do possess the same very general powers and liabilities. It is with this fact that scientific explanation stops. So either the orderliness of nature is where all explanation stops, or we must postulate an agent of great power and knowledge who brings about through his continuous action bodies having the same very general powers and liabilities (that the most general natural laws operate). Once again, the simplest such agent to postulate is one of infinite power, knowledge and freedom, i.e., God.[13]

Swinburne's argument is similar to Thomas Aquinas "fifth way." In his Summa he writes:

> The fifth way is taken from the governance of the world. We see that things that lack knowledge, such as natural bodies, act for an end, and this is evident from their acting always, or nearly always in the same way, so as to obtain the best result. Hence, it is plain that they achieve their end, not fortuitously, but designedly. Now whatever lacks knowledge cannot move towards an end, unless it is directed by some being endowed with knowledge and intelligence; as the arrow is directed by the archer. Therefore some intelligent being exists by whom all natural things are directed to their end; and this being we call God.[14]

The difference between Aquinas and Swinburne over a period of almost 800 years is the far greater knowledge of the physical universe possessed now.

John Polkinghorne, the Cambridge physicist, discusses an argument presented by Lezek Kolakowski that physics is a work of the mind, not God's mind, but our mind. "We are understandably liable to see certain characteristics in the objects we perceive because these objects have indeed been shaped by our minds." Polkinghorne responds to this sharply. "It is hard to exaggerate how implausible such a view is." The physical phenomena we encounter are not plastic to our interpretation,

"They resist our attempts to bend them to our prior exception." He refers to Kant who believed he had shown the a priori necessity of Euclidean geometry. Kant was wrong. "Of course we approach the world from a particular point of view, but it receives its confirmation or necessary correction from interaction with the way things are."[15]

In similar fashion Swinburne refers to the "vast uniformity in the powers and liabilities of bodies throughout endless time and space."[16]

In other words, the universe is something we have to deal with. We cannot explain it in terms of ourselves. Owen Gingerich describes the carbon-oxygen resonance as "a striking example of the remarkable design properties of the universe that seem necessary for the existence of life."[17] He refers to Fred Hoyle's admission that "A common sense interpretation of the facts suggests that a super-intellect had monkeyed with physics, as well as with chemistry and biology, and that there are no blind forces worth speaking about in nature."[18]

Hoyle is not a believer like Polkinghorne, but he is candid enough to admit the power he recognizes in what, in effect, is the teleological argument. It provides a basis for Brian Hebblethwaite's observation, "Much the most powerful general argument for the existence of God is the design argument."[19]

Not everyone agrees, but the claim that our world is the result of a spontaneous, casual, random, purposeless collision of atoms, while it is true of the initial explosion twelve billion years ago, is at least questionable beyond that. Something happened along the way, and we now have an orderly functioning universe. The persistent claim that this is only chance, accident, randomness, given all that we are discovering about the macro and micro constituents of the universe, itself comes under critical scrutiny. Is *that* explanation reasonable? Not to consider the question but to insist that at the root of all things "there is only corruption and the unstoppable tide of chaos." itself becomes something like an act of faith.

The Cosmological Argument

The other empirical argument for the existence for God, or~~ paired with the teleological, is the cosmological, so ~~' considers the cosmos, the physical universe, asks \ and concludes that it did not come from itself. W come from? The only satisfactory explanation i argument, is God. Part of the argument is that the infinite regress. This universe came from something, that something also came from somewhere, and that somewhere came from something else. Unless a stopping place is found the regress goes on and on. Aristotle brought it to a halt by the idea of an unmoved mover. Something creates what is, but is not itself created. It moves things, but is not moved. Aquinas includes this idea in the first of his 'four ways.'

> The first and more manifest way is the argument from motion. It is certain, and evident to our senses, that in the world some things are in motion. Now whatever is moved is moved by another, for nothing can be moved except it is in potentiality to that toward which is moved; whereas a thing moves inasmuch as it is in act. For motion is nothing else than the reduction of something from potentiality to actuality. But nothing can be reduced from potentiality to actuality, except by something in a state of actuality. ... Therefore, whatever is moved must be moved by another. If that by which it is moved be itself moved, then this also must needs be moved by another, and that by another again. But this cannot go on to infinity, because then there would be no first mover, and, consequently, no other mover, seeing that subsequent movers move only inasmuch as they are moved by the first mover as the staff moves only because it is moved by the hand. Therefore it is necessary to arrive at a first mover, moved by no other; and this everyone understands to be God.[20]

Contemporary physics does not reject an infinite regress.

> ...as we understand better and better the very early Universe, we may learn that complexities are to be found at every smaller and smaller level in the remote past. This need not mean that each underlying or previous level is a scale model of the adjacent one (as in the simple models that can be presented explicitly) - it may ultimately prove novel and interesting in various ways - but the infinite regress should be a part of our picture of the cosmological singularity.[21]

Sufficient Reason

Richard Taylor believes that some difficulties with the cosmological argument are created by thinking of temporal order, first and second: first God's creative act, then what he creates.

> To describe God as first cause is only to say that he is literally a primary rather than a secondary cause, an ultimate rather than a

derived cause, or a being upon which all other things, heaven and earth, ultimately depend for their existence." For example, "The sun is the first cause of daylight... this light would be no less dependent upon the sun if we affirmed it had no beginning.[22]

Whether God came first, or the universe and God always existed together, the universe is dependent upon God.

Taylor offers a common sense suggestion. For almost anything that happens people want a reason. I hear a tapping on my bedroom window in the middle of the night. It wakes me, I am alert. What is that, is someone trying to get in? Then I remember: there is an overgrown branch on the tree close to the house. When the wind blows the branch touches the window. I hear the wind blowing so I have not just a reason but a satisfactory or sufficient reason for the tapping on the window. Taylor then proposes that as we require a sufficient reason for everything in the universe why not require a sufficient reason for the universe itself. The "big bang" is not a sufficient reason, for that requires explanation. To stop inquiring is not, according to this, resting with the evidence but avoiding the intellectual challenge of trying to find an answer even though it carries one into the realm of metaphysics.

The two arguments, the teleological and the cosmological are alive because interest in the existence of God is alive. They have frequently been disproved, but they are not dead. As we learn more about the universe they become more reasonable alternatives to other explanations or to none. They illustrate the character of humans that they want to know. If they don't they will try to find out. And they illustrate the nature of empirical inquiry: to be proven wrong does not mean to be finished. It means trying again.

A Suggestion

Science cannot explain itself. We must accept it. We can speculate about where the physical universe came from, but that is the limit. To those who reflect on it, it is an enormous mystery. Physical existence is almost unimaginably complex, and life is dependent upon a delicate balance of fortuitous events not to be taken for granted. We might want to draw the teleological inference that such a balance requires an ordering intelligence. Or we might want to draw the cosmological inference that existence must come from somewhere. Yet we know that a strict scientific view, though not adopted by all scientists, is to accept what is, and not ask the question.

But could we find in this quite astonishing circumstance, in the mystery of the physical universe, not an argument but a suggestion to direct us toward the possibility of some existent that is non-physical?

The question asked of the theist "Where did God come from?" is similar to that asked of the scientist "Where did physical existence come from?" Both have to answer "We don't know." The scientist, however, has the advantage that whatever it is about whose origin he does not know, it is a tangible reality. The theists, or the super naturalists, are at a disadvantage. They are not only unable to indicate the origins of what they believe, but what they believe is not tangible. The theist cannot say, as the scientist can, "I don't know where it came from, but here it is." That is a considerable disadvantage, yet to dismiss the great range of non-material data to which the supernaturalist turns could call into question all use of non-material data. It might be more than the critic may want. The data may be non-material, but it is not unfamiliar. It shares its immateriality with other human experience: of beauty, of love, of moral sensitivity. None of it is tangible as a physical object is tangible, but it plays an important role in life, as important as tangible things. Included in this are religious apprehensions and beliefs.

If this argument has any persuasiveness it brings us to the point at which religious claims may not be utterly distinct from empirical claims. We live in a world that consists of both empirical and of non-empirical facts of existence. The most empirically minded has to deal with both and recognize the importance of both, hence the suggestion that religious claims may not be utterly distinct from empirical claims.

To dismiss the non-empirical is not only an epistemological presumption, it is to dismiss much of life's meaning, of life's joy, of what makes it life. Deprived of its immateriality life is merely the husk of being.

Is it an unwarranted step to include in that immateriality the actuality of something we call religious or spiritual, something that plays a role in human life as important as the other immaterialities we mentioned? Like physical existence, it is there. Scientists give their energies to discovering what they can about physical existence. Where it comes from is the speculative issue that does not have to be answered in order for scientists to go about the business of science. Non-materiality, playing the role it does in life, is also an existent. It also is there. Believers or simply the religiously curious give their energies to discovering what they can about it. Scientists believe they are dealing with a physical reality. Are the religiously curious warranted in the belief that they are dealing with a spiritual reality, given the fact that they too are dealing with data, though of a different kind?

The non-believer may object. On what basis can anyone claim that immaterial, religious concepts have a status comparable to other immaterial concepts such as love, beauty, a moral sense? But the believers could ask: if we grant to them a reality why should we not grant it to religious concepts?

Perhaps it is because love, beauty, a moral sense are located in the perceptions of an individual. They are a reality, but not an independent reality. The claim for religious concepts is that they are independent of the person who conceives them in a way that love or moral senses are not. In other words, they do not have the same status. Their claim to reality must be established apart from the person who makes the claim.

That argument is familiar and reasonable from a Western intellectual point of view. Less so from a non-western. Hinduism does not require a religious concept to be of something separate from the individual. The Ātman (self) is Brahman (the universe). It is immanent, yet not confined to self. If we think in non-western terms the objection loses force.

Yet the critic could make a further objection. Hindus, as much as Christians, Jews and Muslims must still place confidence in something that goes beyond the evidence. What evidence is there for the existence of Ātman or Brahman? According to this, it is not a matter of finding religious elements within the data of immateriality. It is an assumption that they are there, made on the basis of faith.

But granting the unsatisfactory nature of any claim that goes beyond the evidence, what is meant by the term "going beyond the evidence?"

Immateriality, we argued, is a real fact of life. It is evidence. To go beyond the evidence of empirical data to the non-empirical is not going beyond the evidence. It is going beyond the empirical evidence.

The writer of the New Testament letter to the Hebrews declared, "Faith... is the evidence of things not seen." (Hebrews 11:1 KJV) which appears to make the same point. According to this, faith is the consequence of trusting, grasping, acting upon a range of immaterial data, "not seen." Indian religion would have no difficulty there. Does that mean that Indian religion is wrong?

Let me ask this question. What is the relation of these immaterial data to the various consequences of it we call religions? Consider an analogy.

The basic constituents of the physical world are different from the material objects we deal with in our daily life. What these objects are, what we consider them to be depends upon themselves, but also on the ways we interpret the basic constituents consistent with the inherited, learned and familiar context of our life.

Spiritual reality, to the extent it exists, is not the same as theological expressions of it. It is the source from which theologies and religious points of view arise, also interpreted in ways consistent with the inherited learned and familiar context of our life.

The analogy goes like this: As the macro world of physical objects is to the basic constituents of the physical world, so the many expression of religious belief are to the immaterial data we choose to call spiritual reality.

This would be pre-theological and pre-religion. It would be the source, the ground, and the root of what Jonathan Edwards once called the religious affections.

But the critic could object that this analogy takes us beyond the point to which our preceding discussion led us. It appears at least to accept the idea of a spiritual reality, whereas our preceding discussion accepted the idea only as a suggestion. As a suggestion the critic might allow that the analogy has merit. As a proposal it is speculative, all it does is raise further questions, possibly set in motion trains of thought. It is not an argument for the existence of a supernatural. It assumes it. It is therefore as unpersuasive as the other arguments for the existence of God which we examined.

But questions and trains of thought are the essence of inquiry, whether about the origin of the physical universe or about the existence of something beyond it. My proposal, certainly tentative, is that immaterial data has a status comparable to material, and therein we may find confirmation for religious belief. If the existence of this data, which I describe as a spiritual reality, can be sustained, it would provide an explanation for the ground of all religion, and so of the multiplicity of religious beliefs as the many interpretations of it.

The enlargement of human life enabled by religion in its various forms is a reality. What it represents is not agreed upon. Is the enabling religion a reality? Is it something lodged initially in the human heart, and so to be understood in human terms, or is it something other than that, something humans don't create and cannot encompass, but may share?

The Ontological Argument

The other traditional argument, the Ontological, is quite different. It is an a priori argument which, if we recall, does not depend upon facts. Anselm who invented it believed it provided an argument for the existence of God by the mind alone. It is as certain as 2+2=4, and therefore is unassailable, but its weakness is that all it tells us is about itself. Like 2+2 its logic is valid, but it tells us nothing about reality outside of that.

Anselm created the ontological argument in the eleventh century. René Descartes restated it in the 17th century, and it has its defenders now. It may tell us less about the existence of God than the persistence of those, at least in the Western world, who cannot accept the fact that God does not exist. Such persons come to the argument having already accepted what the argument is intended to prove. In that respect it does what Anselm intended. He did not create it for non-believers. Perhaps he suspected that non-believers were not likely to be convinced. He created it to provide an intellectual justification for an existing belief.

The argument runs as follows: I have a concept of God, than which nothing greater can be imagined. But an idea that exists in the mind only is not as great as an idea that exists in both the mind and reality. Therefore, if my idea of God is such that nothing greater can be imagined it must exist in reality as well as in my mind.

If one accepts the premise that one can have an idea of God than which nothing greater can be imagined, and if one accepts the premise that an idea which exists in reality is greater than an idea which exists in the mind only, and if one does not press too hard for a precise definition of greater, then, one could conclude, the argument works. But what does it do? It tells us that the argument is consistent with itself, like a mathematical equation. Within the confines of the argument it is true. But it does not get outside itself to provide information about the actual existence of God. In other words, like an *a priori* argument it is certain, but unrelated to a real world.

Perhaps we should try to understand it not from a logical point of view, but from a psychological. As such it is evidence of a reality, not that God exists, but that for many persons the non-existence of God is unimaginable. These would be among the 94% who answered 'yes' to the Gallup Poll question. It is then not so much an argument as an inner conviction, a personal assurance.

Norman Malcolm asks a pointed question:

> Why is it that human beings have even formed the concept of the
> infinite being, a being, a greater than which cannot be conceived? This
> is a legitimate and important question. I am sure there cannot be a
> deep understanding of that concept without an understanding of the
> phenomenon of human life that gives rise to it.[23]

Malcolm offers the hypothetical explanation that it is from an initial
feeling of guilt, a guilt that is "beyond all measure," a guilt "a greater
than which cannot be conceived" that there arises the desire for a
forgiveness "a greater than which cannot be conceived. Out of such a
storm of the soul I am suggesting that there arises the conception of a
forgiving mercy that is limitless, beyond all measure."[24] Such an
experience can be documented many times within the history of
religion. What arose then was not a new concept but a new experience
of the divine being, a conversion perhaps. Malcolm's example takes us
to a time before the existence of religion, to an initial feeling of guilt
which in its deep concern to find forgiveness, found God. It is one of
the various explanations given for the origin of religious belief. Social
solidarity, loneliness are some others.

As these, including Malcolm's proposal, are hypotheses which
cannot possibly be confirmed or disconfirmed we might suggest
another: that human beings, having emerged from a physical existence,
do not feel themselves complete so long as they recognize only their
physical nature. Why might this be? In some extraordinary way, which
itself may provide data for the teleological argument, physical beings,
men and women, have achieved the ability to think and to imagine, to
develop and present rational and often abstract arguments, to conceive
of what does not exist (as far as evidence is involved) and to explain
and organize their lives around such non-existents to which they have
attached their hope. In that way humans, so they believe, can find
completion. With echoes of Teilhard de Chardin, human beings have
entered the non-physical realms of life and are continuously expanding
them. In the physical realm humans discover that what is exists. In the
non-physical realm humans are creating new concepts about what does
not exist, but might exist.

Is the Ontological Argument An Expression of The Irrepressible?

An explanation of that development is itself a hypothesis which cannot be proven. Maybe it can take its place along with other creative ideas. But there is more to it, because the ideas developed by Anselm of "that than which nothing greater can be conceived" may well be an innate quality of humans as Anselm understood it in eleventh century Western Europe, driving them on in quest of completeness. In this sense the ontological argument is not an argument so much as a description of certain characteristics of humans which seem not able to be repressed, a quality of human life found at least 3500 years ago in the *Rig Veda*. As Charles Moore and Sarvepalli Radhakrishnan explain:

> The *Rg Veda* (the oldest of the Hindu writings) represents the earliest phase of the evolution of the religious consciousness where we have not so much commandments of priests as the out pouring of poetic minds who are struck by the immensity of the universe and the inexhaustible mystery of life.[25]

Some remarkable passages illustrate this:

The Vedic Hymn of Creation

1. Non-being then existed not nor being: There was no air, nor sky that is beyond it. What was concealed? Wherein? In whose protection? And was there deep unfathomable water?
2. Death then existed not nor life immortal; Of neither night nor day was any token. By its inherent force the One breathed windless: No other thing than that beyond existed.
3. Darkness there was at first by darkness hidden: Without distinctive marks, this all was water. That which, becoming, by the void was covered, That One by force of heat came into being
4. Desire entered the One in the beginning: It was the earliest seed, of thought the product. The sages searching in their hearts with wisdom, Found out the bond of being in non-being.
5. Their ray extended light across the darkness: But was the One above or was it under? Creative force was there, and fertile power: Below was energy, above was impulse.
6. Who knows for certain? Who shall here declare it? Whence was it born, and whence came this creation? The gods were born after this world's creation: Then who can know from whence it has arisen? None knoweth whence creation has arisen; And

whether he has or has not produced it: He who surveys it in the highest heaven, He only knows, or haply he may not know.[26]

And from a hymn to the Unknown God with the repeated refrain "What God with our oblation shall we worship?"

I.   As the Golden Germ he arose in the beginning; when born he was the one Lord of the existent. He supported the earth and this heaven. What God with our oblation shall we worship?

II.   He who gives breath, who gives strength, whose command all the Gods wait upon, whose shadow is immortality, is death – what God with our oblation shall we worship?

III.   Who through his greatness over that which breathes and closes the eyes is only king of the world, who is Lord of the two-footed and four-footed – what God with our oblation shall we worship?

IV.   Whose are the snowy mountains through his greatness, whose, as they say, are the ocean and the Rasā, whose are the regions, whose the arms – what God with our oblation shall we worship?[27]

And a passage, evocative of William Paley...

To Viśvakarman [the "all-worker," creator of the universe]

I.   The father of the eye, the wise in spirit, created both these worlds submerged in fatness. Then when the eastern ends were firmly fastened, the heavens and the earth were far extended.[28]

"What God with our oblation shall we worship?" Anselm believed that he knew. "In the beginning God created the heaven and earth." He had his answer. But what assurances did he have of the truth of that? First it was his concept of the creative being and then, set within the great context of "the immensity of the universe and the inexhaustible mystery of life," the intellectual and emotional impossibility (for Anselm) of accepting that what was conceived of, what was imagined and hoped for, did not exist.

This has been described as taking the rabbit out of the hat, having first put the rabbit in, or setting up an a priori argument which was in effect a tautology, the one side equals the other. But Anselm may have been describing not only an intellectual argument but also the actual condition of humans who, despite themselves, find themselves forced to grapple with the question.

Such an explanation depends upon allowing that there could be an intuitive thrust towards non-physical completion. Then it becomes either poetry or a not very convincing logic.

It does seem to me that when we consider the ontological argument we misunderstand it if we discuss it as an example of reasoning only and not as an expression of the man who created it. The argument is inseparably connected with the thought processes and emotional imperatives of Anselm himself.

This provides for me an explanation of why, despite trenchant criticisms, beginning during Anselm's lifetime the argument survives and actually thrives. I believe that we can find in this explanation a better understanding of the other arguments. They are not simply arguments, but the expression of a deeper conviction and of an insistent question that we find throughout recorded history among any people we know.

In the last few decades of space exploration and space travel there has been a great deal of speculation about extra terrestrial life. Much of it is silly, but not all. The statistical probability of other life increases with our increasing awareness of the vastness of the universe. We have good empirical reasons to believe that the physical universe developed from one source, and if there are intelligent beings elsewhere in the universe it is not an unreasonable hypothesis that they progressed through similar intellectual and emotional stages as have we. It is also, perhaps, allowable that if we postulate the need for spiritual completion in humans on earth we may some time discover that a similar need characterizes intelligent being elsewhere. The answers they would reach would undoubtedly be of many kinds. As Alice Maynell wrote in her poem: we will be able to "compare together... a million alien gospels" if we ever meet. She therefore cautions herself.

O be prepared, my soul!
To read the inconceivable, to scan
The million forms of God those stars unroll[29]

Yet throughout the million forms, however different, they would have this in common with one another, with us, and with Anselm: they are answers, though of many kinds, to a common and irrepressible question.

Chapter 2

If There Is A God What Is God Like?

What Do We Know About God?

    We know a great deal from all that has been written, yet, what can we know? God is an infinite being; we are finite. However hard we try, can we reach across that division? When we attempt to describe God in positive ways aren't we simply applying our human notions to a being whose basic qualities go far beyond anything that a human can comprehend? We describe God as good, but the utmost goodness we can conceive of must necessarily fall far short of the actual goodness of God. Our description of God is therefore a limitation, possibly a distortion even though we do not intend that. Both Michelangelo and William Blake attempted to portray God. They did so in dramatic and, to many, authentic ways. But in both cases God is portrayed as a physical being, an awe inspiring older man. Yet he is not physical, so what has been done in these admittedly magnificent paintings? Two great artists have painted what no one can see. They have had to imagine what God is like. We admire their imagination, but still do not know how closely, if at all, what they painted resembles God. When we think less of appearance and more of the qualities and attributes of God we seem to be further removed.

This is not just a Judaeo Christian problem. In Hinduism one of the oldest of the Vedic writings, written between about 1500 and 500 BC, the Brhadaranyaka Upanishad expresses the confusion of a worshipper confronted by the immortal, imperishable, universal self. Yet his confusion is not without a touch of humor.

> He who, dwelling in all things, yet is other than all things, whom all things do not know, whose body all things are... He is the unseen Seer, the unheard Hearer, the unthought Thinker, and the ununderstood Understanderer..."

Yājnāvalkya has already cautioned his friend,

> "Gārgi, do not question too much lest your head fall off. In truth, you are questioning too much about a divinity about which questions cannot be asked. Gārgi, do not over question."[30]

But if we take a theistic view that God is the creator of all things, and if we grant that as a consequence God is the author of our intelligence, we are both bound to ask questions and to recognize that God should expect us to. We may therefore have some confidence that, having asked questions and having formed for ourselves what we believe to be answers, what we assert of God with good intention by means of language is not likely to be completely false. Of course *what* we assert of God must proceed from some knowledge of God which we have before we attempt to put it into words. This is a cause of the criticism, that what we achieve is not an understanding of the nature of God. It is the expression of our own spiritual or theological points of view. Our descriptive language according to this is therefore nothing but the expression of our experience. More than that, not only does our particular experience influence our view of God, but also our personality will affect it. My understanding of God is different from yours, not only because I have had different experiences, but also because I am a different person. To test this one might conduct a survey of the different understandings of God held by the worshippers of the same Christian congregation, and then consider to what extent the particular views reflect the particular personalities of those who hold them.

How Separate is God From His/Her Creation?

Is God so separate from human creation that however hard a person tries no reliable understanding of the nature of God can be achieved? Yet in religions where God is understood to interact with people as their creator, as friend, as parent, as savior, for example in Christianity, Judaism, Islam, Hinduism, it would follow, in ways we often cannot comprehend, that he/she is reaching out to us in a fashion we can comprehend.

Children understand what is taught them by means of what they know. In a similar fashion God teaches us by means of our experiences, our culture, and our personality. We should therefore *expect* some understanding of the divine would be achieved because:

1. It is God's intention this be so, and
2. We are not alien creatures. We have within us some of the same life that animates God.

Here perhaps the Hindu doctrine of Ātman, self, and Brahman, the universe, applies. According to this we are not separated from God at all or, it could be argued that, given God's care for his creation, it is not God's unknowability but our lack of effort to reach out to God that separates us.

Belief, however, is assumed. For those who don't believe, the argument fails; it is irrelevant to anything else we do. The discussion is not addressed to the non-believer, but to the person who is at least willing to entertain the possibility of a true object of belief, and to wonder about the nature of God he/she might be willing to believe.

Complementary Ideas About the Attributes of God

If we consider the religions of the earth we will notice that certain qualities appear and reappear, not identically but complementarily.

In all religions God is more powerful than humans; even lesser deities are more powerful. In all religions the deity is considered to be wiser, to have the capacity and willingness to do well, yet can be frighteningly angry. Although, except for basically destructive deities such as Lamushtu from Mesopotamia, Angra Mainyu in Zoroastrianism, Satan in Judaism and Christianity, their anger is tempered by love and justice, such as the Hindu goddess Kali, or in the Bible, God as an avenging fire.

Having created men and women God is regarded as participating in the life of people, and his qualities or attributes are found in concepts of divinity worldwide.

Geoffrey Parrinder writes that the nature of God in African belief, "can be gathered from the qualities attributed to him. "These correspond generally to many of the divine attributes postulated in other religions. That God is almighty is one of the most obvious assertions, since supremacy implies it. All-powerful is a common name and there are many similar titles: creator, allotter, giver of rain and sunshine, the one who began the forest, 'the one who gives and rots', maker of souls, father of the placenta, the one who exists by himself. "The Omnipresence of God, less commonly expressed, is found in sayings such as 'the one who is met everywhere,' and 'the great ocean whose head-dress is the horizon.' More clearly God is omniscient: the wise one, the all-seeing, the one who brings round the seasons."[31]

Elsewhere Parrinder provides another list of attributes, "Father of babies, Great Mother, Greatest of Friends, the Kindly One, God of Pity and Comfort, the Providence Who Watches All Like the Sun, the One on Whom Men Lean and Do Not Fall." Finally there are mysterious and enigmatic titles: "the Great Pool Contemporary of Everything, the One Beyond All Thanks, the Inexplicable, the Angry One, the Great Spider" (that clever insect who is part of many African stories.)[32]

These descriptions are of interest beyond their connection with African religion; they give some indication of the nature of the relationship between people of all societies and what they believe as God.

Not What God Is (who can know that?) But as the Believer Understands

If there is a God, or spiritual power, responsive to human concern how persons respond will be understood in terms of that concern, and that understanding will, for those persons, characterize God.

The words we use in our attempts to describe God are inadequate so we resort to negation, or analogy or other figures of speech such as metaphor. What is suggested by these African descriptions of God, and is relevant to Western society, perhaps all societies, is that we do not describe what God is (an impossibility) but what God has done for us.

To describe God as "good" is not an attempt to describe the goodness of God as it actually may be. We cannot do that, but we can say, as far as we are concerned this set of characteristics is good, and in our experience of the life of faith God is good in that way. It is an attempt to cut through the theological and philosophical puzzles that focus on the gap between humans and the divine. Perhaps not an attempt to cut through, but to recognize that when people have business with God they go about it without thought of how difficult it might be. They would not turn to God unless they believed they would find, certain attributes expressed on their behalf: goodness, fathering babies, allowing one to lean on and not fall. How subtly they may be expressed, what sophistication they may imply is of much less importance than belief that such attributes exist because they are experienced or hope to be experienced in a believer's life.

Whether in Africa or North America or any other place, attributes refer to what a person who needs that help expects God to do. It is not philosophical, it is practical. Only when God does not respond as expected does disappointment lead to the kind of reflection one might call philosophical.

If we consider the attributes of God, not as they might actually be but as a believer understands them to be, we do not have what some may claim, God made in the image of man but God understood as best as men and women can understand. For each believer that may be different, a difference based first on learned faith, then on faith developed within experience. This we find from region to region in the world, and from faith to faith. Hardly anything is less negotiable for Christians, Muslims and Jews, than that God is one. The first commandment in the Old Testament orders that God alone is to be worshipped, for God is the only true God. Monotheism is a given in these three religions, but not in all religions. Referring to the idea of God in Africa one writer describes it as "diffused monotheism," Evans Prichard writes that a theistic religion need not be either monotheistic or polytheistic. It may be both. It is a question of the level, or situation of thought. Nuer religion (from the South East Sudan) "may be regarded as monotheistic, at another level as polytheistic; and it can also be regarded at other levels as totemistic or fetishistic. These conceptions of spiritual activity are not incompatible. They are rather different ways of thinking of the numinous at different levels of experience."[33] Radhakrishnan has observed that the idea of God is "an interpretation of experience."[34]

Sex

A basic attribute of a person is sex. What sex is God? In the western world God is generally described as male, although one passage in Isaiah refers to God as a mother. (Isaiah 66:13) In recent years many women have claimed that God, the creator of all things, can not be only male, but presumably not only female. Is God androgynous? It is beyond understanding.

But if we want to worship a real being we want a sexual being, at least in the ways that girls relate to their fathers and boys to their mothers. God without a sexual identity cannot be a God for humans – perhaps for angels.

It is the somewhat liberal theological style to refer to God as "she," or "he/she," as I do at various points in this book, and occasionally "it" to indicate that we are not bound by theological conventions.

An obvious problem is that a non-physical being can have little to do with sex, as it is known most intimately by humans. Yet, as creator of humans, he/she must be the creator of sexual intercourse. It might have been simply a mechanical arrangement; instead of that it provides an intensely pleasurable experience. If that was God's doing he gave us means for the highest expression of love and the lowest degradation.

Much Christian devotion is couched in terms of sex. Some nuns wear a wedding ring to symbolize their marriage to Christ.

If Christ were tempted in all points as we are he was tempted by the powerful desire on the part of younger men to engage in the sex act, and the temptation to look at every woman in terms of that. But as a man he could not have been tempted in all points as we are because he would not have experienced the sexual temptations felt by a woman.

If God is male and female has he gone through menopause? No, because he/she is not physical. Similarly, God as male/female has a son but has not given birth. Is that another limitation?

The Old Testament contains a great deal about sex, much of it explicit, some of it unpleasant. In the late eighteenth century Dr. Thomas Bowdler prepared selections from the Old Testament and from William Shakespeare for families with such passages removed. From this we get the term "to bowdlerize," meaning to censor or expurgate. Historically, Jews and Christians have been squeamish about sex hence the appeal of Dr. Bowdler's work. What is called responsible sex requires personal and social discipline. It is surely part of what is included in the New Testament passage 'God endows us richly with all things to enjoy." (I Timothy 6.17 NEB)

For a Hindu the body is an integral part of a human, not to be separated from the spirit but to be enjoyed. The stone sculpture at Khajuraho, India, depicts a god and goddess in close sexual embrace. "Hindu goddesses," writes Capra, "are not shown as holy virgins but in sensual embraces of stunning beauty." Similarly, the "half spiritual, half sensual" wall paintings in the cave temples of Ajanta express, as one writer puts it, "the joyous acceptance of life and delight in the beauty of youth and nature."[35]

The stories of the god Krishna and his affairs with the gopis or young cowherd women are celebrated in poetry by the Hindu saint Nammālvãr. The woman whom Krishna has made love to laments when he leaves her:

Ungracious, graceless Krsna, when you hold my breasts
there is a flood of joy that does not crest in our touch:
it goes beyond the sky, encompassing, submerging my knowledge,
but then it ends like a dream.
Unlimited desire has entered my inmost self, everywhere within me;
when sweet, sweet you leave me and go to herd the cows, I die.[36]

Some have likened Krishna, the manifestation of the god Vishnu, to Christ, eternal and without fault. But Krishna's amorous adventures are quite foreign to what most Christians believe about the character of Christ. For the Hindu *that* aspect of life is a part of life and should be celebrated. The Kamasutra, a manual of erotic and aphrodisiac instruction, is not regarded by Hindus as pornography. It is an account of God-given human pleasure.

Hans Licht, in his *Sexual Life in Ancient Greece* comments that those biased toward the Judaeo Christian view of sex "will only with difficulty be able to understand the idea that there exists any connection at all between erotics and religion."[37] His chapter "Religion and Erotic" is filled with examples of the sexual adventures of the Greek gods and goddesses. Otto Kieffer, writing about the role of sex in religion in ancient Rome notes that "the Christian sees everything sexual as primarily unspiritual and unconscious, as something which must be conquered... in antiquity men still approached sex in an ingenuous and primitive way... in sex they saw something essentially natural, which yet contained and exercised a power which was divine."[38]

This sexual power was often expressed through female deities. In Hellenistic religion Osiris (identified with Hades or Pluto) was God of the Lower World. He represented the birth and death of the year. But his consort Isis was a gentle and loving deity who represented the female principle in nature. Her image seemed to radiate compassion as she was carried through the cities of Egypt in her long white robe.[39] Isis' role seems to have been not altogether different for many worshippers from that of the Virgin Mary, centuries later, whose gentleness balances the fear that Christians may have of a God of justice.

In polytheistic religion we can separate the qualities of God by assigning them to one and the other: male, female, loving, angry, for example. In monotheism we have to try to understand them all in the one being. It might, however, be argued that this is a closer reflection of the ordinary condition of humans. We ourselves are each one person, and to live a satisfactory life we have to find a way of combining the disparate elements within us. We are men or we are women, and yet the difference is best understood not as disjunctive but as complementary. When the Apostle Paul declares that in Christ there is neither male or female (Galatians 3:28) he does not mean that as Christians we lose our sexual identity but that, given the graciousness and openness to others that should characterize a Christian, our sexual identities are enriched in concert with one another. An embrace is an expression of love, but it is also a symbol of the interactive communion which exists (waiting often to be realized and often not realized) between the two complementary halves of the human race.

The Traditional Attributes of God

The attributes of God familiar in the Western tradition are omnipotence, omnipresence, and omniscience. Omnipotence means that God is all-powerful, not only in the sense of being exceptionally strong but being able to do anything. Omnipresence means that God is everywhere at the same time. Omniscience means that God knows all things. Beyond that we say that God is omni benevolent, he is totally good, and that he is infinite, the creator of time but not bound by time.

These attributes are not without problems when we try to understand them in human terms. If God is all powerful then he can do anything, but in fact there are limits to what he can do. C. S. Lewis in *The Problem of Pain* refers to a comment of Thomas Aquinas, "Nothing which implies contradiction falls under the omnipotence of God."[40] God cannot cause a door to be open and closed at the same time. He cannot make 2+2 equal 5. He cannot cause to have happened what has happened, "Socrates never engaging in philosophy," an example provided by Edward Wierenga.[41] "Meaningless combinations of words," writes Lewis, "do not suddenly acquire meaning simply because we prefix to them the two other words, 'God can'."[42] Yes, all things are possible with God, but "intrinsic impossibilities are not things but nonentities. It is no more possible for God than for the weakest of His creatures to carry out both of two mutually exclusive alternatives, not because his power meets an obstacle, but because nonsense remains nonsense even when we talk it about God."[43]

This does not preclude puzzling questions. According to Peter Geach people who try to find Philosophical Truth in "God can do everything," have only, "landed themselves in intractable problems and hopeless confusion."[44] Wierenga believes he can avoid such confusion and endeavors to prove it by discussing and resolving the paradox of the stone. The paradox states that whether God can or whether God cannot create a stone which he cannot lift he is not omnipotent. But Wierenga argues that omnipotence is an enduring property of God. It cannot be lost, so whether he can or cannot create such a stone he remains omnipotent. It is his nature. He cannot be other than he is.[45] If we criticize that as a limitation the answer is, neither an individual nor God can be what he is not, it is a contradiction, therefore meaningless, and does not acquire meaning by the prefix "God can."

These instances are not usually on people's minds when they pray to God for help: a wife who prays that her solider husband will return from the war safely, a child who prays that his sick father will be cured. These requests are well within the omnipotent power of God. It creates an anguishing problem when the soldier husband is killed and the father dies.

Omniscience

Omniscience means that God knows everything. Whatever has happened she knows, to use the feminine pronoun. Whatever has existed, does exist and is happening she knows. She knows what will happen in the future. Nothing is hidden from her, nothing is beyond her understanding.

If she knows the future she knows what I will do. She knows the choices I will make. If so, are they truly choices? If God knows I will choose 'x' she knows I will not choose 'y.' Do I have the option, at the moment of choice, to decide to choose 'y' anyway. Am I not determined by God's foreknowledge to choose 'x.' The answer is no. Prescience does not imply compulsion. What I choose is not determined because God knows my choices ahead of time. If at the last moment I decide to choose 'y' instead of 'x' God will have known that. Boethius, the fifth-sixth century Roman philosopher, wrote in his *The Consolation of Philosophy*, written in prison while awaiting execution, "the future events which God foreknows will all undoubtedly come to pass, but some of them proceed from free choice."[46]

William Rowe argues that knowledge of a future event cannot be true or false. It can only be known as true or false when it happens or doesn't happen. God therefore cannot know a future event because, until it happens, it is not an object of knowledge. "Knowledge is of what is true, and if statements about the future are neither true nor false, they cannot then be known."[47]

This would be correct for human beings, but not for an omniscient God. I cannot claim to understand his omniscience, but I can understand, that whatever there is to be known, past, present and future, is known by God. His omniscience goes beyond the event. He knows what will happen, "For God's gaze," writes Boethius, "anticipates everything that is to happen, and draws it back and recalls it to his own knowing in the present."

According to Boethius God does not have foreknowledge as we understand the term "God's status is abidingly eternal and in the present, his knowledge too transcends all movement in time. It abides in the simplicity of its present, embraces the boundless extent of past and future, and by virtue of its simple comprehension, it ponders all things as if they were being enacted in the present."[48] In this respect God is outside time but that does not limit his comprehension of time. As creator, time is part of his creation.

Omnipresence

Omnipresence means that God is everywhere at the same time. When I was a little child I got the idea that God was in everything, including trees, and gained great satisfaction from kicking a tree because then I was kicking God! The God who is everywhere at the same time, that is, omnipresent, is everywhere as a distinct and independent being at the same time.

An obvious problem is that God is not a spatial being so thinking of him in space at one point or simultaneously at every point appears contradictory. He cannot be at any point in space because he is not spatial. George Galloway proposes that God is the condition of space "for he brings into being the world of interacting individuals and the medium in which they interact, and it is out of this co-existence of individual elements that the idea of spatial order is developed."[49] For Galloway God is, "the active ground of all existence... [He] is everywhere in the sense that he makes his working everywhere felt."[50] He likens the ubiquitous presence of God in the universe to the presence of the spirit in a body" certainly, everywhere felt, and present in every part. How that can be is certainly as mysterious as the other two attributes, yet a widespread belief in omnipresence suggests, even if it does not imply, some empirical or experiential basis. Whether warranted or not, except by faith, we can pray to God in Rochester, New York, or London, England, or Dehra Dun in India and believe that God is listening, not at a distant high point in the sky, receiving simultaneous messages from across the world but in the present "closer than brother" listening to me personally.

Where Did We Get Our Ideas About the Attributes of God?

But where did these ideas come from? How do we know or claim to know about the attributes of God? Were they revealed in dreams or visions; were writers inspired to set them down as a record of the nature of God? Are they the work of human imagination, created like poems and passed into the tradition as true descriptions?

Why ask the question? I suppose for the same reason that the question, "Does God exist?" is asked or, as E.A. Burtt put it "Why do civilized cultures have any religion at all?"[51] Human beings are curious; they want to know. Not knowing, not, at least, trying to know troubles them, especially if the object of the question, the reality and character of what they believe is of importance. It is metaphysical, yet practical in the lives of almost all people whose thoughts turn to whatever realm of their existence is not confined to today, and whose concept of their lives is not landlocked.

Our attempts to understand God could be described as passing though three stages. The first is often overlooked, and taken for granted. We can understand it as a question: how did humans arrive at a concept of God? How did our earliest ancestors, the first pre-hominids with undeveloped brains, still concerned like animals primarily with survival, grasp the elusive idea that outside, above, beyond, not to be contained by anything they knew, there was a something, maybe like the stars in the sky, the moon and, when fire had been invented, like fire, which had the power to enhance life with its inexplicable, intangible yet invigorating warmth? Was it a revelation, or an achievement of the imagination? Even if the latter, it is still remarkable, for while the work of the imagination can be attributed to the person who imagines it, it has a human origin. Imagination itself is mysterious. Where it comes from and why it came defies reduction, yet does not quite lead to creation.

The second level, having arrived at the concept, is whether that concept is true. Is it an objective reality with an existence independent of ourselves? Is it a product of our imagination, or was it given to us to believe? This we discussed in the earlier chapter, God?, where we considered attempts to prove the existence of God.

The third level, if we regard God as an objective reality, is to ask, what kind of reality? What power does it have, what characteristics? If we deal with it we need to know, and so we consider the attributes of God. According to certain critics all that we can mean by such attributes are those qualities we admire among ourselves, and which we project upon our concept of God and, by so doing, create a being from whom we can draw the qualities we need. It is a kind of spiritual Ponzi scheme. There are no independent benefits, only what we have already put in. If the object of our worship truly exists we are still engaged in spiritual make-believe. We don't know that object. We would only imagine what he/she would be like by what we would like him/her to be. While man initially, was made in the image of God, God, latterly, is made in the image of man.

This argument appears to have force. God is revealed as a human creation. But one wonders, if there is a God, the character of that God is not likely to be so different from the character of men and women as to bear no resemblance. To the contrary, one would expect there to be a deep complementariness. And if men and women are to draw a portrait of that God, where else can they turn except to those qualities which they admire and hope for in one another?

The idea of omnipresence arises from the desire, and hence perhaps the belief that wherever a believer is, God is there, and for however many believers there are, God is with them. Omniscience arises from the desire we have for answers, and the belief that if there is a creator God he/she must be able to provide those answers. Omnipotence arises from the fact that God in every society is conceived of as having more power than humans as an infinite being with infinitely more power.

Does this explain away God's traditional attributes as no more than human creations? I'd say not. Humans have no means to describe anything other than by a human language rooted in human ideas. This does not mean that what is described in human terms is not consistent, at least in some small way, with divine reality, if divine reality exists. If such reality exists one would expect it, as originator of all things including humans, to possess those qualities which support humans and make their relationships with one another, and with God, instructive and enjoyable. And belief in these attributes expresses a view, not only that God may have these characteristics, but also that, shared by the finite and the infinite, they are universal.

It is a view with which, in part, the unbeliever might agree. A view that certain values may have an identity and endurance not dependent upon human inventiveness alone. As the origins of the concept of God, even in an atheistic universe, are still mysterious, so are the origins of the qualities of God which we call attributes.

Chapter 3

Mysticism, Religious Experience

The topic of mysticism, or more broadly, religious experience provides the second approach (as I suggested earlier) to considering the question, 'God?' It flows easily from the topics of death and what might follow death, which we will consider in a following chapter. We don't understand the one, even though none of us can escape it, and the other is beyond our human comprehension, except when we can break through the barrier that separates us as humans from the supernatural.

The word, mysticism, is derived from the Greek muo, or muein, to close or to shut the eyes. It suggests the absorption of a person in his or her self, a distancing from the surrounding world. The mystic looks within rather than without, and so proceeds in a way that is seemingly contrary to the manner in which we ordinarily behave.

At the beginning of her book *Mysticism*, Evelyn Underhill writes, "So remote…are those matters from our ordinary habits of thought, that their investigation entails, in those who would attempt to understand them, a definite preparation, a purging of the intellect."[52] Mysticism has an aura of strangeness about it, and indeed it is strange from the point of view of ordinary day-to-day life. Yet it is attractive. Like a homeless child, standing in the street, looking through a window at the lights and the warmth and the affection of the family inside, separated by a thin pane of glass a sixteenth of an inch thick. He could be a thousand miles away, so might we. "Here we have no lasting city," state the scriptures (Hebrews 13:14 RSV). A great many people feel like that, like spiritual waifs. We do not belong, and yet we would belong. The attraction of the mystical experience is that by means of it we could belong. Plotinus wrote:

> What then is our course, what the manner of our flight? This is not a journey for the feet; the feet bring us only from land to land; nor need you think of coach or ship to carry you away; all this order of things you must set aside and refuse to see: you must close the eyes and call instead upon another vision which is to be waked within you, a vision, the birth-right of all, which few turn to use.[53]

Plotinus (205-270 AD), who wrote this, had a loyal band of followers, many of them wealthy and influential, Roman senators among them, who found the murderous tensions of their political and civil life more than they could bear. They turned to Plotinus' teachings. They closed their eyes to ordinary life and opened them to the promise of unity with the One, the ultimate level of spiritual reality.

Robert Cole reports an incident in his book *The Spiritual Life of Children*. An Islamic woman explains, "My children, when they are quite young, want to *see* Allah, and Mohammed as well. If I had pictures of them--their faces--the children would be *so* happy! I tell them that not everything appears on the tube (television). I tell them we must close our eyes sometimes, not always try to see more and more."[54]

Life is the potentiality actualized of physical constituents. It has reached the point at which the physical can reflect within itself upon what it conceives to be non-physical, and in fact posits, like Plato, two worlds, a sensory world of phenomena, and a world of ideas, of concepts, of the spirit. As I ponder on this it seems to me to be increasingly remarkable, and suggests that existence itself--which we take for granted because of its ordinary dailyness--is mysterious. We have only to close our eyes for a moment to begin to be aware that our dailyness is not ordinary at all.

C.D. Broad's Analogy

Here I would be at odds with C.D. Broad who compares religious sensitivity to appreciation of music.

There are a few people who are unable to recognize or distinguish the simplest tune. But they are in a minority, like the people who have absolutely no kind of religious experience...Let us, then, compare tone deaf persons to those who have no recognizable religious experience at all; the ordinary followers of religion to men who have some taste for music but can neither appreciate the more difficult kinds nor compose; highly religious men and saints to persons with an exceptionally fine ear for music who may yet be unable to compose it; and the founders of religions to great musical composers such as Bach and Beethoven.[55]

While I agree with most of this, I disagree with the view that even small minorities "have absolutely no kind of religious experience." If we understand by religious experience some sense of the unordinariness of our existence, that is part of the life of everyone, not *a* part, as perhaps the study of computer language is a part of our education, but an aspect of our character as human beings. Our manner of life may subvert that aspect, but it can erupt unexpectedly at crucial moments, as it did in the life of Ebenezer Scrooge (in Charles Dicken's *A Christmas Carol*) when he came to realize that his daily existence as a wealthy but embittered banker was a false cloak he had woven around himself. I do not think his visions of Marley, of his childhood and courtship, his pursuit of wealth, and his fear of the future were the first time he had them. They were the inner tensions that eventually erupted and destroyed his unreal life.

Such experiences are not limited to particular kinds of people, because people are of the kind who naturally have such experiences.

This aspect of character creates an affinity between humans and various kinds of artistic expression. Thus mystical or religious capabilities are at the heart of our appreciation of beauty as Plotinus wrote, "Harmonies unheard in sound create the harmonies we hear and wake the Soul to the consciousness of beauty."[56]

It is not that some people are prone to mystical or religious experiences. We all are. A number of my students have shared such experiences with me. They represent the quieter and less spectacular examples. Robert Coles in his book provides instance after instance of children's sensitivity to religious ideas, which could suggest a natural affinity, although the children whom he interviewed had already grown in a context of North American Indian, Roman Catholic, or Protestant belief.

The history of mysticism witnesses to outstanding individuals, those who are known as "the possessors of spiritual genius, the pathfinders to the country of the soul. These starry names are significant not only in themselves but also as links in the chain of man's growing spiritual history."[57]

The Mystic Like the Scientist Wants to Know

The driving force for the mystic, as for the scientist, is the desire to know. The mystic may be more like a scientist than a theologian, which is why mystics often have trouble with theological authorities. The mystic seeks to know in terms of personal insights not only according to rules or theological dogma. Near the end of his life, Meister Eckhart was charged with heresy, and after his death Pope John XXII who denounced him for "wishing to know more than he should" condemned some of his teachings[58]

The great mystic endeavor is to know God, to know how to achieve unity with God. The Bible has declared that no one can know God directly; there must always be a distance between the Creator and the created. Yet the New Testament teaches otherwise. In John's gospel, Christ, speaking to his disciples about his return after his death, declares "because I live you too will live; then you will know that I am in the father, and you in me, and I in you" (John 14, 20-21 NEB).

The Apostle Paul describes a mystical vision:

> I am obliged to boast. It does no good; but I shall go on to tell of visions and revelations granted by the Lord. I know a Christian man who fourteen years ago (whether in the body or out of it, I do not know--God knows) was caught up as far as the third heaven. And I know that this same man (whether in the body or out of it, I do not know--God knows) was caught up into paradise, and heard words so secret that human lips may not repeat them. (2 Corinthians 12 1-4 NEB)

This search for ultimate knowledge through personal experience is found in various traditions. For example, in the Upanishads: "The real which is at the heart of the universe is reflected in the infinite depths of the self. *Brahman* (the ultimate as discovered objectively) is *Ātman* (the ultimate as discovered introspectively) *Tat tvam asi* (That art thou) Truth is within us. 'When we realize the universal Self in us, when or what may anybody fear or worship?'"[59]

The Katha Upanishad declares: "The *Ātman* cannot be known by the senses, by reason, or by much learning but only by intuitive, insight, or direct realization."[60] And later:

> What is soundless, touchless, formless, imperishable,
> Likewise tasteless, constant, odorless,
> Without beginning, without end, higher than the great, stable--
> By discerning That, one is liberated from the mouth of death.[61]

Meister Eckhart (born in Germany about 1260) endeavored to teach people that there was no simple communion with God. It had to be "a complete fusion of man's nature with the nature of God." "God must become I," Eckhart declares, "and I must become God."[62]

He believed that essentially God and man are one. His intention was not to exalt man nor reduce God but to point out the intimate relationship between the divine creator and the created being. Men, he believed, have too low an estimate of themselves. They are too preoccupied with their sinful nature. One could think of Hans Christian Anderson's story about the ugly duckling, derided by the other ducks until it grew into the swan it really was.

"There is a faculty in the soul," writes Arthur McGiffert, "by which a man may know God directly." He refers to Eckhart.

> I have a power in my soul which is always sensible of God. I am as certain as I live that nothing is so near as God. God is nearer to me than I to myself. My existence depends on God's being near me and present with me. He is also present with a stone and a stick of wood but they know it not. If the wood knew about God and were conscious how near he is, as the highest angel is conscious of it, the wood would have the same blessedness as the angel. Therefore man is more blessed than a stick of wood, because he recognizes God and knows how near God is. The more conscious of it the more blessed, the less conscious of it the less blessed he is. He is not blessed because God is in him and is so near to him, or because he has God, but only because he is aware of God and knows how near he is and that he is dear to him and

present with him." The faculty by which one knows God is not merely human like the senses, or the reasoning power, but divine. "The eye wherewith I see God," Eckhart says, "is the same eye wherewith God sees me. My eye and God's eye are one eye--one seeing, one knowing, one loving.[63]

Let Us Value Ourselves

"Admiring pursuit of the external" wrote Plotinus " is a confession of inferiority; and nothing thus holding itself inferior to things that rise and perish, nothing counting itself less honorable and enduring than all else it admires could ever form any notion of either the nature or power of God."[64]

The mystical path for Plotinus was not abnegation, nor was it exaltation, but a proper awareness of the value of human life as an aspect of divinity. The Stoics, whose founder Zeno lived 300 years before Christ, taught that the universe is divine, and that men and women, as part of that universe, are divine within it.

Sextus-Emipiricus, the skeptic, who lived in the third century after Christ wrote, "Zeno says that the universe is the most beautiful product executed according to nature, and in all probability a living being, endowed with soul, both intelligent and rational."[65]

Seneca, a contemporary of the Apostle Paul, asked, "And why should you not believe that something of divinity exists in one who is part of God? The whole universe which contains us is one, and is God; we are his associates and his members."[66]

The Stoic concept of God was ambiguous for they were materialists, yet they granted to humans the highest stature, and in an age when slavery was normal declared that no one is a slave by nature.[67] All partake of the divinity and rationality of the whole and so all people are fellow citizens, an exceedingly radical idea when Roman citizenship was highly valued and closely guarded.

The Stoics are not in a religious mystical tradition, but their affirmation of human value is not unlike that which we have seen in the other traditions, so although the word mystical conjures up an image of persons who are different, esoteric, not in the main stream, mysticism offers the most practical of good advice, (in current parlance, that we are all right, even OK,) if we recognize the qualities, the potentialities of human personhood, and act on them. Consequently, mysticism can appeal not only to those attracted to the contemplative life but those for whom life is a gift to be appreciated and used, a challenge to be responded to.

Not all are of this opinion. In concluding his discussion of mysticism, Robert H. Thouless writes that it is customary to discuss the value of mysticism, but that will depend upon our attitude to religion as a whole. "If we judge it from a this-world point of view, we must remember that for the mystic the alternative is probably mental ill health; even if we do not like mystics, we certainly prefer them to lunatics." He notes that mysticism often tends to incapacitate its subject for activity in this world. However, if man's highest activity is to love God, "mysticism may have a value of its own entirely independent of any usefulness it is found to have in this world."[68]

If the potential of mystical experience is a natural part of human character, is at the core of human character whether or not a person is willing or even able to express it, and if the expression of this character through various kinds of mystical experience is of positive practical value, why is mystic experience so often incomprehensible and difficult, if not impossible to explain? According to William James, one of the four marks of mystical experience is its ineffability. The Upanishads expressed this long before.

"Incomprehensible is that supreme Self, unlimited, unborn, not to be reasoned about, unthinkable."[69] And a contemporary theologian, in a sermon on "Our Experience of God" writes, "Our experience of God is bound to be different from our experience of any particular thing in the world."[70]

But if anything is to be effective in our lives we must surely understand it, at least in part. What we don't understand, can't comprehend, is disconnected from our lives.

Can Everyone Be A Mystic?

I find that thinking, reading, studying, trying to write about mysticism is not like trying to think, read, study, or write about other things. It is possible of course to describe mysticism and tell the stories of various individuals, Eckhart whom we have referred to, or George Fox, or the near contemporary Sadhu Sundar Singh. But there is a gulf between, in this case, the person describing and what is described, and there seems no way of bridging the gulf except by striving to become a mystic oneself. Yet it is hardly what one decides to do as we can decide to become a doctor or an engineer. Although, if it is correct that the potential of mystical experience is present in everyone, there cannot be a sharp distinction between the mystic, a small minority, and the non-mystic, the great majority.

I would call it a difference in degree, not of kind. As individuals we can be at any point on that continuum at any moment of our lives, in simple meditation and prayer, spasmodic and fitful though it may be, or by following a spiritual discipline. The difference will be in complexity and intensity. The similarity must be that, at whatever level, the individual is acting sincerely and therefore unpretentiously, for whom grace at meals or advanced meditation are regarded as natural. I would qualify Evelyn Underhill's conclusion that the mystics who have "run on before us urged by the greatness of their love have a sublime encounter of which we are incapable."[71] To an extent, yes, but we may be more capable than she seems to allow even for those with only a vestige of personal faith.

Harold Bloom discusses this, referring to the work of Henry Corbin who "deplored the Western gap between sense perception, with its empirical data, and the intuitions or categories of the intellect." In the post enlightenment world, poetic imagination "works in that void" but for the most of us they are fictions. Corbin regards this as the realm of actual reality. Bloom agrees, "Between the sensory and the intellectual world, sages always have experienced an intermediate realm, one akin to what we call the imaginings of poets. If you are a religious believer, whether normative or heterodox, this middle world is experienced as the presence of the divine in our everyday world."[72]

He quotes Emerson "It is by yourself without ambassador that God speaks to you."[73] Bloom's book is an appeal to all people to recognize "the way of gnosis." The knowledge of God within, which institutional religion has been suspicious of, is actually the heart of true religious experience.[74]

The Fringe of Feeling

Friedrich Von Hugel, whom Nicholas Lash discusses in his *Easter in Ordinary*, describes this as "the fringe of feeling" which lies between reasoning, logic and abstraction, and instinct and intuition. The one too specific and remote, the other "too particular, too evanescent." The fringe of feeling is woven out of our total experience of race, family and individual life. It is by this "apparently slight, apparently far away, accompaniment of a perfectly individual music to the spoken or sung text of the common speech of man, that I am, it would seem, really moved and won."[75]

A Constructivist View

One of the weaknesses of religious experience is that while its truth is compellingly evident to the individual who has it, it carries no or little evidentiary weight to others. Jones may be absolutely certain that God spoke to him this morning, but his certainty alone is not sufficient to validate the claim. If he has a reputation for trustworthiness we are more likely to give him credit, even for such a 'strange' tale. If he had been a disreputable character, drinking, gambling, cheating, and so on, and then reformed, so that after his alleged encounter with God he became a changed person, no more drinking, totally trustworthy we might say there must have been something about that encounter. Yet it is still possible that he imagined it, and what he imagined brought about the changes in his life. The argument is difficult if not impossible to turn back. Unless one is willing to believe, there is nothing, or very little, to compel belief. "In plain language, what is being said is just this: Unless you can manage somehow to believe without evidence, that is, without objective evidence, you cannot get any evidence. Unless you really believe in fairies, you will never see any."[76]

What the mystic claims to have experienced is a construction of his/ her imagination fed by all the elements that created it. At the beginning of his book *Mysticism, Mind, Consciousness*, Robert Forman makes this observation:

> Over the last quarter of a century, scholars--who are rarely mystics-- have come to generally agree that it's not a Who but a what that plays the key formative role in mystical experiences. The "what" is the mystic's background: his or her beliefs, expectations, hopes, wishes, needs, questions, etc. In academic shorthand these are commonly referred to as the mystic's conceptual "framework" or background "set." This approach to religious experience, along with a range of relatively minor variations and shadings with which it is taught, is called "constructivism". Constructivism is the view that in significant ways the mystic's conceptual and linguistic scheme determines, shapes, and/or constructs his or her mystical experiences.[77]

As Wayne Proudfoot explains "Any bodily changes or feelings may be accounted for in religious terms when the subjects past experiences and present context make such an account plausible and compelling. The common element in religious experience is likely to be found, not in a particular physiological or mental state, but in the belief held by the subject about the causes of that state."[78]

Forman notes that the insight we construct within our own reality has been enormously influential in Western humanities and social sciences. But he proposes to challenge it "For I am, in effect, asking in this book, is there a limit to the constructivist model of human experience? Are there any experiences, types of experiences, or phenomena that a human being may consciously undergo, which may plausibly be said to be not determined or constructed by the subject's set?"[79]

His answer, developed through his book, is that yes, there are such experiences or phenomena and so he does not accept the consequence of the constructivist approach, namely that "mysticism becomes virtually an epiphenomenon of language and culture."[80]

The constructivist view provides a clear, simple, and to the skeptical mind reasonable explanation of mystical – or more broadly – religious experience. But as Forman argues throughout his book it runs counter to the experiences of mystics themselves. If one approaches these experiences from a constructivist position one has already decided that they can be explained only in terms of prior influences. Not a recommended type of argument. If one keeps an open mind and is willing to grant that such experiences are *sui generis* we are faced with the task of explaining them and then interpreting them in terms of those who have them. If the experience is pure in the sense of having no specific intentional object we can accept it as "a procedure for unveiling certain deep truths of human existence."[81]

When a religious claim is made the deep truths will be divine truths and have great authority for the mystic. The philosopher needs to consider the proper way to respond. Epistemological bias is bound to affect judgment – compare the attitude now in the West toward dreams and that in the time of Joseph in the second millennium before Christ recorded in the Old Testament. Dreams are not taken seriously by most people in the West as a source of knowledge. We may find that our attitude to mysticism is constructivist. It may then be difficult to regard it apart from all that has constructed it. It is a philosophic challenge not to jump to conclusions one way or the other.

Transcendence

Stephen Carter has, in effect, taken on this challenge in his *The Culture of Disbelief*. "It turns out," he writes, "that America is bursting with desire to talk about religion but often afraid to do so." People write to him about the casual acceptance of "anti-religious bigotry, tolerating nasty comments about, say, Roman Catholics or Southern Baptists that they would never countenance were they made about women or African Americans."[82]

Carter's book describes mainly recognizable religious behavior and beliefs, yet his comments apply to the 'strange' beliefs and behaviors which do not fit into traditional understanding: the writings and the utterances of the spiritually possessed, those for whom the core of their belief is transcendence. Bloom asks in his *Omens of the Millennium*, What is transcendence? "It means," he writes, "climbing beyond the material universe and ourselves." It is dismissed by materialists as an illusion, yet it has an "uneasy existence in many of us, and a more secure hold in a scattering of individuals through the ages: mystics, visionaries, sages, men and women who have a direct encounter with the divine, or the angelic world..."[83]

These comments are echoed again and again in other writings. For example, W.T. Stace's *Religion and the Modern Mind*:

> My contention is that all religion is ultimately mystical, or springs from the mystical side of human nature. All religious men are therefore mystics in greater or less degree. There is no sharp line between mystic and non-mystic. Those who are commonly recognized as mystics, and who so recognize themselves, are only those whose mysticism is explicitly realized in the full light of consciousness. In the ordinary religious man that mysticism is implicit, lies below the threshold of consciousness, only faintly stirring the surface waters of the mind and not recognized as what it is either by himself or others.[84]

Dennis O'Brien, in his somewhat offbeat *God and the New Haven Railway*, puts it this way.

> The miraculous, the fascinating, and the spooky are entertaining distractions, but they do not speak to the daily anxiety of the human heart. If God is not an interesting oddity but the ground of our life meaning, then He or She must somehow be sensed in the everyday.[85]

Brian Hebblethwaite echoes this, in a book published three years before O'Brien's comments. For him the experience of God, through indirect, is similarly encountered in the everyday.

> What then do we mean, when we talk about experience of God? I do not myself think that we finite human creatures can really claim to experience God directly; even mysticism seems to require some medium through which God makes himself known, such as nature, which for some poets and mystics comes to mediate a sense of the divine, of ultimate, unchanging being permeating all things. I think I can understand that dimly, but I do not know what it means to say that we might experience God directly. Nor do I think that there is some particular peculiar kind of experience that we can pin-point and isolate as being experience of God as opposed to experience of the world or other people or myself. Rather it is these ordinary things -- world, people, self -- that take on a new dimension of depth, that can come to disclose to us the presence of God and the reality of God, so that we find ourselves wanting to say that we experience God in and through nature, in and through the other, in and through the depths of self-knowledge.[86]

Plato believed that there is a more real world behind or beyond the phenomenal world we ordinarily encounter. Many believe that they catch glimpses of it, and want to find out more. Others catch those glimpses and are simply puzzled and put them aside. In all societies in all times there is a sense, not of discovery, but of something to be discovered if we knew how to look, or if we had a key to unlock the door, or a teaching, such as the Gnostics and others believed they had. It is this sense that makes the topic of mysticism and religious experience surprisingly relevant to our ordinary life. William Wordsworth captures something of it in his poem, "The Two Voices."

> Moreover, something is or seems
> That touches me with mystic gleams,
> Like glimpses of forgotten dreams--
> Of something felt, like something here;
> Of something done, I know not where;
> Such as no language may declare.

In England and America such indirect and evanescent experiences are unusual, tantalizing, mysterious. But if we move from our familiar surroundings to other surroundings, not familiar, we may have a better, or at least a different understanding. Recently I attended a service in a Russian Orthodox Church in St. Petersburg, and I was struck, as I have been at other Orthodox services, in other parts of Russia and Eastern Europe, by the depth of feeling of the worshippers. Most of them were ordinary people moved at a level I do not ordinarily encounter in the western world. Orthodox belief is such that the mystical element is never far away, in this instance a service in a church in a weed strangled graveyard. The music, the liturgy, burning candles constantly replenished, great and small icons each symbolizing an aspect of the faith, believers praying before them and the solemnity of two corpses lying in open coffins in the midst of a continuously changing crowd of worshippers, was a world apart from the streets through which we had walked to get there. When I left and walked through those same streets again I felt I was leaving behind an environment quite different from that of my daily life. But it was not one to which I could not return, and that I take is the special genius of the Orthodox Church.

Can A Genuine Religious Experienced Be Induced?

One of the four characteristics of mysticism identified by William James is passivity. The others are, ineffability which we have discussed, noetic, that something is learned from a mystical experience, and transiency, a mystical experience lasts a very short time. Forman challenges this characteristic in his book providing various examples of sustained mystical experiences, including his own. The fourth characteristics is passivity. Mystical experience is passive because the subject does not induce it, it comes unsought. Neither Ezekiel nor Isaiah were looking for their great experiences before they had them. But in certain instances experience, described as religious, is deliberately induced by the use of drugs.

In his book *The LSD Story*, John Cashman asks, "Does LSD, in truth, cause a mystical or religious experience?" To those who answer "no" he relates two experiences, quoted by Huston Smith, one drug induced, the other not. It is difficult to tell which is which.

Suddenly I burst into a vast, new, indescribably wonderful universe. Although I am writing this over a year later, the thrill of the surprise and amazement, the awesomeness of the revelation, the engulfment in an overwhelming feeling-wave of gratitude and blessed wonderment, are as fresh, and the memory of the experience is as vivid, as if it had happened five minutes ago. And yet to concoct anything by way of description that would even hint at the magnitude, the sense of ultimate reality...this seems instantaneously and with such complete force of certainty that it was impossible, then or since, to doubt its validity.

All at once, without warning of any kind, I found myself wrapped in a flame-colored cloud. For an instant I thought of fire...the next, I knew that the fire was within myself. Directly afterward there came upon me a sense of exultation, of immense joyousness accompanied or immediately followed by an intellectual illumination impossible to describe. Among other things, I did not merely come to believe, but I saw the universe is not composed of dead matter, but is, on the contrary, a living Presence; I became conscious in myself of eternal life...I saw that all men are immortal: that the cosmic order is such that without any peradventure all things work together for the good of each and all; that the foundation principle of the world...is what we call love, and that happiness of each and all is in the long run absolutely certain.[87]

Of a large group of Princeton students, who were asked to read the two accounts and decide, approximately two thirds got it wrong. The first account is the drug induced. The oblique reference to Romans 8.28 in the second account might have provided a clue. But when the accounts are so similar does the manner in which they occur make a difference? If the experience is the end in itself, perhaps it doesn't. But the first subject writes of the gratitude felt at the sense of ultimate reality, not unlike the second account which refers to eternal life, the foundation principle, and love.

Is a drug-induced experience like sending a letter to oneself? Peyote has been used for centuries by Mexican Indians, and during the last century increasingly by Native American Indians of North America.[88] It provides consolation and illumination. But is that any different from what Marx meant when he described religion as the opium of the masses. Opium was cheap and easily available in the nineteenth century. It gave people a sense of well being, false, as their situation was not improved. According to Karl Marx that is the way religion works.

Do we draw the line at drugs? What about inspiring church music which has deepened the worship of many congregations? What about candlelight, extraordinarily impressive and uplifting in Orthodox services? At Easter time a whole town or village will be filled with little lights that the worshippers carry. In many Roman Catholic churches, and High Church Anglican, incense is used. In Buddhist worship, bells, in African worship, dancing to the almost hypnotic rhythms of drums. What is allowable and what is not allowable? Harvey Cox discusses this in his book, *The Feast of Fools*:

> The time may come when we will recognize that the various substances we smoke, swallow, or swill to induce particular states of consciousness are all devices that in a perfect world of fulfilled human beings, no one would need. But no one lives in such a world. We are beset by noise, interruptions, and banal chores. We sometimes want to contemplate or celebrate, but the world is too much with us. So we use the substances nature has placed in the grains and grasses. Often we misuse them. But the fact that something is misused does not mean it should be banned.[89]

What we need, he writes, "are dependable data" on the harm that these substances could cause. Yet the data alone would not be sufficient. Wine is used at communion services; it is a known intoxicant. Is that dangerous? We have to balance possible harmful effects with tradition and good sense.

But possible harmful effects are only one of the issues we need to address in connection with mysticism and religious experience. As we saw in the parallel between a "normal," that is non-induced religious experience and a drug induced religious experience, the effects were almost identical. Do we judge the character of such an experience by what causes it, or is what causes it not important, only the effects? Or, putting it another way: Is the religiousness of the experience dependent upon the individual who has it or can it be conferred only by divine power? Or do they work together, somehow complementing one another? If they do, what does the one contribute to the other? Is there any way we can know this? Ernest Troeltsch believed that by one interpretation of mysticism it can be regarded as something that is humanly cultivated. Does that include drugs?[90]

Such questions indicate how complex, baffling and contradictory the topic is and yet, despite that, how compellingly attractive.

Chapter 4

Problem of Evil

A Theological Problem

The problem of evil as philosophers and theologians discuss it is a theological problem. The problem of evil as such, that is, other than as a philosophical or theological problem, affects everyone. It becomes a problem when untoward events disrupt peoples' lives: a young father in good health suddenly gets cancer, small twins wander into the street and are struck and killed by a car, a student about to graduate from college is casually murdered outside a restaurant near the campus. We call these evils. They are hard to bear. They happen unfortunately all the time. Generally we can't anticipate them. Cancer has an empirical cause, but how and why it happens in particular instances is too often not known. Hardly anyone could have prepared for two small children to run into the street. The student was completely surprised. Who could have known these things, flagged down the car for example, or warned the student not to have gone to the restaurant at that time? Few people have such foresight. But God, who is all-knowing, all-powerful, and all-loving, does. Yet he/she allows these things to happen. That is the theological problem of evil, the contradiction between what one might reasonably expect of God, given the characteristics we believe that God has, and what he/she assumedly allows to happen.

The problem can be expressed simply:

> God is all-powerful
> God is all-loving
> Evil exists.

If God is all-powerful and all-loving evil should not exist. Had we the power we would certainly use it to save someone whom we love. We don't have the power; we don't save the person we love. God has the power, and is supposed to be all-loving, but the person we love dies. It can be a wrenching experience. Not many things are more painful than to be let down by someone we trust. When that happens it is hard to trust the person again. When God lets us down, it may be hard to trust God again.

Ways of Dealing With The Problem

Various attempts have been made to deal with the problem. Consider again the three terms of the equation.

> God is all-powerful
> God is all-loving
> Evil exists.

It is possible to deny one or both of the two premises, to deny that God is all-powerful and to deny that God is all-good. Either denial would deal with the problem of evil. If not all-powerful God is like a parent, all-loving but limited. If not all-loving God would not always want to prevent an evil. Rejecting either premise would resolve the problem.

If we turn to the conclusion, and declare that evil does not exist, the problem becomes moot. It might be hard to go along with that, but it is an option.

For those who want to resolve the problem without diminishing the power of God, without making the claim that God is not all-powerful or not all-loving, we can employ what are known as theodicies, a term coined by the German philosopher Gottfried Leibniz, literally it means, God victorious. By means of a theodicy we can still claim that God is all-powerful and all-loving, and that evil exists, and yet resolve the problem.

We therefore have a choice. We can change the terms of the equation or we can construct a theodicy. Let us consider first how effective the attempts have been to change the terms of the equation.

Challenging The Terms of The Equation: God Not All-Powerful

The nineteenth century philosopher, John Stuart Mill, denied that God is omnipotent. His argument was beguilingly simple. As we saw in the chapter about proofs for the existence of God the argument from design has been well regarded. Mill was not persuaded. Writing in his *Three Essays on Religion*, he asks, what is meant by design? Design means, "…contrivance, the adaptation of means to an end. But surely," he argues, "…if God has to contrive something he is limited in power. If he were all-powerful he could snap his fingers and it would be done. The fact that he doesn't do that suggests a limitation. Perhaps Satan limits God's power, or perhaps the materials of the universe are too difficult to work with, so, although we can agree that the author of the cosmos is wise and knowing, he is not all-wise and all-knowing."[91]

Mill's objection has a common sense appeal. Why would God design something if he could simply cause it to be? If he doesn't cause it to be when he assuredly could, given his omnipotence, then perhaps, although he is powerful, he is not all-powerful.

Yet we might look more closely at the term "design" that Mill criticizes, for whether the design we perceive in the universe was created in an instant, or worked out over a period, it is still a design, complex, intricate beyond imagining. The word 'design' is both a noun and a verb. Mill is criticizing it as a verb; God would not have to go about designing anything if he were truly an all-powerful God. That is possible: we do not know for sure what God has done or would do. But he may have created a design, the noun, in the way that Mill declared he should have done if he were God. When we examine the universe we see the interconnections between its parts; from our point of view they must have been designed. From God's point of view they are a design which he may not have designed, being God.

Another approach to this problem, to God's apparent failure to deal with evil in the world because he lacks the power, was made by A.N. Whitehead. He argues that we must think of God's activity in the universe in some other way than it is traditionally thought of: God creating the universe, "by the word of his might."

According to Whitehead "the nature of God is dipolar. He has a primordial nature and a consequent nature." The first has the character we ordinarily ascribe to God; the second is that aspect of God that is in continuous evolution. Each is understood in terms of the other. The primordial nature is in a process of completion by the consequent nature. As Whitehead explains it, "The consequent nature of God is the fluent world become 'everlasting' by its objective immortality in God. Also the objective immortality of actual occasions requires the primordial permanence of God."[92] The world is in a constant process of completing God's primordial nature. All events are included in this, those we call good and those we call bad. The worst that happens is dismissed into triviality. Everything that happens, including what we call evil "is transformed into a reality in heaven, and the reality in heaven passes back into the world." God is God, but not yet fulfilled. He is in a process of fulfillment. As a result, as evil strikes and we cry to God, though he may not be able to help us in the ways we want, "God is the great companion – the fellow sufferer who understands."[93]

Whitehead was an eminent mathematician who collaborated with Bertrand Russell in writing *Principia Mathematica*. He later developed his theory of process theology or process philosophy which we have very briefly described. He lost his son in the First World War, which may have stirred his interest in metaphysical and theological matters. His ideas have been, and continue to be influential. They do indeed offer a way of dealing with the problem of evil. God as a "fellow sufferer" cannot be held responsible for evil as can God the omnipotent being who has the power but does not use it. Yet he is totally sympathetic to human concerns.

My personal response to this is one of quiet puzzlement, which may reveal my own lack of understanding. Process theology, however impressive, is an invention, a product of the imaginative thought of a notable thinker. Whitehead did not claim to be a prophet. He was a philosopher trying to deal with a tremendously difficult problem. We may, therefore, at least as philosophers, question his solution. What evidence is there at all for the dipolar nature of God? One might also ask what evidence is there at all for the omnipotence of God? Whitehead asked that question and proposed his hypothesis, but how much does it help us? If God is the fellow sufferer, what is the status of evil? It must be more powerful than God for God cannot control it. Is it an arbitrary phenomenon, a series of random occurrences over which no one has control? If so evil has no explanation. The problem of evil has been resolved, if one can call it that, by making God irrelevant to it.

Whitehead's thesis about the suffering of God is not entirely new. Christian theology teaches that Christ suffered on the cross; Christ is God, therefore God suffered. In this sense he is the "fellow sufferer who understands." The New Testament makes that point specifically. Referring to Christ, the author of Hebrews writes:

> For ours is not a high priest unable to sympathize with our weaknesses, but one who, because of his likeness to us, has been tested every way, only without sin. (Hebrews 4.15 NEB)

Again, as Christ is God, this statement must refer to God. "I and my father," said Christ, "are one" John 10.30. But Whitehead was not presenting his ideas from within Christian theology. His concept of the suffering God was of a God still not complete. According to Christian teaching the Christian God is complete, is perfect. It's a basic difference.

The Buddhist teaching known as "dependent origination" is suggestive of Whitehead's thesis. It is that whatever is - is dependent upon something else for its existence. God therefore cannot be an uncreated independent being but is in a continual process of creating and being created. [94] Here I would have to temper my puzzlement about Whitehead out of respect for Buddhist tradition. Nevertheless, Buddhist ideology should not be less vulnerable to criticism and questioning than Christian ideology.

A further issue, that is, an issue for me, is the claim that all events on earth, good and bad, are "transformed into a reality in heaven and the reality of heaven passes back into the world." Heaven, if one uses that term with its many associations, is presumably a realm of values. But in this understanding it makes no distinction between good and bad. It is therefore like Spinoza's view of good and bad: everything is what it is. But Spinoza made no claim about a divine being, Whitehead does. If there is such a being, even dipolar, one would expect it to have a moral sense, not only in suffering with and understanding those who suffer, but in trying to do something to alleviate and prevent the suffering.

Is God Good?

The other premise in the problem of evil is that God is good. If that could be shown to be not so the problem of evil is solved. In the Babylonian story of the flood (which was earlier than and probably provided a basis for the biblical story) the gods became irritated with the noise that humans were making and decided to destroy the human race by a great flood. Those gods were not good; they were selfish and capricious. If God is like that no wonder human beings suffer.

Is God like that? Surely not. But Jeremiah, out of the depths of his physical and spiritual anguish compared God to a deceitful brook. In a country where water is precious a brook must be reliable. If it fails that is a calamity. God is not supposed to fail, but he chose Jeremiah to be a prophet, promised to help him and then left him. He was a deceitful brook. When C.S. Lewis grieved over the death of his wife he wrote, "Meanwhile, where is God?" For him it was one of the most disquieting symptoms. "When you are happy, so happy that you have no sense of needing Him you will be--or so it feels--welcomed with open arms. But go to Him when your need is desperate, when all other help is vain, and what do you find? A door slammed in you face... The conclusion I dread is not "so there's no God after all" but "So this is what God's really like--deceive yourself no longer."[95] But neither Jeremiah nor Lewis gave up their faith in God. It was a momentary anger at a time of great stress. They did not continue to think that God was "really" like that. Apart from Satan cults, it is difficult to think of God as deliberately not good, or as evil. If such a being exists it is not very successful because despite the many incidents of violence one can find many more examples of caring

Does Evil Exist?

The next move, having considered that God is not all-powerful and that God is not always good, is to deny the fact of evil, to claim it does not exist. This view is not as strange as might appear. Christian Scientists believe it. The basis of their faith is Mary Baker Eddy's *Science and Health with Key to the Scriptures.*[96] In it she writes "evil is but an illusion, and it has no real basis. Evil is a false belief." Elsewhere she writes "Sin, disease, whatever seems real to the material sense, is unreal in the divine science." Every now and then one reads about sick children who have been made wards of the court because their Christian

Science parents refused to allow them to receive what the court regarded as necessary medical treatment. The tone of these news items is generally critical of the parents, incredulous that so obvious a matter of common sense would be rejected. But at the end of *Science and Health* are numerous testimonies to the efficacy of Christian Science teaching: "Freed from Many Years of Suffering," "Relief from Intense Suffering," "Hereditary Disease of the Lungs Cured," and so on. I don't believe the theory, but I do respect the faith.

Benedict Spinoza (1632-1677) the Dutch Jewish philosopher, who was excommunicated for his radical opinions, believed that the world is a deterministic system. Everything is what it is. He referred to everything as God, but it was not God in the Judaeo Christian sense. As we come to understand this God, or everything, we will realize that evaluative terms such as "good" and "bad" are meaningless, for they refer to what ought to be rather than what is. What we *call* good and bad are not intrinsically good or bad, they just are. In other words neither good nor evil exists.

It is a persuasive theory. Beyond a certain time the worst events subside into the morass of moral equanimity. We do not feel strongly about the atrocities of the Thirty Years War, or of the Crusades. Historians are apt to write about them in terms of their larger significance: the Crusades, opening up a backward Western Europe to the culture and scholarship of the Islamic and Byzantine East, and the Thirty Years War as part of the political development of central Europe. Those who keep alive their moral outrage about the past, such as present day Serbs, create further moral tragedies for themselves and others.

Gottfried W. Leibniz (1645-1716) a slightly younger contemporary of Spinoza, taught that we should accept what happens because ultimately, in the purposes of God, it is for the best. Voltaire parodied this in his *Candide*. His wretched young hero goes from disaster to disaster, but continues to believe with his naïve faith that it is for the best. If we believe that whatever happens is for the best, evil is not really evil. Does this solve the problem? After the event we can usually see some positive benefits no matter how bad it was, but does that neutralize the evil, so that what happened wasn't evil? My friends whose daughter was murdered established a foundation to help troubled young people from turning to violence. As a result much good has come from a brutal act. But is the murder any less evil? Leibniz's theory does not answer that question. Murder is evil, though it may lead to good. To say it isn't may simply be an evasion of the central issue. If God is good, if God is all-powerful, why does he allow such things?

Theodicies

To attempt to deal with the problem by changing the terms of the formula, to deny that God is all-powerful, or totally good, or to deny that evil exists may be of help in trying to solve the problem of evil, but is not without its own difficulties.

We can try to solve the problem without diminishing God's character, without claiming that he/she is not all-good or not all-powerful, and without denying the existence of evil. If we try that we may use what is called a theodicy. The term is a transliteration of two Greek words meaning, "God victorious." When a theodicy works it shows that despite the existence of evil God's power and his love are not compromised.

Is Sin The Answer?

What may be the oldest theodicy is that evil is punishment for sin. When Christ came upon a man, blind from birth, the disciples asked, "Who sinned, this man or his parents?" (John 9.2. NEB) Job's comforters were sure he had done something terribly wrong to be so afflicted. They became increasingly angry when he denied it.

Adam and Eve were expelled from the Garden of Eden because they disobeyed God. Evil then is the consequence of human misbehavior. The Apostle Paul developed this into what became a major doctrine.

"It was through one man," he wrote, 'that sin entered the world, and through sin death, and thus death pervaded the whole human race, inasmuch as all men have sinned." (Romans 5:12 NEB) This teaching, presented with conviction by St. Augustine and hundreds of years later by John Calvin, has had what some believe to be a baleful influence upon the Western church. Yet it is found not only in Christianity.

The number of rebirths and the quality of subsequent lives in Hinduism are determined by the quality of present life. In Africa, when a person is disrespectful of ancestors, elders, or one another, or commits a crime he may become ill and have misfortunes such as Job suffered. Among the Tutsi cattle herders of Rwanda the myth of expulsion from the heavens because of human disobedience explains the origin of the human condition: "suffering, toil and separation from God.'[97]

These traditions express what may be a universal belief, that behavior has consequences, and bad behavior has bad consequences. Yet the consequence may not be such as to make impossible a change for the better. The teaching of Paul, interpreted by Augustine and Calvin, was that the sin of Adam infected the whole human race, and there is nothing a human can do to avert punishment for that. This provided an explanation for human sinfulness. "All have sinned and come short of the glory of God." But it did not explain why many people do not behave as sinners. Their lives are kindly, gracious, concerned with other people, and the argument that they really are sinners by nature is unconvincing now. The British monk, Pelagius, who lived at the same time as Augustine, argued that humans do have the ability to live a good life, even a perfect life. From Augustine's point of view that was heresy; he challenged it strongly and prevailed. Pelagius' teaching was condemned. But the contemporary philosopher and theologian, John Hick, argues along similar lines with what he calls the Vale of Soul Making theodicy.

The Vale of Soul Making

According to Augustine man sinned and is now corrupt. This, Hick describes as the "majority report." But another theologian, Irenaeus, who lived about two hundred years earlier than Augustine, proposed what Hick calls the "minority report," This report turns on an interpretation of Genesis 1.26. "Let us make man in our image, after our likeness." (KJV) Everyone is created in the image of God, although everyone fails to live up to it, but everyone is created in the likeness of God as a potential. It is a potential they are able, in fact are intended, to actualize. How can they do this? According to Hick, through suffering. That is the explanation of evil and its justification, in other words it is a theodicy. Evil is not a contradiction of God's love, nor is it a sign of God's weakness. It is a divine policy by which a believer is trained, in a way that harsh and even brutal military training prepares a soldier for combat. The process can be painful. "The picture with which we are working," writes Hick, "is thus developmental and teleological. Man is in process of becoming the perfected being whom God is seeking to create. However, this is not taking place – it is important to add – by a natural and inevitable evolution, but through a hazardous adventure in individual freedom."[98] This adventure is what Hick calls "The Vale of Soul Making," adopted, Hick explains, from a letter of the poet John Keats to his brother and sister written in April 1819. "The common cognomen of this world," Keats writes, "among the misguided and superstitious is 'a vale of tears' from which we are to be redeemed by a certain arbitrary interposition of God and taken to Heaven – What a little circumscribed straightened notion! Call the world if you please "The Vale of Soul-making.'" In this letter, Hick explains, Keats sketches a teleological theodicy. "Do you not see, he asks "how necessary a World of Pains and troubles is to school an intelligence and make it a soul?"[99] Evil is therefore a process of God teaching us what we cannot learn in any other way.

I learned a very great deal from the loss of my first wife. I doubt I could have learned it in any other way. And perhaps it was necessary for me to go through that experience to be the kind of person I now am. But did she have to suffer for my education? The Vale of Soul Making is a theodicy, which, to a certain extent, provides an explanation for the evil that happens to us. But in the past few months there have been terrible examples brought to us by radio, and television and newspapers from Kosovo in Serbia, affecting men and women, many of them old, some even in hospitals, and children. The question I find myself asking is, can one really suppose that God sanctioned such behavior for the purpose of soul making? Are those Kosovars whose bodies are slowly being recovered from mass graves experiencing a richer spiritual existence in heaven than they would have done had they been allowed to live out their lives with their families? I cannot answer 'yes' to that. In my study I have a small book of photographs assembled by the French photographer Luc Delahaye.[100] The first three were taken by him in a street in Sarajevo in September 1996, the other photographs are copied from obituaries in the journal *Oslobodenje*. All were killed in the city streets, including the three whose photographs he had taken first, men, women, boys, girls, and even little children mostly by grenades and sniper fire. The book is dedicated "au morts de la guerre en Bosnie." I find it deeply moving, so did my American students when I showed it to them. Such dreadful things go so far beyond what I conceive of as required by soul making that I cannot accept it as an adequate explanation of the evil in the world.

The Free Will Defense

This little book of photographs makes it difficult for me to accept another theodicy known as the "free will defense." When God created people he might have created them so that they would always do what was right. Had he done so they would not be truly persons and they would not be in the image of God. An essential characteristic of God is that he makes choices. If men and women were made in God's image they must have the power to choose. A person without the power to make choices is not fully a person. But in creating men and women with free will God had to take the chance that sometimes they would do what was wrong, that they would sin. That happened. Adam and Eve did what they were told not to. God thereupon punished them. He did not want them to sin. He did not cause them to sin. It was their choice. Evil then can be explained as the disciplinary consequence of willful behavior. As the prophet Hosea put it, referring to the Northern Israelites, "They have sown the wind and they shall reap the whirlwind." (8.7 KJV)

But it does not always happen. The Psalms record many complaints about how the righteous suffer while the wicked get away with it. In an ancient Egyptian poem at a time of great social unrest (about 2240-2000 BC) the writer complains how everything in life is backwards and he is the victim.

> To whom shall I speak today? There are no righteous men. The land is
> left over to the workers of iniquity.[101]

The prophet Habakkuk writing many centuries later (about 612 – 597) laments

> Thou whose eyes are too pure to
> look upon evil,
> and who canst not countenance
> wrongdoing,
> why dost thou countenance the
> treachery of the wicked?
> Why keep silent when they devour
> men more righteous than they?
> > Habakkuk 1:13 NEB

A criticism brought by J.L. Mackie is that God could have created a world in which everyone freely chose to do the good. In that case the possession of free will would not be an argument for the existence of evil, for it would not follow that having free will would lead to wrong behavior and thence to punishment (evil). But the issue is moot. With free will, men and women already have a choice between good and bad. Any man or woman exercising choice could always do what is right. If all people so decided it would then be a world without sin and therefore, according to the argument, without evil.[102]

Pelagius believed that humans were capable of this. Augustine was convinced they were not. The possibility is there. But if Augustine had too low an estimate of human nature Pelagius had too high. Human beings sin, God punishes. That is the free will defense of evil in a world governed by a God who is both all-powerful and all-good.

If we return to the passage in Habakkuk we find in it another criticism of the free will defense. The righteous who were suffering were not suffering because of their willfulness. They just suffered at the hands of willful people who were getting away with it. As I pick up the little book of photographs on my desk and leaf through the pages I see no arrogance, or anger, or willfulness in any of those faces, certainly not in the face of a little boy who looks about five years old. And were I to see someone about to engage in potentially self-destructive behavior and could do something about it I would at least shout 'stop!' or 'go back' or something like that. God sees it all and does nothing. Why? To respect the willful person's independence? That does not seem to be consistent with the caring character of God.

Is It Just God's Will?

If none of these theodicies work we might say simply, "It's God's will." We don't know. As a Muslim in Britain explained when asked about a devastating earthquake in Iran that killed forty thousand people, "God is manager of the universe; he knows best." Eight hundred years ago St. Bonaventure (d 1274) wrote, "if anyone asks why God did not make a better world or make this world better no answer can be given except that He so willed and that He Himself knows the reason."[103] It is a mystery. We don't understand, we will never understand. We must simply accept his will.

One person who did not accept it is Harold Kushner. After many diagnostic tests he and his wife were told that their little boy, Aaron, was suffering from *progeria*, an aging disease. He would "never grow more than three foot high, would have no hair on his head or body, would look like a little old man while still a child, and would die in his early teens."[104] That is what happened. The experience was more painful because Kushner is a Rabbi. His life is committed to the cause of God. One might suppose that God would support his ministry, not make it so terribly hard, and, if he wanted to do that, surely not at the expense of the child. Rabbi Kushner was familiar with all the arguments we have discussed in this chapter. None of them fully answered his questions; so he provided his own answer. Yes, God is good, but he can't do everything. He loves and cares; yet he is limited in what he can do, "by the laws of nature and by the evolution of human nature and moral freedom." Kushner gave up trying to find the meaning for his son's suffering and death. He concluded that the bad things that happen to us have no meaning. We have to give them meaning. "The question we should be asking is not, 'why did this happen to me? What did I do to deserve this? That is really an unanswerable pointless question. A better question would be, 'Now that this has happened to me what am I going to do about it?'"[105]

It's a sensible approach, not unlike Epictetus' advice in his Enchiridion. "What disturbs men's minds is not events but their judgment on events. For instance, death is nothing dreadful; or else Socrates would have thought so. No, the only dreadful thing about it is men's judgment that it is dreadful."[106] Epictetus was a Stoic who did not have a theistic belief. Kushner is a Jew who does. The Hebrew God is ultimate and has a beneficent plan and purpose. "Shall not the judge of all the earth do right?" (Genesis 18:25) Kushner's position, while understandable as the result of his grief, is inconsistent with his theological commitment as a Rabbi. How he works that out must be part of a continual spiritual, theological and intellectual struggle, not more obviously contradictory than that of an acquaintance of mine, an Anglican Minister who officiates at services, yet has publicly denied the objective reality of God.

Like proofs of the existence of God which do not prove but express the natural human desire to want to find out, the explanations and theodicies designed to deal with the problem of evil do not really deal with the problem of evil. They do however provide at least possible answers for those who are unwilling to reject God, but want to respond to the dire things that happen with more than grief, anger bitterness or incomprehension.

Chapter 5

The Problem of the Problem of Evil

The failure of God to act when called on, the enormity of the evils that take place, has created an immense problem for faith. This is the view of John Hick. He writes, "The reality of evil in its many forms presents theistic faith with its most serious challenge."[107] Elsewhere he makes a similar point. "The fact of evil constitutes the most serious objection there is to Christian belief in a God of love."[108] In a text by another writer: "The problem of evil is perhaps the most powerful objection ever raised against belief in God, and it cannot be dismissed lightly."[109] Michael Peterson in his recent, *God and Evil,* observes:

> Some thinkers believe that unless Christian believers have an acceptable solution to the problem of evil, they have no right to hold their distinctive theological position or to ask others to adopt it. Philosopher T.W. Settle argues that grappling with the problem of evil is a "prolegomenon to intellectually honest theology." Thor Hall proposed that the ability or inability to generate an answer to the vexing problem of evil is the litmus test of the "reasonableness of theology." Hall says that Christian thinkers must "be capable of handling honestly the actualities of human existence (realities which we all know) while at the same time providing a framework for explicating responsibly the essential affirmations of the faith (affirmations which are given within the historical tradition)."[110]

The last comment is important. The historical tradition of most of the Western world is Judaeo Christian. In that tradition God is one, and is supreme. Similarly in the Islamic world. But with one God there is, or appears to be, a contradiction. The deity is understood as totally good, well intentioned and all powerful, yet does not eliminate evil. With the power to do so, why not? Hence the problem of evil. The problem does not exist in polytheism. Different Gods can be held responsible for different behaviors. A God of love can be credited with the positive things that happen; a vengeful God can be blamed for the evil things.

The problem of evil does not exist when a person has more than one life. In Hindu teaching the fortunes of our present life are determined by behavior in a previous life, and behavior in this life will determine the kind of life we will have after our next rebirth. This provides a reason for the evil that happens, not unlike the ancient explanation that evil is the result of sin found throughout the Old and New Testaments. It is in theism, the assertion of one God, with the belief that humans have one physical life only, that the problem exists.

Numerous explanations have been proposed to account for the problem, as we have seen. Many are ingenious, perhaps might even work, despite my doubts, although that may depend more upon the nature of an individual personality than the quality of the arguments; one argument might appeal more to one person than another. It might be claimed that although no one argument is convincing, all of them together suggest at least that the problem is not intractable.

But I want to take a different approach because the dire warnings referred to earlier are quite wrong. Hick's statement "The reality of evil in its many forms presents theistic faith with its most serous challenge." may be true in particular instances, but it is not generally true.

After the bombing of the Federal Building in Oklahoma City, in April 1995, in which large numbers of people were killed including children, the survivors, and many of those who live in a city described as "deeply religious and heavily Baptist,"[111] did not turn against God. They did not say, "We have worshipped you. We have honored your name. We have respected and trusted your teachings, and you have let us down. We're through with you." They did not say that. They turned the lights on in the Liberty Bank building so that throughout the night four huge white crosses shone across the city. They went to the churches to pray in round-the-clock prayer chains. For reasons inexplicable in terms of the problem of evil they rallied to God, the God who, if he exists, if he is all-powerful, if he is all-loving, if he knows everything, could with the slightest exercise of his power have prevented the explosion. Why was this? Could it be something similar to a recent news report about a boy, badly abused by his adoptive parents, who still did not want to be taken from them and placed elsewhere because they were his parents, and to be parted from them in a safe place was worse in his mind than to be with them, even with abuse.

The charge that the people in Oklahoma City were irrational (they closed their minds to the problem of evil which had struck them, they were too shocked to think clearly) has to be proven. This is not an isolated instance. During the Second World War, Londoners, many of whose churches were destroyed by enemy bombs, did not turn against God who might have deflected the bombs or prevented them from exploding to save his own places of worship. They came to their church the following morning, cleared wreckage from the nave the best they could, and gathered for worship on Sunday, not stricken in faith but stronger. Visiting Bosnia recently I heard many stories of continuing, even strengthened faith in the face of evil. In light of this I would say that the problem is not the problem of evil but the problem of the problem of evil.

Oklahoma City's faithfulness appeared not to be rewarded. Four years later, in May 1999, a tornado struck the city destroying about 1000 buildings, killing almost 40 people in the State, injuring hundreds of others. People in the city responded quickly. They explained that they were prepared for this tragedy because of what they had learned from the other, and some made a distinction. The explosion was the action of an individual, what philosophers and theologians call a moral evil. The storm was a natural disaster, or a natural evil, not attributable to human action. This enabled some to handle the storm emotionally better than the bombing. But the storm, like the bombing, caused undeserved suffering, which was well within the power of an almighty, a loving God to have prevented. Yet again, none complained that God should have prevented it, especially in view of what they had suffered before.

Another terrible incident in this country occurred recently in Littleton Colorado, where two students entered their school with guns, killed thirteen other students and then themselves. The police and school authorities were blamed for not heeding warning signs and taking some preventative action. But God was not blamed. In fact one student, confronted by a killer who asked her if she believed in God was shot to death, point blank when she said, "Yes, I do believe in God." She has been described as a martyr to her faith. She wanted to become a doctor, to help people. Wouldn't it follow that out of self-interest God would preserve the life of a young Christian woman like that, cause the gun to misfire? He/she didn't, and has not been blamed. The young student's death has become an occasion for honoring her faith with the confidence, not only on the part of her parents, that her 'martyrs death' is consistent with the idea of a God of Love.

And most recently, the September 11, 2001, terrorist attach on the World Trade Center in New York City, and the Pentagon in Washington, DC: once again the reaction of people across the country has been prayer.

These terrible incidents are examples, just a few among many, of how untrue it is that the fact of evil "constitutes the most serious objection there is to Christian belief in a God of love." Evil strikes people; they still love God. So it would seem to follow that the philosophical and theological arguments of academic discourse are beside the point. By far the majority of people in Oklahoma City, Littleton, New York City, and Washington, DC had never heard of the arguments. Many would be mystified or even irritated by them. What then is the value of these arguments?

The issue is not only theoretical. It can be discussed objectively, and theoretically. But evil, the subject of the discourse, is neither theoretical nor objective. It is a real, dreadful fact of life felt by those it strikes in a keenly subjective way. People have to be able to surmount it, to go on with their lives. They look for help from those who love them, their family and their friends, and realize that what has happened cannot be explained by anyone they know. They look beyond people, beyond this natural realm. They look to some concept of the supernatural.

What does this mean? That they have a mature faith which ordinarily we would associate only with outstanding believers? They would not claim it for themselves. Perhaps it is that what we turn to as our last recourse we have to believe. We are otherwise bereft. Better a world filled with iniquity, with unfairness, with evil, but with some slight possibility that somewhere is an explanation, than a world without God where we are on our own with no other help than we and others like us can provide.

Why not rest with that? Evil is a problem by itself. It's a greater problem when linked with theology. We usually can't do anything about the worst evils. The people in Oklahoma City and Littleton had no way of preventing what happened. They were victims. But we do not have to be victims of theology. We can reject the theology and live without it, which would not mean living an unethical life or selfish life. It would be an independent life, one without illusions. But to keep the theology when evil strikes makes the evil worse. Why keep it? The problem of evil is the contradiction between what we might reasonably expect of God and what he/she assumedly allows to happen. The problem of the problem of evil is that the dire consequences of this for personal religious faith, widely proclaimed, do not follow. A third contradiction which we might describe facetiously as the problem of the problem of the problem of evil is that while the issue is created by theology and could be resolved completely by rejecting the theology people don't.

The question is why? Is the mainly unreflective, emotional reaction to inexplicable evil something which we should try to understand better than we do? Is this an intuitive route to knowledge, one that is foreign to the intellect? Is this what Søren Kierkegaard meant when he wrote "The thing of being a Christian is not determined by the *what* of Christianity, but by the *how* of the Christian."[112] Is this what Radhakrishnan meant when he described the character of religious experience?

> The experience itself is felt to be sufficient and complete. It does not come in a fragmented or truncated form demanding completion by something else. It does not look beyond itself for meaning or validity. It does not appeal to external standards of logic or metaphysics. It is its own cause and explanation. It is sovereign in its own rights and carries its own credentials. It is self established (*svatahsiddha*), self-evidencing (*svasamvedya*), and self-luminous (*svayamprakāśa*). It does not argue and explain, but it knows and is. It is beyond the bounds of proof and so touches completeness. It comes with a constraint that brooks no denial. It is pure comprehension, entire significance, complete validity. [113]

Returning to the original problem. How can we explain God's apparent silence and inaction in the face of evil? One way is to minimize evil. The Apostle Paul, writing to the Christians at Rome (8:18), declares that the suffering of this present time are not to be compared with the glory that is to come. And to the Corinthian Christians "Our troubles are slight and short lived, and their outcome an eternal glory, which outweighs them far." (2 Corinthians 4.17 NEB)

According to Epicurus, however intense our suffering it cannot last a long time. And the longest time it can last is a very short time compared with the length of history, compared with the twelve billion year span of the universe. What God allows, in terms of evil, is insubstantial overall, however bad we think it is.

Yet to ameliorate the concept of evil is not to eliminate it. A hurt hurts for a second or a lifetime. Unfairness is a wound, and though my wound is insignificant compared with a world full of wounds, it is my wound. It hurts me. God is my God. Doesn't he care for me?

In trying to work this through over the years I find some help in thinking about a ship on a voyage. At the onset, the sea is calm, the ship clean, and its crew optimistic. Perhaps it sets out with balloons and streamers and bands and a crowd of friends and relatives wishing the best for a safe and prosperous voyage. Soon the ship is in open water, no sight of land. The ship is on its own. Eventually, inevitably, bad weather comes and the ship is subject to two challenges, one is the sheer force of the weather. It can be a frightening experience in even a large vessel, to be at sea in a powerful storm. A fifty thousand-ton ship can be like a cork, a plank, thrust back and forth and up and down, struck by waves as destructive as torpedoes. Some storms will overwhelm any ship, and down it goes. That is the external challenge. The challenge of a force beating on a ship. The other challenge is closely connected to it. The storm will discover the ship's every weakness. If there are faulty rivets they will go, and perhaps because of the added strain, other rivets will go, and the ship will open up. If a bulkhead is not secure it will be smashed. If important equipment is not tied down it will be washed away. If the navigation is faulty the ship might be pushed over by the wind if the captain becomes confused or loses his nerve, the ship is lost. The winds and waves don't have a grudge against the ship; the bad rivets are not themselves at fault. All that happens is a series of events which, when they come together, determine whether that ship will survive the storm or won't. If it survives it may have to be decommissioned, or rebuilt, or perhaps end up in good shape and after minor repairs, carry on with other voyages.

I try to apply this to my thinking about God. Will it work? Each of us is like that ship. We start our lives, as the ship begins its voyage with everyone's best wishes. But soon at sea, we are on our own. Even as a child we are on our own. Parents can protect us only from certain things, the children for example in Kosovo, or grade school children in Sarajevo whom my wife and I met when we visited Bosnia. The same two forces will work upon us: external forces, (the sheer power of them can overwhelm us), and internal weaknesses: lack of preparation, lack of self discipline, vanity, selfishness, not knowing our direction in life, not being clear about standards of behavior. The storms of our life will find them and we can be wrecked because of them.

Where is God in all this? He is like our friends who bid us farewell and wish us the best, but once we have gone they cannot help us much. In these days they can send weather reports, navigational aids, another ship or even a helicopter to pick up survivors. It doesn't amount to a lot. Mostly we are on our own in the water.

Can't God do more than that? He/She chooses not to. We cry for help. He/she does not answer. We ask for protection; we don't get it. We are on our own at sea. We are required to accept the vicissitudes of life just as the ship has to accept the vicissitudes of wind and weather. Why would God do that, not help us, abandon us? Does God abandon us? He is beyond the weather. We believe he created it, but he chooses not to control it for specific individuals. It is an argument we can use to explain natural evil; volcanoes that destroy villages, earthquakes, forest fires, all those things still described as 'acts of God.' God is ultimately responsible, but were he to prevent earthquakes and volcanic eruptions the earth would be blown apart. There is a natural order. Gravity keeps the earth and its planets in equilibrium. It also causes the death of someone who slips and falls when climbing a mountain. We grieve for the mountaineer but would not want gravity to be suspended, even for the mountaineer. The physical universe operates in accord with a natural order, and we describe untoward events caused by earthquakes and so on as natural evil.

But there is an order in the processes of life. A motorist who speeds is likely to crash and be killed. Someone who drinks too much is likely to die from alcoholic poisoning. Adam sinned by disobeying God who had created him perfect. The word perfect in Greek also means complete. God therefore created Adam a whole person. Included in that wholeness was all the potentiality which he could actualize. One of those potentials was to disobey God. His disobedience was the actualization of that potential. The list of human failures, which Augustine enumerates, and before him the author of Ephesians and long before that in the Bhagavad-Gita[114] are as natural to human society as gravity and other physical forces are to the physical world. Moral evil then is really a species of natural evil.

As we do not expect God to interfere with the natural processes of the physical world, although sailors do pray for good weather, why should we expect God to interfere in the natural processes of the human world? We do not blame him for bad weather even after we have prayed for good weather. Why should we blame, or be surprised by the evil that happens in the human world?

Why has God set it up this way? Someone can read to us "Who has known the mind of God and who has been his counselor?" (Romans 11:34 RSV) Ultimately it is a question of why aren't things different from what they are. Why am I not someone else? Why was I not born three years ago with seventy, eighty years ahead of me? Why was I born when I was born, with only a few years ahead? We don't ask those questions seriously because they are useless. Similarly, why is God what he is? Why does he choose to do what he chooses to do? Why did he create a world with good and evil and not a world with just good? In a letter to the mother of a young Union soldier, badly wounded, whom he had sat with and cared for in a hospital until he died. Walt Whitman wrote, "Such things are gloomy – yet there is a text, 'God doeth all things well' – the meaning of which, after due time, appears to the soul."[115]

If he/she exists, if we believe in God as a creative being, he created an existence and we are part of it. We have God's given gifts, God's given strengths and we can have faith. We have the option of using them as we toss on the sea. They won't protect us from evil, but they can enable us to deal with it better. We may need spiritual seamanship, moral navigation. We may need to take charge of ourselves, not lose our nerve. The interplay of human plus and minus, the wretched, the exalted, the generous, the mean, are all part of what we have to deal with during the course of our lives. What persists is not human good but human goodness, not human life but human hope. Pain won't end, but human ability to overcome pain won't end. It is in the goodness, and the hope, and the overcoming that people with faith seek God's help. And for those who seek there will be a response, even if the source of that response cannot be understood or clearly identified with any spiritual being or power.

If we go under, then what? If we make it to port, what then? If God is everlasting, God will be there. If God is all loving his love will extend. If there is a more-exceeding weight of glory we will achieve it, and the difficulties of this life will take their place in an eternal perspective.

And if we have no faith in God we will still have lived the best way we could.

Chapter 6

Death and After Death

Life Without Death?

Can we imagine life without death? Much literature would lose its point: Emily Dickinson's poem *"Because I Could Not Wait for Death,"* Virginia Woolf's essay *"The Death of a Moth,"* Tolstoy's *The Death of Ivan Ilich*, Dicken's *A Tale of Two Cities*, Walter Pater's *Marius the Epicurean*.

The dramatic and reflective focus of all of these is death. Without death what would their meaning be? Can we imagine people going on forever, our great, great grandparents with us still, and we with our great, great grandchildren, the generations of the Stone Age, the Bronze Age, and the Atomic Age living side by side?

Physical consequences would be one thing: old people never retiring and young people having to struggle against incumbents to find a place in life. One can try to visualize a world made unlivable by life, struggling with all its power to invent a thing called death as a solution to its ills. Perhaps that is bizarre. People for the most part love life; they want to hang on to it as long as they can. But what would be the mental, the emotional, and the spiritual consequences of life without death? For while death casts a shadow it imposes upon life a seriousness, a solemnity, a discipline. It is the bell buoy that calls our attention to the depths and dangers of the sea.

For some people death is the end. They don't believe in existence after death. But for the majority death seems to demand explanations about what happens after. Some regard these explanations as real knowledge, others as hypotheses, for still others a low level hope that surfaces at moments of crisis.

The most familiar explanations in North and South America and in Western Europe are based on teachings in the Bible. But other societies have other explanations: India, China, Africa, Sri Lanka, Indian tribes and the Inuit in Canada. If we turn to the ancient world we find differences between the Greeks, the Egyptians, the Canaanites, the Mesopotamians. The diversity is so great, and the followers of one tradition so often positive they are right and the others wrong, that the skeptic may ask: Why accept any of them? Yet despite the differences, those who believe have this in common; they want to know what happens after death, not only because of fear or superstition, but because of the natural disposition which humans have to want to know. Our modern world is a consequence of that, so is the corpus of philosophy, growing all the time, so is every branch of human interest, including metaphysics and, as part of that, questions about death and what there might be after death.

Negative Views About Surviving Death

Concern with death is inseparably connected with concern about "surviving death." But what does "surviving death" mean? It is puzzling. Other than by faith, that often used phrase is obscure, even meaningless.

"To many contemporary philosophers it seems that claims to survive death must be described as nonsense statements, and that the philosopher's job is to lay bare their nonsensical character."[116] To a believer this could be regarded as an extreme statement, but it is not the only one. Peter Atkins is equally blunt.

> I believe, by showing that the characteristically human capacities which we lump together for convenience of discourse as 'human spirit' or 'soul' are no more than states of the brain, and likewise that extension of the idea of a soul to expectation of eternal persistence is already quite plainly explicable in terms of a deep-seated desire to

avoid, and the inability to come to terms with, the prospect of ones own annihilation.[117]

A.J. Ayer rejects all religious claims because it is not possible to find empirical justification, or even the possibility of empirical justification to support them "...the notion of a person whose essential attributes are non-empirical is not an intelligible notion at all."[118]

Elsewhere he writes "If a mystic admits that the object of his vision is something which cannot be described, then he must also admit that he is bound to talk nonsense when he describes it."[119]

Ayer and the others are on strong ground when they criticize religious claims generally or belief in continuing existence in particular. Despite much effort there is little, if any, proof of the kind ordinarily used in the world. Even to acknowledge this lack of proof is an important step, writes D.M. McKinnon, "toward curing oneself of the illusion that the stumbling speech of those who speak of immortality and survival (I except here the physical researchers) is expressive of an attempt to gain knowledge of fact without the discipline of experiment and reflective analysis."[120]

McKinnon is critical of the lack of empirical data and the illogicality of the arguments. "To put it very crudely, just what is it that is at stake for a person in this matter of immortality? What is it that is bothering him? Of course, you can show the queerness, the confusedness of the way in which the bother is expressing itself, when it does so by means of the traditional language of survival, and so on. You can discredit this means of expression by showing the logical confusions into which it plunges; but does that settle the perplexity, the issue in the mind of the bewildered person?"[121]

A.J. Ayer's claims about the importance of empirical verification have themselves been criticized. Not that they are simply wrong. (In most cases we determine if something is true or false or doubtful by checking the empirical data.) The fault of the verificationists was to assert that if a claim could not be verified empirically, or there was no way to determine how it might be verified empirically, the claim made no sense. It was nonsense. But that assertion is too hard. Meaningful claims can be made which do not meet the verificationists' criteria: claims about art, claims about music, claims about personal emotions such as love, claims about religion, and included in those, claims about continuing existence after death. Such claims may not be substantiated. For example, how can we substantiate that James McNeill Whistler painted finer portraits than John Singer Sargent or that Benjamin Britten is a greater composer than Aaron Copeland? A good deal of personal opinion is involved, even though those who make the judgments are knowledgeable in art and music. But such claims are not nonsense. Similarly, the claim made by Richard Swinburne "The soul is the essential part of me and it is in its continuing in existence which makes for the continuing of me."[122] What empirical proof could be brought to support such a statement? Yet it is not nonsense, as Swinburne's extensive writings on the topic of religious faith show clearly.

What Do We Mean By 'Spirit' 'Soul' 'Heaven' 'Survival'?

Nevertheless, McKinnon's objection to claims about continued existence that they are illogical or logically confused, are not as easily turned. Consider one example he uses in this article. We talk about the soul, or spirit surviving the body. I have been to many funerals where the minister spoke about the soul of the dead person, now freed from his/her illness, or other human impediments, and able to enjoy the fullness of heavenly existence in the presence of God. The congregation can picture the dead person possessed now of health and beauty, engaged in heavenly activity in the company of those who had "gone before." I remember one funeral service for two young men, good friends, who had been fooling around on the lake in high powered boats--at night--trying to come as close as they could to a collision but to just miss one another. Unfortunately, they got too close and collided. The two boats went down with the two young men. It was a difficult funeral, but in his homily the minister said that the two were now in heaven, no doubt stirring it up quite a bit with their high spirits. The congregation laughed but, of course, no one asked him to explain the logical difficulties in what he said. Yet, even for a believer there are some.

As in the case of the two boys, or young men, actually teenagers, their parents, their family, their friends were thinking of them in heaven as they were on earth. A man who has lost his wife and believes that she still exists in a spiritual realm will think of her as she was, her face, her hair, her build, even the kind of clothes she wears, all those characteristics of her bodily existence. But her body, her physical self is either in a grave or has been cremated. So what is it that is in the heavenly realm?

In his letter to the Christian community in Corinth the Apostle Paul attempted an answer.

> But, you may ask, how are the dead raised? In what kind of body? A senseless question! The seed you sow does not come to life unless it has first died; and what you sow is not the body that shall be, but a naked grain, perhaps of wheat, or of some other kind; and God clothes it with the body of his choice, each seed with its own particular body. All flesh is not the same flesh: there is flesh of men, flesh of beasts, of birds, and of fishes--all different. There are heavenly bodies and earthly bodies; and the splendor of the heavenly body is one thing, the splendor of the earthly, another. The sun has a splendor of its own, the moon another splendor, and the stars another, for star differs from star in brightness. So it is with the resurrection of the dead. What is sown in the earth as a perishable thing is raised imperishable. Sown in humiliation, it is raised in glory; sown in weakness, it is raised in power; sown as an animal body, it is raised as a spiritual body. (I Corinthians 15: 35-44 NEB)

As there are different kinds of body on earth, fish, birds, animals, men, so there are different kinds of body in the larger realm, the material and the spiritual. But what Paul has done is to define something by a term which itself needs defining. If we are quite sure that we know what a spiritual body is our question is answered. The word which Paul uses here in Greek for body, in the term 'spiritual body', soma, is used by him, elsewhere, to indicate a physical thing subject to death (Romans 7.24). Yet in Romans 12.5, he writes of the church as the body of Christ. In this instance he is using the term, soma, metaphorically. Body for Paul can therefore be spiritual, physical, or not a 'body' at all. It means that 'spiritual body' is more of an evocative term than a descriptive term. If the two teenagers now have spiritual bodies the most we can say for certain is that they have an identifiable presence of some kind. Whether or not it is like their human presence we don't know, so we have to decide for ourselves whether the metaphor represents what actually is the case or whether it represents the closest we can get in our imagination, formed by our earthly experience, to what might be the case. As McKinnon would ask, "What exactly are we talking about?" when we refer to a person's spirit?

Another problem of comprehension, or of language, is that we talk quite readily about a person's soul (or spirit), but what do we mean by that? Descartes believed that a human consisted of two parts: a spiritual and a physical linked to one another through the pineal gland. In that way the spirit which is not physical can affect the body which is. Similarly, the body can affect the soul. This doctrine, known as dualism, meaning that a human consists of two parts, the physical, which concludes its existence on this earth, and the spiritual, which continues to exist after the body had died. But where is the spirit in the living body? Again we speak figuratively, "He is in high spirits," "His spirits are low today," "He gave a spirited talk." We refer to the "human spirit." But no one has ever found traces of a distinct entity--a spirit--in a body.[123]

Another problem is the location of the spiritual realm, heaven, or whatever it may be called. If the two teenagers now in heaven are stirring it up, where is it? The minister's comment indicates a place. Despite extensive exploration of outer space no trace of it has been found, (not surprising, considering the huge size of the universe). But is it even in the universe? The universe had a beginning; it appears likely to be moving toward a physical end. Heaven is not physical, it is eternal. Is it therefore outside the physical universe? That is hard to answer. The universe is everything. What can be outside of everything?

Beyond trying to imagine where heaven might be is the difficulty of trying to imagine in any realistic way what heaven could be like. The popular image of harps and celestial architecture is as false, if we think about it, as the picture of retirement of an elderly couple sitting on the balcony of a luxury condominium, drinking martinis, looking at a beautiful sea. That would last a week, or a month. Well, there's television, the local movie house, bridge clubs, and beauty parlor, all of which are thin fare, if the only fare, for life. Life must either be used in constructive ways (even by the elderly as long as they have their faculties) or it will deconstruct. The same applies to heaven where the problem is intensified. There, it is forever. Karl Rahner makes a sensible suggestion. Explaining that death brings man a kind of finality he adds that this statement "excludes neither man's further development after death, nor suggests a lifeless concept of the future life with God."[124]

I know of a woman who lost her baby daughter two or three days after she was born. I met the mother many years later who told me wistfully that that week, if she had lived, her daughter would be 21 years old. I mentioned to her this passage from Rahner. She found it helpful. It gave her the hope to believe that her daughter would not be eternally a two-day-old baby, but now was a young woman, though a spirit. Surely a wonderfully comforting thought, yet one that is scarcely open to empirical or logical examination.

Does "eternal" mean, going on and on without stop? That explanation reflects our linear thinking: an unending passage of time. Yet eternity is outside time. It belongs to a different realm of understanding. Because we have never experienced it, eternity is beyond our comprehension except in time related terms that are inconsistent with a non-temporal entity.

These are some of the considerations we face when we use words like spirit, soul, heaven, and eternal life, not glibly as McKinnon charges, but often without thought. We assume that our faith-based understanding is equivalent to understanding.

Not Difficult To Be Critical Of Religious Claims

Reviewing these arguments I'm of the opinion that it is not difficult to be critical of religious claims. Religious claims are generally not made on the basis of logic, more likely they are statements of faith. Evidence is often lacking, or is second hand, or rests on assumptions. I remember years ago hearing a speaker who outlined the empirical basis for the claim that Christ rose from the dead. The scriptures relate how he was seen and heard by one person (John 20.15) two people (Matthew 28.1 and Luke 24.13) and a number of people. (Acts 1:1-9) He even ate and swallowed food (John 21:12-13) I was impressed, and so were others in the audience. It was a convincing argument providing that one accepted the historical reliability of the scriptures. It would not be difficult for a historically minded critic to attack the whole argument on that basis. But I wonder often what might be accomplished by doing that.

Just as in our discussion about the problem of evil I pointed to a gap between philosophical arguments and how people actually deal with tragedy, so here too, a gap exists in our discussion of eternal life. The philosophers claim that the problem of evil is the major impediment to belief, but it isn't. We could argue that the empirical inadequacy and illogicality of claims about eternal life show convincingly that claims about soul and immortality are nonsensical. But they don't. I wonder then whether, while reason and evidence are important, reaching conclusions about religious claims on the basis of reason and evidence alone is not premature. As I mentioned earlier, a great deal in life lacks evidence and traditional rational support, yet is not inconsequential, not trivial, not to be rejected as unworthy of a mature mind. If that is so what do we do? Is it possible to look for explanations which are not illogical but are grounded on a base from which logical understanding, at least on this issue, develops? Might it be what Sri Aurabindo calls "the fundamental truth of existence,"[125] or that knowledge of the truth which Plato sought?

At the funeral service for John F. Kennedy Jr., killed with his wife and her sister in a tragic but needless plane accident, his uncle, Senator Ted Kennedy, gave the eulogy. In closing he said this "We pray that John, Carolyn and Lauren will find eternal rest, and that God's perpetual light will shine on them." In the face of such instinctive hope philosophical objections fall to the ground, except that separate from personal grief, it is surely proper to ask such questions.

African Understanding Of Death

African religion is not of one kind, anymore than Western religion is of one kind, even Western Protestantism. But granting that, some general statements can be made. "Africans," writes Steve Biko, "are a deeply religious race." They believe in God, however understood, and they believe that God is "always in communication with us."[126]

In these respects African views about religion and Western views are similar. Yet there are differences. The Judaeo Christian tradition thinks of a person's soul or spirit leaving the body at death and traveling to "another shore," as an Anglican prayer puts it. The dead person is the "departed" and except for visions and for spiritualistic phenomenon all that remains, though often strong, is a memory. In African religion the dead are departed but they play an active role in life. "What is of importance here is not the afterlife itself but the way in which the dead continue to be involved in this life among the living."[127] Benjamin Ray explains "There is little speculation about "last things"--that is about the nature of the afterlife or about immortality or final judgment--for there are no "last things" towards which human life is headed...Thus, the afterlife and the notion of personal immortality have meaning only in concrete terms in relation to the present life of the community"[128]

In African religion a death creates a "moral and social gap" which must be closed by means of ritual and social adjustments. These are for the benefit, both of the remaining family and of the dead person to enable him/her to find a secure place in the spiritual community.

Among the Ndebele, immediately after death a brother digs a grave in uncultivated ground. The corpse is taken out of the house through a hole in the wall. It must not be carried out through the door of the house. "This probably symbolizes," explains John Mbiti, "the belief that the deceased person has not 'gone away' from, or completely left the homestead; he is in effect still present."[129]

The role of spirits and what is known as the living-dead is important in Africa. They represent a realm of being separate from God intimately related to the living community. Mbiti uses two Swahili words "Sasa" and "Zamani" to represent the two stages of human existence. Sasa is "now", as it is lived month-by-month and year-by-year on earth. As a person gets older he approaches the end of his Sasa period and moves toward the Zamani. The two overlap even when a person has died, for the surviving friends and relatives remember him and so in a sense keep him alive. When the last person who knew him on earth dies he is no longer in the Sasa period and enters the Zamani period. He becomes completely dead.[130] The idea is credited to the Africans but it is common everywhere. I had an elderly relative who died just short of her hundredth birthday. She would often tell me stories of her girlhood, in particular about a great aunt whom my relative remembered as irrepressibly vivacious. This lady was born about 1830; my elderly relative died in 1990. She was the last of those who knew the aunt. Now there are a few like me who remember her by hearsay, eventually none will be left, and she will be absolutely dead.

The open way in which Africans recognize the fact of death, the rupture it causes and the need to engage in specific rituals to accept it and adjust to it, are psychologically healthier than some of the self conscious evasions practiced in North America. Medical technology has created an assumption that doctors are supposed to save people and keep them alive, and if that does not happen something must have gone wrong. This attitude is curiously like the view among primitive people that death is never natural, that it is caused, generally, by someone's evil intentions.

Very Ancient Views About Death

Recent studies have revealed an awareness of the significances of death and the need to deal with it and its aftermath as early as eleven thousand years ago. In the ancient settlement of Abu Hureyra, near the Euphrates river in Syria, bodies were taken to a charnel house and leftthere until the flesh had rotted. The skeleton was then buried (a second burial) not infrequently with beads and other goods. The archeologists' account (2000) quotes form an earlier work (1907) as representing their own conclusions about the views of this very ancient people, that the death of a human, even then, was "more than just a biological event," that secondary burial "presupposes a belief in soul and in an afterlife."[131] How valid such a belief was is a continuing questions, but it seems we have to go a long way back before we find humans who had no ideology of death

Empirical Data

One criticism of claims about a future life is the lack of empirical data, yet there is data of a kind if one is willing to accept it. What we call "ghost stories" are common in Africa, not uncommon in England, and quite uncommon in the US, which suggests that they thrive within a context of belief. The familiar claim of spiritualists, (familiar in England,) "life after death proved" probably does not "prove" much because those who give it their attention are already inclined to believe. Some stories appear to be current across societies. Mbiti tells of a group of men collecting honey in the forest who heard the sound of cattle and sheep being driven towards them by shepherds and herdsmen. But there was nothing there. The men left their honey and fled.[132]

A few years ago at a dinner in Winchester, England, a builder told us about how people at a certain place would hear the sound of Roman soldiers marching, their cries, the tramp of the feet, the noise of their equipment. Winchester was once an important Roman city. The builder had been engaged to do some construction. He dug into the ground several feet and discovered the remains of a Roman road. No one knew that it was there, but it was exactly where, allegedly, the Roman soldiers could be heard.

Another story told by Mbiti is about a man who, before he died, told his wife not to sell a plot of land he owned. But she did. The new owner built a house and then complained that he and his family were attacked by invisible clubs and stones. Finally he left, sold the property back to the wife who moved in and the spiritual harassment stopped.[133] On one occasion I was traveling through Kingston, just outside London. As we passed a church my companion remarked casually that the diocese couldn't get any one to stay in the parsonage, next to the church, because furniture is thrown about, curtains torn down, the people in the house are disturbed and sometimes hit by a poltergeist. My informant described this to me as if it were quite ordinary.

The Society for Psychic Research has attempted to apply empirical criteria to such stories. One which stands up to examination most successfully is that of an RAF pilot, shortly after the First World War, who had just landed and visited his friend on the air base to tell him about his flight. They had a brief conversation and he left. The friend then learned that shortly before the pilot spoke to him his plane had crashed, and he was killed.[134]

Whom did he talk to? Why would he imagine it was his friend? Was this imagination after the fact? We have a right to be skeptical. But if we conclude in advance that the story is untrue we are not skeptical but biased. How should I take the experience told to me by a colleague, who is a Presbyterian minister now retired, who lost his wife shortly before? He told me that he had seen his dead wife twice. Should I put it down to an understandable grief and the manner in which we can at times imagine as real what we very much want to be real. He has a Ph.D. in psychology, which suggests that he knows how the mind can play tricks on itself. I was biased in favor of wanting to believe his story. My own wife had died a year before. I felt envious that he saw his wife twice. I had not seen my wife once. Are such visions given only to certain people? How does one qualify? Or am I too skeptical, analytical, and dubious even though with another part of my thinking I am ready to believe? Does wanting something a lot not mean that the imagination will make one believe it has happened? Would this suggest that my friend's seeing his wife could be an actual occurrence: he did not imagine he saw her, he saw her?

A Spiritual Imagination?

Animals do not reflect upon death and what might follow after death. Why do humans? Among those arguments for the existence of something which cannot be fully explained in terms of its physical origins alone is the spiritual imagination, and the distinction that we draw between imagination in its fictional sense and imagination which carries with it a conviction of truth.

As Emily Dickinson put it in one of her poems:

Each Life converges to some Centre--
Expressed--or still
Exists in every Human Nature
A Goal--

And she concludes:

> Ungained--it maybe--by a Life's low Venture--
> But then
> Eternity enable the endeavoring
> Again.[135]

Perhaps the Centre is not more than our desire to discern what is a deep puzzle to us, and so our imagination constructs hypotheses, some of which are fantastic, but some of which seem to provide an explanation and so encourage our beliefs. At the same time, with the same mind we ask how realistically do these explanations merit belief? The gift of humanity is its ability to think about its own condition, but it is a gift that can be a burden. Perhaps anything to do with faith is a contradiction. It is both about what is always just outside our comprehension, and it is deep within what most of us feel compelled to hope for.

The issue of death brings out these contradictions as sharply as possible. They are felt most keenly not only because death concerns our own existence but it concerns our living relationship with those we love. At the conclusion of a funeral I conducted for a woman whom I had known, her daughter came to me and asked, "Is that it? Is it all over? Is mum gone?" Once a man admitted to me that when he prayed he prayed to his recently dead wife rather than to God. Given his denominational background, certainly it was unorthodox, but he knew her, he could visualize her. He felt confident that were there a heaven or any such place she would be there, she would listen to him and try to help him, the very characteristics described of God in Exodus 3.

Karl Rahner states plainly, "There is no eternal return of all things; there is only a history, given once and for all. There is no migration of souls which would make but a provisional effort of this life, open to complete revision at a later date, which in turn, for better or worse, might be repeated."[136]

In India one finds quite a different belief. "The Hindu holds that the goal of spiritual perfection is the crown of a long patient effort. Man grows by countless lives into his divine self-existence. Every life, every act, is a step which we may take either backward or forward. By one's thought, will and action one determines what one is yet to be."[137]

The sharpness of separation at death is therefore muted in the Hindu tradition although I doubt whether husband or wife, parents or children feel much less pain. In the Bhagavad-Gita we read

> You have spent your sorrow on beings who do not need it
> and pay lip-service to wisdom.
> Educated men do not sorrow
> for the dead nor the living...
>
> Just as a person changes from
> childhood to youth to old age in the body,
> He changes bodies.
> This does not upset the composed man.
>
> He is never born.
> He never dies.
> You cannot say of him
> He came to be
> And will be no more.
> Primeval, he is
> Unborn,
> Changeless
> Everlasting.
> The body will be slain,
> But he will not.[138]

Like the Stoic Epictetus, who taught in his Manual that we should simply accept the fact that those we love are mortal, and not be troubled when they die, death is something over which we have no control. His advice to us is, not to be disturbed by it, a hard teaching to follow in actual experience.

Resurrection, the After Life: What Sense Do They Make?

Earlier in this chapter we addressed some of the logical problems connected with claims about life after death. For example, we talk about an immaterial soul yet think of it in material terms. We refer to heaven as if it were a place, yet place implies physical extension, boundaries, location, contrary to what we know or think we know. If we believe in resurrection what is it that is resurrected? The British artist Stanley Spencer painted a number of imaginative pictures of the general resurrection, which showed people climbing out of their graves in English country churchyards. Their bodies look the same as when they were alive wearing the same clothes. But that is not possible, their bodies would have decayed, their clothes perished. What are climbing out? Spiritual bodies? St. Paul's description doesn't help. What is a spiritual body?

In his introduction to a volume of readings entitled *Immortality*, Paul Edwards provides a comprehensive but concise account of the numerous theories attempted to explain continuing life.[139] There are several of them: reincarnation, resurrection, astral bodies, epiphenomenalism and so on. (Richard Taylor provides a shorter account in his *Metaphysics* with a set of clever drawings to illustrate them.)[140] Edwards goes on further to discuss spiritualism, near death experiences, and metaphysical arguments. He does so objectively yet with a slight touch of satire at various points. One might suppose, if God really exists he/she won't object to a little academic humor at his/her expense (or perhaps His/Her expense).

The conclusion is that no attempt to provide an explanation of immortality is without logical flaws. If one's mind is not already determined ahead of time, they are an obstacle to belief. Upon reflection the position of Epicurus may be a sound one: We have one life, at death we are gone. Let us make the most of it, use it constructively, and cultivate friends. "I bequeath myself to the dirt," wrote Walt Whitman, "to grow from the city I love." (New York) "If you look for me, look under your foot soles." Is that not a grand enough conclusion to an earthly life? The alternative, (belief in life after death and belief in gods) according to Epicurus is not only delusive it is self-destructive. People burden their lives with unreal and thereby unnecessary fears. To continue with such beliefs is irrational.

Is There Another View?

I find the argument appealing. Yet another part of my mind cautions me not simply to dismiss the huge number of people over a great stretch of history, including many in the present time, for whom belief in some kind of continued existence after death is not irrational, is not thought of as a delusion, is not regarded as self destructive, but is regarded with seriousness and with various levels of belief.

William James and Alexis DeTocqueville wrote about the tyranny of the majority, when large numbers of people believe something and it becomes the truth for everyone. The dissenting minority is at a disadvantage against the majority.

But as both James and DeTocqueville argued, because most people believe something that does not mean what they believe is true. Darwin had a problem, after the publication of his *Origin of Species*, not only with theologians but also with respected fellow scientists who, on the basis of their training and practice, could not accept his theory of evolution. In the twelfth century the dominant view was belief in God and in an after life. Those who challenged it were dealt with harshly. In the twenty-first century a dominant view if not the dominant view is belief in science, along with much skepticism about an after life.

But acknowledging this, can we take the risk that, if there is some element of life not explainable in empirical ways, it may make itself known through an intuitive conviction? When the conviction is widespread can we claim for it at least an element of truth?

Young Jim in Willa Cather's novel, *My Ántonia*, has lain down on the warm earth in the late summer's afternoon of a summer's day. He watches some little red bugs crawl around him. He keeps as still as he can.

Nothing happened. I did not expect anything to happen. I was something that lay under the sun and felt it, like the pumpkins, and I did not want to be anything more. I was entirely happy. Perhaps we feel like that when we die and become of part of something entire, whether it is sun and air, or goodness and knowledge. At any rate, that is happiness; to be dissolved into something complete and great. When it comes to one, it comes as naturally as sleep.[141]

Let us ask some questions. Humans want to survive. Yes. But why? They have an instinct for survival. What does that mean? They want to survive as naturally as they blink their eyes when something gets too close. But again, why is this? It is part of the instinctual, psychological makeup of human beings. Animals have that instinct too, yet they don't reflect on it as we are doing now. Unlike animals, we not only want to survive, we consider why we want to survive, and how, and in so reflecting reach a point at which survival becomes symbolic of other concerns perhaps as important. Thought about survival moves us to thought about our existence, and within that framework of ideas we encounter issues about God, and immortality, and meaning, and worthwhileness and purpose. Survival becomes associated with all of these issues to such an extent that, while they are not dependent upon it, they are informed and vivified by it. So to dismiss concerns about survival from our thinking, as Epicurus urged we do, is not to remove a delusion, (its not as clear as that,) or to rid our life of self destructiveness (it may not be self destructive), but to reject a concept which provides some explanation of matters of importance in life. How it provides an explanation is not necessarily clear even when we are endeavoring to use it as an explanation, as if in doing a calculation to reach an answer we had to create a method of calculation as we went along.

Where we come to is the edge of our understanding, to the edge perhaps of any possible understanding, although we could have used traditional intellectual methods to get there.

My conclusion is that when an issue is of exceeding importance to us, when we have exhausted all obviously rational means of finding an answer, we don't subside into frustration or intellectual or emotional apathy. Instead we make use of what means may yet be available to us, and if those means are intuitive, figurative, perhaps revelatory we don't reject them on those grounds. We use them to whatever extent we can, and then perhaps combined with that enterprise the ordinary processes of rationality. If St. Paul wrote, "by all means win some" that is, in all ways attempt to convert people to Christ, then by all means let us strive for understanding when the understanding we strive for is integral to our lives, even though the skeptic (an unkind skeptic) may charge us with attempting to cover our intellectual nakedness with only rags of rationality.

Chapter 7

Miracles

A Philosophical Puzzle

Several philosophical puzzles are associated with the topic of miracles, but the most puzzling is why people are attracted to them. Attracted, enamored, deceived, fooled? What persuades them? In the great temple of Sarapis, in the ancient city of Alexandria, worshippers who entered were greeted with a fanfare of trumpets, sounding of their own accord, the altar fire miraculously bursting into flames, an image of the god moving forward to welcome his visitors. These and other remarkable events assured those who saw them that Sarapis was a great god indeed. None of the worshippers seemed to know that what they saw and heard was the work of three clever engineers, Ctesibius, Philo of Byzantium and Hero, who produced these effects by an ingenious use of hot air, lodestones, and invisible wires.[142] Those were ancient people, we might say, what more can we expect? In fact, a lot more. Archimedes, one of the greatest of mathematicians, lived during that period. Eratosthenes, who determined the circumference of the earth and came close to a correct answer, Aristarchus of Samos who, two thousand years before Copernicus, proposed that the earth revolves around the sun, and the poet and librarian, Callimachus, who devised the first library catalogue, were active at this time. On the one hand huge numbers of people irrationally committed to astrology, easily susceptible to fake miracles, on the other, high levels of scientific, literary, artistic, dramatic and philosophic achievement.

What we are saying about this distant period we could say of our own. *The New York Times* reported that a committee had been established to expose fraudulent paranormal phenomena. It would use scientific techniques to debunk miracles. But three years later, whatever the committee's scientific techniques may have accomplished, people still believe in miracles. A report in the *San Francisco Examiner* "Priests' hands credited with miracles" describes the healing power of a Roman Catholic priest. "One day this month, more than 1000 penitents jammed a small San Francisco church to attend his most recent healing service."[143]

A Question for Philosophy or Psychology?

Before we try to discuss the topic of miracles philosophically, the question to deal with is the one we asked at the beginning of this chapter. Why are people, not only in ancient times but also in our own, so attracted to them? Perhaps the question is psychological rather than philosophical, and has more to do with how and why people think than what they think. But the philosopher is interested. Are we dealing with an innate tendency or with acquired habits? Is the attraction that people have to the mysterious and the miraculous the result of fear of what is unknown, together with the contrary yet irresistible impulse to know what it is? Is it as natural a part of our humanity as gravity is of the earth, and inclines us to believe what ordinarily is impossible? Or are we taught to believe in the magical and the miraculous, not perhaps deliberately but by our culture and the belief of those we know who accept them? These questions precede philosophical discussion as similar questions precede philosophical reflections on the problem of evil. People go about their lives after a disaster despite logic, despite philosophical considerations, as if they were drawing from a deeper level of awareness than philosophy.

In the case of miracles, as with the problem of evil, the philosopher has two tasks. One is with the set of philosophical difficulties as generally discussed by philosophers working with the subject. The other is the task of relating an intuitive and inarticulate awareness to a process of disciplined thought. For those who have it such awareness is not learned, it is a gift of life. It is so powerful it may make the process of thought appear irrelevant. Who considers premises and logical arguments when moved by the power of God?

Yet for the believer, the intellect is a gift of God. It was given to be used, and because each of us is a whole person it is meant to be related to other aspects of our life, not separate from them. We are emotional, we are intellectual, we are intuitive and we are rational. To live life in a satisfactory fashion, to live it, if we are believers, in a manner that is pleasing to God, we must find a way to be both emotional and intellectual, intuitive and rational.

These considerations might encourage us to be more charitable when trying to account for what we regard as the gullibility of those who lived in the Hellenistic age, and those who live now. The yearning desire in those days for ataraxia, or peace of mind, is not unknown in the twenty-first century, particularly in less secure parts of the earth, but even in Western Europe and North America. Imagination is a product of intelligence, and the gullibility that arises from our yearning is the product of our finitude. Our trust, so often betrayed, is the product of hope in what seems to meet the need that cannot be met, we think, in any other way.

Few People Who Don't At Some Point Hope for A Miracle

No doubt there are those who have never, at any point, wished for a miracle. But the experiences of life are such that few are untouched by the temptation to want something to happen somehow against all rational, empirical probability, to want a miracle that will transform sorrow into joy, or just ameliorate the sorrow. When we are young miracles don't seem impossible. When we are very young we don't distinguish between the miraculous we wish for and the reality we have to deal with. Often, perhaps mostly, we get over that. We become sensible, until life turns on us and crushes the certainties we had depended upon.

So we go to the Sarapeum and draw confidence in the power of God to help us when doors open mysteriously and an altar fire bursts into flames, or when, in answer to the Gallup Poll interviewer, we say yes, we believe in miracles, and listen expectantly to the next miracle report we hear.

Two Further Questions

Apart from the question of what is a miracle, as discussed by Hume, further questions arise. If we believe in miracles at all, but are denied one in a moment of need, yet miracles appear to be available to others, we ask, "Why them?" It's the same kind of question asked about Christ's miracles of healing: why *that* blind man, or was it chance? But what is our moral estimate of a God who deals with human suffering by chance? We pray in faith, yet our prayers are not answered. Why? Shouldn't we be given some reason, or are we, though God's children, like employees of a nineteenth century factory, whose owner can fire us at will without explanation?

The anterior question about miracles, their reason, their arbitrariness, hang like a cloud before we begin to discuss them philosophically. Yet philosophical questions are not unimportant, and so to them we turn.

"Miracle" Often Used Casually

The word miracle is often used casually, perhaps carelessly. "It's a miracle she passed her exam." She hadn't studied until the last moment. "It's a miracle he didn't get a speeding ticket." He drove a four-hour trip in three hours. The word, so used, means no more than very unusual, unexpected, and surprising.

Yet Miracles Are Generally Thought Of In Connection With Divine Power

But when people are asked "Do you believe in miracles?" one of the regular questions asked by the Gallup Poll, and a great number say 'yes,' they are thinking of something more specific, as if they were answering the question: "Do you believe that God – or some divine power – works miracles?"

If the persons do not have anything from their own experience to draw upon they might refer to what they had heard, perhaps about healing at Lourdes. Some years ago I was traveling on a train in France which was bound for Lourdes, though that was not my destination. There were many obviously sick and handicapped passengers, and many of them were excited about their pilgrimage and the possibility of being healed. It is estimated that a million pilgrims travel to Lourdes each year. A medical and ecclesiastical commission investigates cases of healing. Not many are authenticated, but some are, so that some pilgrims allegedly are cured. I think it is that sort of thing people have in mind when asked about miracles. If they were Christian scientists or knew about Christian Science they might be acquainted with the many examples of miraculous cures described at the back of *Science and Health with Key to the Scriptures*.

But mostly, in the United States, people would think of incidents from the New Testament, of Christ turning water into wine (anticipated by Hero and his colleagues in the Sarapeum), or Christ's healing a blind man (John 9), or raising Lazarus from the dead (John 11).

Miracles As Violations Of The Laws Of Nature

What characterizes these incidents is that ordinarily they could not happen. Water cannot suddenly change into wine. Wine is fruit juice which requires time to ferment. Similarly, dead people cannot be brought back to life. They stay dead. To claim that water is suddenly changed to wine or that a dead man is brought back is to claim that the laws of nature, substantiated countless of times, have been violated. This is the view of David Hume.

In his book *An Inquiry Concerning Human Understanding*, Hume wrote, "A miracle is a violation of a law of nature; and as a firm and unalterable experience has established these laws, the proof against a miracle, from the very nature of the fact, is as entire as any argument from experience can possibly be imagined."[144]

J.L. Mackie made the further point that if a miracle is a violation of a law of nature it is "maximally improbable."[145] Miracles, he concedes, may be possible, but the likelihood is remote. Usually a miracle claim can be explained by "the familiar psychological processes of a wish fulfillment."[146] The evidence against a miracle happening is much stronger than the evidence for it happening. "A wise man," wrote Hume, "proportions his beliefs to the evidence." His conclusion is that "In the case of miracles evidence against their happening is very much stronger than evidence for their happening." He provides a now famous norm. "That no testimony is sufficient to establish a miracle, unless the testimony be of such a kind that its falsehood would be more miraculous, than the fact, which it wishes to establish."[147] Not raising Lazarus from the dead would be more miraculous than raising him.

How many people would be convinced by that? "The trouble with miracles," wrote Matthew Arnold, "is that they never happen."[148]

Yet Those Who Believe Are Not Without Recourse

Yet those who believe in miracles are not without recourse. Augustine argued that miracles are not contrary to nature; a great many things that occur in nature are miraculous to us because we do not understand them. Even the skeptic does not claim that they are unbelievable. Why then should the skeptic declare that divine miracles are unbelievable when it is simply that they are beyond understanding?[149] Aquinas elaborated upon this. The order imposed on things by God "is based on what usually occurs *in most cases*, in things, but not on what is always so... divine power can sometimes produce an effect, without prejudice to its providence, apart from the order implanted in natural things by God."[150] God who created all things has the power to bring about unanticipated changes (unanticipated by humans) in what he created.

A violation of a law of nature, it is argued, would have to be a non-repeatable instance. If it could be repeated it would likely not be a violation but a further understanding of the law. Yet that may not always be the case. The law of gravitation is that a force, gravity, pulls objects in certain directions. If I drop something it falls to the ground. When I pick it up I have, in a sense, violated a law of nature. I have gone against the law of gravity. But I have not disrupted that law, even though I pick objects from the floor frequently. When I lift my feet to walk I violate a law of nature. I have the power to pick something up from the floor and to lift my feet. I don't have the power to raise the dead or to turn water into wine. But if I had that power I could use it just as, having the power to lift my feet, I lift my feet. Granting that power to God, which a believer could, it is not difficult to accept violations of the law of nature, such as we describe, as miracles.

The obvious criticism of this is that I am not violating the law of gravity by picking up something that has fallen. I am working within it. These examples are instances of the law, not violations of it. Yet the difficulty of any argument for miracles may direct our thinking to John Polkinghorne's approach (discussed later in this chapter) that the miraculous must be understood as a sign of a deeper or wider rationality underlying the whole rather than as a divine *tour de force*. We might use Polkinghorne's suggestion to construct an analogy. As the relation of an object falling and my picking it up is that of a wider, or deeper, gravitational reality that provides an explanation for two apparently contradictory forces, so the wider reality Polkinghorne refers to in connection with miracles could provide an explanation of the incompatibility of a law of nature and its violation. The problem here is that the law of gravitation is testable. It is something we have empirical knowledge of from within the physical universe. We have no such knowledge of a wider or a deeper reality. It is a metaphysical hypothesis. But does that mean it is unacceptable?

A Strong Argument Which Is Weak

A few years ago a letter was published in the *London Times* from fourteen scientists, some of them members of the Royal Society. It addressed the issue of science and belief in miracles.

From the President of the Linnaean Society and others

Sir, In view of the recent discussion about the views of bishops on miracles we wish to make the following comments.

It is not logically valid to use science as an argument against miracles. To believe that miracles cannot happen is a much an act of faith as to believe that they can happen.

We gladly accept the virgin birth, the Gospel miracles, and the resurrection of Christ as historical events. We know that we are representative of many other scientists who are also Christian standing in the historical tradition of the churches.

Miracles are unprecedented events. Whatever the current fashions in philosophy or the revelations of opinion polls may suggest, it is important to affirm that science (based as it is upon the observation of precedents) can have nothing to say on the subject. Its "laws" are only generalizations of our experience. Faith rests on other grounds.

Yours etc.
Sam Berry,
E.H. Andrews,
Martin H.P. Bott
R.L.F. Boyd,
Denis Burkitt,
Clifford Butler,
E. Roland Dobbs,

J.T. Hougton,
M.A. Jeeves,
J.B. Lloyd,
Colin A. Russell,
Douglas C. Spanner,
David Tyrell,
G. Barrie Wetherill,
As from: 4 Sackville, Sevenoaks,[151]

This letter proves that Hume was wrong in one point. He wrote, "it forms a strong presumption against all supernatural and miraculous relations, that they are observed chiefly to abound among ignorant and barbarous nations..."[152] The social context of these letter writers could hardly be described as either.

However, the letter makes a claim of some importance which may actually weaken the defense the letter writers intended. Science, it affirms, can have nothing to say on the subject (of miracles). "Its 'laws' are only generalizations of our experience. Faith rests on other grounds." An unassailable argument, but exceedingly weak. What are the grounds: various kinds of revelation, inward assurance, intuitive certainty? These are undoubtedly compelling for those who have them, but not necessarily for anyone else. We discussed this issue in connection with religious experience. I cannot deny that your experience is as you say you experienced it. Nor can I challenge your belief in miracles. You believe, that's up to you. I can, however, challenge the objective reality of what you claim from your experience. I can also challenge the reality of miracles without challenging the fact that you believe in them. The letter above is an expression of a point of view – perhaps it was not meant to be anything more – not a defense of the validity of miracles.

"A Much Wider Reality"

The topic of miracles has been given attention by the scientist whom we referred to. For many years John Polkinghorne was professor of mathematical physics at Cambridge University. Some years ago he and his wife discussed what God wanted him to do with the rest of his career. He decided to give up his teaching and enter the Anglican Ministry. Since then he has written numerous books discussing the relationship between science and religion. In his *Science and Creation*

Polkinghorne writes, "I am groping for an understanding which does justice both to what science can tell us about the world and also to our experience of a much wider reality than that which science could ever claim to explain."[153] This is a challenge to thoughtful persons on both sides of the believing divide. Polkinghorne is a Christian, familiar with the critical arguments. As a scientist he writes, "The quest for sufficient reason and a comprehensive understanding of the world drives the physicist to seek unified theories, which consolidate the forces of nature into a single grand scheme." But in his view: "Physics needs metaphysics for its intellectually satisfying completion."[154]

Fred Hoyle, who is not a theist, seems almost to support this. In the *Cal Tech Alumni Magazine,* he writes.

> Would you not say to yourself, "Some supercalculating intellect must have designed the properties of the carbon atom, otherwise the chance of my finding such an atom through the blind forces of nature would be utterly minuscule." Of course you would... A common sense interpretation of the facts suggests that a superintellect has monkeyed with physics, as well as with chemistry and biology, and that there are no blind forces worth speaking about in nature. The numbers one calculates from the facts seem to me so overwhelming as to put this conclusion almost beyond question.[155]

Science Stimulates Metaphysical Questions

Rather than eliminate metaphysical concerns, the immensity of scientific knowledge raises further questions about the nature of existence which cannot be answered within science itself. We live in a physical universe, we know a great deal about its origins. But we do not know why it is what it remarkably is, and why the apparently non-physical constituents of our existence: thought, emotion, imagination, and affection, play such a huge role in our otherwise physical lives. If we are willing to concede that this is not only a mystery, but also an intellectual, experiential challenge, we might be able to accept explanations of miracles as divine interventions. Polkinghorne takes this position.

> The scope of the creative activity of the 'potentialities and potencies of God' is not to be limited to the readily discernible regularities of common occurrence. Nothing I am saying denies the possibility that God's relationship with his creation exhibits particular aspects in

particular circumstances. What is conventionally called the miraculous is coherent within the picture here presented, provided it is understood – as surely theologically it must be understood – as a sign of a deeper rationality underlying the whole, rather than as a divine *tour de force* bearing an arbitrary relation to the rest of the world's process. The possibility of miracle is part of the openness of creation to its creator, who in his steadfast love is neither tyrannical nor cruel.[156]

Do Our Presupposition's Affect Our Conclusion?

We are discussing the definition of miracles as a violation of the law of nature. If a particular incident happens, water into wine instantly, we say that that is not possible from what we know about physical laws. Yet even with such an obvious case we need to remember, as Augustine reminded us, that there is much about nature we do not know, and our way of reading what happens in nature may be affected by the presuppositions we bring to it

Questioning The Distinction Between Miraculous and Non-miraculous

William Temple, an early twentieth century philosopher and theologian, who in his last years was Archbishop of Canterbury, questioned the distinction made between the miraculous and the non-miraculous, a distinction taken for granted in much discussion of the topic.

> If the Personal God thus indwells the world, and the world is thus rooted in Him, this involves that the process of the world is itself the medium of His personal action. It is commonly assumed by those who use freely the terms Immanence and Transcendence that God as immanent is unchangeably constant, while God as transcendent possesses a reserve of resource whereby He can from time to time modify the constant course sustained by His immanent action. This seems to be a mere reflection of the wholly unphilosophic dichotomy of events into normal and miraculous. The naïve religious view is that God made the world and imposed laws upon it, which it invariably observes unless He intervenes to modify the operation of His own laws.

Temple rejects this view. The dichotomy implies that God is bound by his own laws and cannot change them unless he breaks them. God is not bound in this way. Constancy in general is good, but a refusal to adapt, whatever the circumstances, is "mulish." In fact, God is flexible in the ordering of his laws.

> Our contention is that an element in every actual cause, and indeed the determinant element, is the active purpose of God fulfilling itself with that perfect constancy which calls for an infinite graduation of adjustments in the process. Where any adjustment is so considerable as to attract notice it is called a miracle; but it is not a specimen of a special class, it is an illustration of the general character of the World Process.[157]

In this way a miracle is not a violation of a law of nature. It is the result of God working with nature.

Miracles As Natural Events

John Macquarrie also questions the common understanding of miracles, which pits it against natural order. This traditional concept of miracle "is irreconcilable with our modern understanding of both science and history."[158] A true miracle is not a special *kind* of event but God's presence in the event. That cannot always be observed. He objects to the way in which a natural event, used by God as a miracle, is turned into a spectacular sign. This obscures and discredits the genuine miracle.

He uses the example of the crossing the Red Sea which is a spectacular event in Exodus but may well have been simply the Israelites crossing when the tide was low and with a strong favorable wind. When the Egyptians followed them their chariots stuck in the sand and mud, the waters returned, many Egyptians were drowned and the Israelites escaped. God was in this, so making it a miracle, without dramatic supernatural phenomena.

He explains that "some particular concrete events stand out in a special way in the experience of individuals or communities as vehicles of the divine action, and such events are miracles." He uses the notion of "focusing" as a useful idea for explaining miracles. "God's presence and activity are everywhere and always, yet we experience these intensely in particular concrete happenings, in which, as it were, they have been focused."[159]

Some Miracles Therefore Do Not Violate Laws Of Nature

Hume's definition of a miracle as an event which violates a law of nature does not apply to those alleged miracles which do not violate these laws. As Macquarrie interprets it, the crossing of the Red Sea would be an example. Winds and tides acted normally, but God used them for his purposes so, it is claimed, it was a miracle.

J.L. Mackie discusses an example from the Second World War. It does not violate natural law, yet it was regarded at the time as a notable miracle. After Hitler's rapid advance through Europe in 1940 the remnants of the British and French armies, about 300,000 troops, were forced into a small enclave on the French coast at Dunkirk. The situation was extremely grave for Britain. Churchill and his Chiefs of Staff thought that about 45,000 might be evacuated. But a combination of overcast skies, which hindered the activity of the Luftwaffe, and calm water, which enabled many small boats to cross the channel and pick up soldiers, enabled almost all the men to be evacuated. To many people in Britain it was a miracle. When it appeared that the men were trapped, King George VI called for a day of prayer; large numbers attended churches all over the country, even those whose faith was not particularly strong. It seemed that God had answered these prayers with an extraordinary miracle.

J.L. Mackie, however, considers that the overcast sky and the calm waters at that crucial time were no more than a meteorological coincidence.

> Even if we accepted theism," he writes, "and could plausibly assume that a benevolent deity would have favored the British rather than the Germans in 1940, this explanation (that it was a miracle) would still be far less probable than that which treats it as a mere meteorological coincidence... instances of this sort are utterly without force in the context of the fundamental debate about theism itself.[160]

Yet from the perspective of the theist, and what we now know about the truly evil nature of the Nazi regime, God had very good reasons to intervene and prevent the Nazis from achieving their goal of conquering the whole of Europe, including Britain.

R.F. Holland provides yet another example. A child is riding his toy motor car on a railway line near his home. A wheel of his car gets stuck in the line. He does not hear his mother calling him from a distance. He does not hear an approaching train. He cannot see the train because it is round a curve, and so the driver cannot see the child. It seems that the child will inevitably be run over and killed. But the brakes of the train are applied and the train stops a few feet away from the child. To the mother this is a miracle. What happened was that the driver of the train fainted, his hand fell from the control lever and the brakes were applied automatically.[161] Saving the child's life was purely a coincidence, as the weather conditions which favored the escape of the British and French troops at Dunkirk were a coincidence, according to Mackie.

But does that make either event less of a miracle? Is it not at least possible, from the point of view of faith, that God was behind these events? In the case of Dunkirk we know that the Nazis made a tactical error by deciding to destroy the troops from the air instead of launching a full-scale attack on the ground. Was that entirely their own doing? Could there have been some other influence at work?

Neither the believer nor the unbeliever can be proven right or wrong. According to the critic, the explanation of these miracles is coincidence. But to the believer, that coincidence is evidence of the hand of God. If we accept the interpretation it would enlarge the range of miracles. What about the person who at the last moment decided not to travel on the Titanic? I have a friend who was booked by his travel agent to return to the United State on one plane rather than another. The plane he was booked on was less convenient; the other plane was the one he ordinarily would have taken. But that plane was blown up in the air by a terrorist and all the passengers were killed. The other plane, the one my friend traveled on, arrived safely. Was that a miracle? The man's friends were inclined to think so. However, there were loyal friends and relatives of those who were killed, why did God not help them?

Miracles and Prayer

All of the miracles discussed so far, to the extent that they were truly miracles, with the exception of Dunkirk were enacted by the initiative of God. But people pray to God for help. You have not, states the scripture, because you ask not. (James 4:2) "Ask and you will receive, seek and you will find." (Matthew 7.7 RSV) The importunate widow was ignored by the judge until she insisted on his giving her attention. (Luke 18:1-7)

Why do we have to call upon God to get his attention? Why, being omniscient, does he not know what we need before we ask? The scripture says he does. "Your Father knows what you want before you ask him." (Matthew 6.8 RSV) Intercessory prayer therefore is unnecessary, or exhibits lack of faith. The chapter on the problem of evil suggested that people are much more on their own than believers imagine. So prayer for a miracle may not only have no influence with God but also be pointless. Perhaps it is not the consequence of prayer but the fact of prayer. Sometimes when we are in trouble just talking with a friend helps, apart from whether or not the friend can do anything more specific to help us. That may be the case with God. So we share our concerns without expecting special favors although we do hope for them (a miracle) on occasion.

Yet what is hard is that sometimes God's response appears to be arbitrary.

Why Is God Arbitrary?

When the legendary Japanese Emperor Sujin was troubled about the condition of his country he called upon the Kami, the indigenous gods of Japan, to find out what was wrong and how to put it right. After initial difficulties they told him. He did what he was told and peace and health were restored to the nation.[162] But the Judaeo Christian tradition is not as straightforward.

We cannot assume an answer however hard we pray. Too often the response is silence. Life goes on at its worst. To H.H. Farmer, a miracle, whenever it happens, is a revelation from God.[163] But such revelations are rare. If and when they are given it is to a person or persons in a particular time and place, and what is a miracle to one may not be to another. So even as we interpret the will of God 'theologically,' as Farmer puts it, our interpretation may be wrong. We may be having to invent an answer to support our belief in God against the disappointment of his failure to respond.

Yet to write in general terms about the sensitive and intricate relations between God and humans can be misleading. A person may regard an incident as not a miracle and as a miracle at the same time. We may reject with our mind yet grasp with our heart, and were we to explain to any but the most sympathetic our tale would be regarded as delusive, confused, perhaps even as a sign of mental illness.

Two Categories of Miracles

Miracles can be divided into two categories: those that people hear about and even see, and those they experience in ever to faint a way, particularly in moments of stress. The first category both calls for philosophical analysis, particular attention being given to evidence and coherence, and to the kind of superstitious wonder exhibited among the worshippers of Sarapis by what they saw.

The second category includes those experiences, most of which are not extraordinary, but may be so to those who have them, and as such will stir their lives deeply. Let me tell you a story about someone I know.

My friend's wife was dying of cancer. Because she had only a short time to live she was at home, no longer receiving hospital care. Her oncologist who treated her for over two years had relinquished her as a patient, but he said that he would like to stop by some time to see her. He had not yet done so. The cancer was such that it was difficult to breathe, even with oxygen, and there was phlegm, making it even more difficult. The fear which both she and her husband had was that she would choke to death.

One morning was particularly difficult; no one else was in the house. Her current doctor and her former oncologist were not reachable by phone. Both husband and wife believed in prayer. The wife said to her husband, "I want you to pray that my doctor (the oncologist) will come here as he said he would." The husband hesitated. His wife continued, "I don't want you to pray. 'If it be your will,' or anything like that. I want you to pray to God right out. 'Bring the doctor here, make the doctor come. I need him now.'" With some agony of mind the husband prayed out loud as his wife asked him. It was the most intense and anguishing prayer of his life. After he prayed he didn't say anything. He sat by her bed. She was quiet. A few minutes later the phone rang. It was the oncologist. "I was thinking about you," he said, "I have the time, would you like me to visit?" Of course. Whatever trials of faith the husband has had since, that incident remains as a clear shining light.

Miracles In Various Religious Traditions

Miracles can be found in many religious traditions. Both Islam[164] and Zoroastrianism[165] believe in the resurrection of the dead. As mentioned earlier, the Shinto Kami can answer prayer directly, in this instance, healing a disordered nation.[166] The worship of Isis and Osiris wrought many miracles of healing in the ancient world, so their adherents believed.[167]

In African Religion's and Philosophy

John Mbiti reports an incident, the results of which he claims to have seen.

> When I was a schoolboy a locust invasion came to my home area. An elderly man, who was a neighbor and relative of ours, burnt a 'medicine' in his field, to keep away the locusts. Within a few hours the locusts had eaten up virtually everything green including crops, trees and grass, and then flown off in their large swarms. Everybody was grieved and horrified by the great tragedy which had struck us, for locust invasions always mean that all the food is destroyed and people face famine. Word went round our community, however, that the locusts had not touched any crops in the field of our neighbor who had used 'medicine'. I went there to see it for myself, and sure enough his crops remained intact while those of other people next door were completely devastated. I had heard that a few people possessed anti-locust 'medicines', but this was the first person I knew who had actually used such medicine and with positive results.[168]

There are scholars from Africa and elsewhere who treat such stories, even when attested by an eyewitness, with deep suspicion. Schoolboys may see things yet misremember what they saw. Mbiti was a clergyman and a professor of theology and comparative religion by the time he wrote his book several years later. While not accusing him of deception, how far can his account be trusted? Yet is the extent of our mistrust the result of critical evaluation, or is it expressive of a disbelieving attitude toward anything that cannot be explained in normal empirical ways? The philosopher must put that question to himself. I regard it as a requirement of a philosopher of religion that the question at least be asked.

The Miraculous And Community Attitudes

The issue of miracles was not a problem in earlier days. It is not a problem in contemporary societies, such as in tribal Africa and in parts of Asia. In the western world miracles are a problem. We spend time asking whether the concept of miracle even makes sense. D.Z. Phillips notes in his book on prayer...

> In New Testament times, the question was not about the reality of miracles, but about whether specific miracles were of divine origin. No one disputed the fact that Jesus performed miracles; what they disputed was his claim that the miracles were signs of divinity.[169]

Why did people in those days not question the reality of miracles, but do now? Phillip's explanation is that *"the truth,* of a miracle is decided by the religious community... when a community has retained a belief in the miraculous, what a miracle means is self evident to that community."[170]

Many people claim to believe in miracles in the west, but one can no longer find an unambiguously widely shared belief in the miraculous. Even when allegedly found, they are generally questioned, puzzled over, inhibited. According to Phillips, for New Testament miracles to be accepted as miracles today there must have been "a continuing and abiding tradition of the miraculous in succeeding religious communities throughout the centuries. In very many traditions this has not been the case."[171]

Perhaps the widespread attention being given in the United States to religion and personal spirituality[172] is an attempt to revive that tradition, to give more attention than a technological society has allowed to what are perceived as essential spiritual values, and to the possibility of a normal, rather than a strange and rare, interaction between the human and the divine. That would include miracles, but surely not exclude continuing questions about them.

Chapter 8

Science and Religion

The Need For Modesty, Yet the Need to Understand

The non-scientist who writes on the topic of religion and science is wise to be modest, and to be careful not to imply more knowledge than he has. Yet it doesn't follow that the non-scientist should not express an opinion about science or its relation to religion. Non-scientists greatly exceed the number of scientists. They are part of that huge population to whom scientists address their findings. The world at large is affected by what scientists do. It is therefore important that the scientists and the general public engage in conversation, that non-scientists find out as much as they can about science, and, indeed, that scientists make themselves aware of the consequences of their activity beyond the scientific community.

The non-scientists, especially those who have religious interests or religious faith, will certainly wish, I would say should wish, to understand as best they can in what way science is of importance to understanding religion. Likewise scientists should try to understand how their work bears upon religious claims.

Two Objectives of This Chapter

The chapter will attempt, first, a description of scientific developments which appear to this writer to have a bearing upon what religious people believe. Second, it will attempt to reflect upon these developments.

The topic, science and religion, can be discussed in terms of itself, but even as we do so it cannot be confined to itself. Science relates to every aspect of our physical existence; religion, even for those who reject it, relates to every aspect of our metaphysical existence from which the physical cannot be excluded.

Religion and Science, Antagonists?

Religion and science are often thought of as antagonists. Andrew White's famous book, *A History of the Warfare of Science and Theology in Christendom*,[173] published in 1896, expresses a view, still widely held, that when a scientific development appears to contradict a religious claim the religious claim must be defended, often by declaring that the science is wrong. In the opinion of their time, Galileo and Copernicus could not be right because man is that being for whom all other things are created. He had to be central, and the earth, his home, had to be central also, distinct, pre-eminent, not spinning around with the other planets as if it were no better or different. Copernicus and Galileo therefore *had* to be wrong.

Similarly, during the nineteenth century, many in the religious community felt they must take a stand against Darwin. The Bible says that men and women were created in God's image. Darwin proposed that the existing forms of life on earth evolved from other, less developed forms. He did not claim that men and women descended from apes, but the blow to human self-esteem was unbearable.

Yet A.R. Peacocke reminds us that reaction to Darwin at the time in theological and ecclesiastical circles "Was much more positive and welcoming than the legends propagated by both popular and academic biological publications are prepared to admit."[174] Whereas the scientific reaction was much more negative than is now supposed. It is a reminder to be wary of stereotypes. John Polkinghorne, speaking of course for present attitudes, observes that "Science and theology have a fraternal relationship and are complementary, rather than antithetic, disciplines." Similarly, Ian Barbour, in his book *When Science Meets Religion*, writes "Some of the most creative work today involves collaboration between scientists and theologians in drawing from the ongoing experience of a religious community while taking seriously the discoveries of modern science." [175]

The reason behind this would appear to be straightforward. Science is an activity which endeavors to find out how things are. One scientist will reach one conclusion, another will reach a contrary conclusion. The objective is to find out which is right, or whether neither is right, or neither is wholly right, nor wholly wrong.

Religion similarly tries to find out how things are. It too reaches conclusions. To that extent the two approaches have "a fraternal relationship." But historically theologians have not been as open minded as scientists (although many scientists have been closed-minded). The truth theologians seek is a truth about existence. Those who think they have found it won't readily give it up. Yet theologians are now more open minded, at least in the Judaeo-Christian tradition. They could perhaps agree with a scientific point of view expressed by Howard J. Van Till.

> The goal of scientific theorizing is not to prove by appeal to empirical data and unassailable logic alone, one theory correct and all others false. Rather, the goal is to construct a theoretical account that is, in the context of all relevant empirical data at hand, and within the bounds of certain presuppositions regarding the character of the universe and its formational history, the most adequate account conceivable at a particular time. [176]

It may still be difficult for a believer to accept that as applying to his or her own religion. During the nineteenth century for a theologian to admit he was looking for "the most adequate" account of Christian truth could incur ostracism, banishment, or scorn. David Strauss, who held a teaching position at the Seminary of the State University of Württemberg, published his *Life of Jesus Critically Examined* in 1835. The reaction was so hostile it almost ended his career. F.D. Maurice was dismissed from King's College Cambridge in 1853 because he questioned the doctrine of eternal damnation. The Presbyterian minister William Robertson Smith was dismissed from his clerical office in 1881 because he had contributed an article to the Encyclopedia Britannica on the Bible in which he declared that the Bible contains the word of God, but is not literally word for word, the word of God. [177]

Since then the theological outlook has changed, though not entirely. A series of books entitled *New Theology* is representative of the experimentation which characterizes much theological thinking, or what we might now call post-theological thinking. In volume eight Robin Scroggs writes,

> We are thus in no secure place. We have found no single authoritative standard from the past of what to say or how to live. Neither have we a secure self-understanding erected on the basis of our immediate experience. We in fact find ourselves in the abyss of a continual uncertainty, but we are kept from falling into chaos by the very tension between past and present. Our specific spot over the abyss is the result of our own individual dialogue. We have no assurance that where we happen to be is the best or final place to stand. And this means that the dialogue is never done, nor dare we get so rooted in any one place that we become complacent or fearful of moving.[178]

Here indeed scientist and theologian share common ground.

What caused this change in theological thinking? No one instance, but several factors reinforcing one another. Important yet difficult to identify in specific ways is a new cast of critical thinking present most obviously in the Western world which challenges authority. Since Viet Nam and Watergate the American public has become distrustful of military and political leaders – for good reason many would say. Those who identify themselves as religious are far more critical of their church hierarchies. While authority is still conferred, a prevailing view is that it should be earned, that those in authority should prove by their behaviour that they belong there. When people feel free to criticize they are more ready to reach their own conclusions about matters which only a few decades ago they might not have questioned.

Another reason for changes in theological thinking, among Christians at least, is that they are not isolated in the way they were from immediate contact with other faiths. Hans Küng refers to the "challenge" of world religions,[179] but many see their encounter with these religions as an opportunity that provides new understanding of the Christian faith and new insights to those looking for religious truth.

A third reason for changes in theological outlook is the increasing pace and volume of scientific discovery, and the effect of this upon religious thinking. A great number of books have been published in the last decade on science and religion,[180] and the high rate of publication continues. In the past many Christians regarded the findings of Copernicus, Galileo and Darwin as a threat. Now the work of the scientist is likely to be welcomed as an opportunity, or as a possible step toward validating belief, or at least questioning non-belief. It is not surprising, writes A.R. Peacock...

> ...that the intellectual beauty, coherence, and all-embracing scope of the present scientific perspective on the universe that the physical (let alone the biological) sciences have vouchsafed us in the last few decades provokes even in quite hard-headed scientists a response of awe, almost of the sense of the 'mysterium tremendum et fascinans' beloved of theologians. Many of the former would indeed, all rhetoric apart, echo the remarks with which Hoyle concluded his broadcast lectures on the nature of the universe in 1950: 'When by patient enquiry we learn the answer to any problem, we always find, both as a whole and in detail, that the answer thus revealed is finer in concept and design than anything we could ever have arrived at by a random guess.[181]

The huge sales of Stephen Hawkins *A Brief History of Time* are a clue to the widespread public interest in the topic. My main aim in writing my book, Hawkins explains...

> ...was to tell people about the progress that was being made in understanding the laws that govern the universe. I thought that others would share the excitement and sense of wonder that I had felt, if the basic ideas could be explained in a simple way.[182]

Indeed, others do share the excitement because what is being learned has led and continues to lead to serious theological questions.

Three Scientific Examples

Consider three instances in which recent scientific developments have implications for our understanding of religion. Or, putting it the other way, religious teaching has been made more understandable and perhaps more believable by these recent developments in science. The three instances are the interrelation of all things, intention versus accident and RNA as an enzyme.

The Interrelation of All Things

This aspect of science has been brought to public attention by a widely published, widely read book, *Fritjof Capras' The Tau of Physics*. He wrote the book to describe the parallels between contemporary physics and eastern mysticism.

> The basic oneness of the universe is not only the central characteristic of the mystical experience, but is also one of the most important revelations of modern physics. It becomes apparent at the atomic level and manifests itself more and more as one penetrates deeper into matter, down into the realm of subatomic particles. The unity of all things and events will be a recurring theme throughout our comparison of modern physics and Eastern philosophy. As we study the various models of subatomic physics we shall see that they express again and again, in different ways, the same insight – that the constituents of matter and the basic phenomena involving them are all interconnected, interrelated and interdependent; that they cannot be understood as isolated entities, but only as integrated parts of the whole.[183]

Another scientist, Gary Zukav, quoting from Henry Stapp, expresses the same thought.

> In short, the physical world, according to quantum mechanics, is: … not a structure built out of independently existing unanalyzable entities, but rather a web of relationships between elements whose meanings arise wholly from their relationships to the whole.

The new physics sounds very much like old eastern mysticism.[184] The basis of all Hinduism, writes Capra…

> is the idea that the multitude of things and events around us are but different manifestations of the same ultimate reality. This reality, called *Brahman*, is the unifying characteristic which gives Hinduism its essentially monistic character in spite of the worship of numerous gods and goddesses. *Brahman* is the ultimate reality; Ātman is the individual reality; …the idea that *Ātman* and *Brahman*, the individual and the ultimate reality, are one is the essence of the *Upanishads*.[185]

This is expressed again and again in Hindu writings.

Verily, this whole world is Brahma... Containing all works, containing all desires, containing all odors, containing all tastes, encompassing this whole world, the unspeaking, the unconcerned - this is the Self of mine within the heart, this is Brahma. Into him I shall enter on departing hence.[186]

Capra makes his point with great effect. The parallels he describes are impressive. Yet we may ask what do they tell us other than that aspects of eastern religious philosophy mirror characteristics of quantum physics? Hindu teaching developed long before science, so it is not dependent upon science. Nor is science dependent upon eastern religious teaching. The nature of physical matter is what it is, and is independent of religious philosophy. What is the relationship? One could argue that if God created the heavens and the earth one might expect the spiritual realm to be similar to the physical realm. That does not follow necessarily, but the parallels described by Capra could possibly be evidence. If Brahman is everything, the development of quantum physics simply reveals what long ago was implicit in non-western religious teaching. The findings of science are thereby confirming the ontological claims of religion – to those of course who accept the ontological claims.

Many do, and they, like Peacocke are impressed, in words quoted earlier in this chapter, by the "intellectual beauty, coherence, and all embracing scope of the present scientific perspective on the universe" which provokes in them a sense of awe.

Perhaps the parallels are an intimation that while in the western world we refer naturally to the physical world and the spiritual world, even when we don't believe in it, there may not be such a distinction. What confronts us, or surrounds us, is neither. Eastern religious concepts and quantum physics may mirror one another, or they may not. They may *be* one another, as for example, Brahman, seen from two perspectives.

Is this speculative? From a western point of view, possibly, yes. Yet it might not be so within the framework of African philosophy. Consider this comment.

...the natural-supernatural dichotomy has no place in the African conceptualization of the universe. The thinking is hierarchical with God at the apex and extra-human beings and forces, humans, the lower animals, vegetation and the inanimate world, in this order, as integral parts of one single totality of existence.

And later, in the same chapter, "there is no radical or categorical difference between the spiritual and the material."[187] Is this just wrong, or should we retain ideas we may call speculative, yet some Africans regard as a true interpretation of the nature of existence? Unless the appeal of Capra's book is no more than the attractiveness of coincidence, we should keep our minds open while scientists uncover the further complexities, the simplicities if not the mysteriousness of our physical environment, haply until they may reach a conclusion.

Intention Versus Accident

The second scientific concern with implications for religion is that of intention and accident. Owen Gingerich asks a question, "How can, or does, God act within the physical world?"[188] Gingerich is a scientist, a professor of astronomy and history of science at the Harvard Smithsonian Center for Astrophysics; he is also, as far as one can tell from his article, a theist, or someone for whom theism is persuasive.

Gingerich continues, "If we grant an integrity to God's creation that embodies an orderly and stable universe, then perhaps we should look carefully into the structure of our physical world for possible insights into the way God might interact with the created cosmos."[189]

From one perspective it does not appear that God interacts at all. According to Peacocke,

A notable aspect of the scientific account of the natural world in general is the seamless character of the web that has been spun on the loom of time: the process appears as continuous from its cosmic "beginning," in the "hot big bang," to the present and at no point do modern natural scientists have to invoke any non-natural causes to explain their observations and inferences about the past. Their explanations are usually in terms of concepts, theories and mechanisms which they can confirm by, or infer from, present-day experiments, or reasonably infer by extrapolating from principles themselves conformable by experiment. In particular, the processes of biological evolution also display a *continuity*, which although at first a conjecture of Darwin (and, to be fair, of many of his predecessors), is now thoroughly validated by the established universality of the genetic code and by the study of past and present species of DNA nucleotide sequences and of amino acid sequences in certain widely-distributed proteins.[190]

The irrelevance of 'non-natural causes' was argued by Jacques Monod in *Chance and Necessity*. According to him the coming into existence of the human species was a pure accident. Like Epicurus long before, no direction or purpose or meaning beyond itself was involved.

But having declared that "non-natural causes do not have to be invoked to explain the observations and inference about the past," so taking the position it seems of Monod, Peacocke argues that chance is given too much credit. Referring to developments in theoretical and molecular biology and physical biochemistry of the Brussels and Göttingen schools he argues that it is "the interplay of chance and law that is in fact creative within time, for it is the combination of the two which allows new forms to emerge and evolve – so that natural selection appears to be opportunistic... it is chance operating within a law-like frame work that is the basis of the inherent creativity of the natural order, its ability to generate new forms, patterns and organizations of matter and energy."[191]

The issue which concerns the theologian is whether this ability is intentional or whether it is the result of a non-cognizant potentiality. As Gingerich puts it, the question is not "creation versus evolution, but intention versus accident."[192] Both sides argue persuasively. "We discover a universe," writes Gingerich, "with an extraordinary cosmic history, that prepares a very special stage for human history, with powerful hints of intention and purpose."[193]

A response to Gingerich's kind of argument, used by other writers, pointing to the complexity of the factors which made possible the existence of life, is similar to that employed by those who object to determinism. Determinists claim that our lives are so ordered that given A, B has to occur. But critics of this note that after the event it is always possible to identify a deterministic series of cause and effects, which one can never predict. Where we are now we can say we had to be and it could be none other. That is because it is none other, but it might have been something other. Similarly, with arguments which move from the condition of present existence to an intention which brought it about. We should indeed stand in awe of this universe, which becomes more awe-inspiring year by year as more and more of its complexities are discovered. But we are not required by what we observe to conclude the role of intention, or some creative power possessed of such intention. We may conclude that, but it would be a personal, psychological decision, not the final step in an argument. The development of the universe is a seamless web. According to Daniel Dennett,

> No 'intelligent supervision' is necessary... No episodes of miraculous special creation in the course of time are needed in order to actualize novel forms. No imposition of form by an act of supernatural assembly is needed. Why not? Because the universe has all of the requisite capabilities for self-organization and transformation. There are no gaps in the formational economy of the universe. And, if no gaps, then what need for a Creator?

He rejects the anthropic principle, the claim that the extraordinarily delicate balance to be found in the universe which makes possible the existence of human life could not have been an accident. It had to be designed.[194] He believes that what appears to be designed is not. It is an accident, it could quite well have been other. It appears to be intentional only because we interpret it that way. But Holmes Rolston in response asks whether Dennett could not draw a more agnostic conclusion from his own premises, namely...

> ...that he does not know whether there is an invisible hand shaping possibility spaces, supporting the information searching, even supply information here and there, amidst the "uncanny" processes of natural selection.[195]

It is a weak argument: "Isn't it possible that another explanation could be given?" For almost anything another explanation could be given. But we would want to know how compelling is that explanation, on what is it based, what is its logical force. The issue may be that, lacking the data to choose one or the other, it becomes a matter of preference, not casual or arbitrary, but held perhaps so strongly as to be unconscious. Thus a person is led to choose one option rather than another when it is not clear which should be chosen.

But is it necessary to choose one or the other, the spiritual hypothesis or the physical hypothesis? Could we examine the matter not as a spiritual seeker or a skeptical naturalist, but simply as a seeker looking for knowledge, and perhaps as a finite being in a finite environment encountering the spiritual without religious commitment or even religious interest, and simply doing what we could to understand it, looking for spiritual intention and purpose in the same objective way we look for physical causation? This would not be inconsistent with the African beliefs referred to earlier, or to the Hindu concept of Brahman. Again, are these ideas wrong, or is it incumbent upon us to consider them more sympathetically than perhaps those of us in a Western intellectual culture have felt inclined to do?

RNA as an Enzyme

The third scientific issue with implications for theology is the discovery of RNA as an enzyme; namely that RNA has the capacity to replicate itself a process that can be simulated in the laboratory. These findings are supported from the evidence of molecular fossils. Dr. Thomas R. Cech who discovered this was awarded the Nobel Prize in 1989.

In his Introduction to a book in which Cech describes his discovery Holmes Rolston III writes,

> Two critical prints are of intense biological and philosophical interest in the natural history of the earth. The first is the origin of life; the second the origin of human life.[196]

We now know, to a considerable degree, how life began. What we, as an advanced form of life, have become, and what we may be is a responsibility which presses heavily given the knowledge we have about our origins. "Science," continues Rolston, "has made us increasingly competent in knowledge and power, but it has also made us decreasingly competent about right and wrong."[197]

The origin of life and the origin of self-reflective human life are about two billion years apart. During that great span of time something remarkable happened. "Biology," explains Rolston, "touches metaphysics... When out of non-living nature there arises living nature, when out of amoral nature there arises moral human life, the conclusions seem to exceed the premises; there is more out of less."[198]

Cech describes the consequences of his discovery. What scientists have seen in modern living things "is that nucleic acids cannot copy themselves, but must be copied by protein enzymes." But RNA can play both roles; "both the information carrying capacity and the ability to catalyze chemical reactions."[199] Cech asks,

> ...is the self-assembly of RNA chemically plausible? ...considering the atmosphere of the primitive Earth to have contained water vapor, carbon dioxide, carbon monoxide, methane, and ammonia and/or nitrogen, then in the presence of an energy source, such as sunlight or lightening, a number of small molecules like hydrogen cyanide, HCN, are formed. These then undergo spontaneous reaction with other HCN molecules, again in the presence of some radiation like sunlight. We can simulate all of this in the laboratory, and remarkably, two of the major products of these very simple reactions are two of the four nucleic acid constituents that we see in all living organisms today.[200]

We have all the ingredients, he explains, "...and we are ready for the great moment in evolution, the origin of life."[201]

Life is Inevitable

One of the more familiar paintings from the Sistine Chapel is of God touching Adam's inert hand to give him life. Cech's discovery provides a scientific explanation of what was happening. With life Adam could move on, be his own person, begin making decisions. In the biblical story, however, it was God who provided the instant of beginning life. Now we know it was the catalyst of RNA. How did it happen? Given the necessary combination, the "building blocks" as Cech calls them, an energy source, and sunlight or lightning, the process of replication begins.

Was this an accident, "a lucky juxtaposition, an extremely unlikely event?" No, according to Cech, one conclusion from his experiments is that life is likely, perhaps even inevitable. The discovery that RNA can be an enzyme "provides more evidence that life is to be expected as a consequence of chemical principles."[202]

This offers a different account of the early universe from accidental, spontaneous, and chaotic. Cech writes, "At least from the perspective of a biologist, I have given an account of how possibilities did, in times past, become actual. When this happened, life originates with impressive creativity, and it does not seem to me that possibilities floated in from nowhere; they were already present, intrinsic to the chemical materials."[203]

That would mean life is not a rare or an improbable event. "If you have very common gases, such as were present on the primitive Earth, and suitable energy sources, such as sunlight and lighting, then nucleic acid molecules will arise by these chemical processes..."[204] Life could be extinguished, as in Neville Chutes novel, *On the Beach*, and begin again. Various scientists have referred to this. Christian de Dure, a Nobel laureate writes,

> Life was bound to arise under the prevailing conditions, and it will arise similarly wherever and whenever the same conditions obtain. There is hardly any room for "lucky accidents" in the gradual, multistep process whereby life originated... I view this universe [as]... made in such a way as to generate life and mind, bound to give birth to thinking beings.[205]

"This universe breeds life inevitably."[206] The evolution of life is "a logical consequence of natural chemicals."[207] "The evolution of life... must be considered an *inevitable* process despite its indeterminate course."[208]

What are we to make of this from the religious point of view? Here is something that just is; we can only accept it? Or do we want to keep asking questions which cannot be answered? Led to the very origins of life is it possible just to say "Oh, so that's it." and go on with what we are doing. Or, as we are led more and more deeply into the "mystery of existence" with huge surprises thus far, can we expect more to come? In the conclusion to his book *A Brief History of Time* Stephen Hawkins discusses the possibility of discovering a complete theory of the universe. It should eventually be understandable in principle by everyone. Then all of us will be able to take part in the discussion of why we and the universe exist. "If we find the answer to that, it would be the ultimate triumph of human reason - for then we would know the mind of God."[209]

An impressive and provocative ending, but was Hawkins serious? He must have been aware that to conceive of knowing the mind of God one has to admit that there might be a God whose mind could be known. Perhaps without intending, he illustrated that at the end of all discussion we come to the same place, not perhaps because we want to, but lacking other explanations for what touches our life most deeply we turn to the one which never yet has been completely proved, but never yet has been proved entirely false.

As the facts of our physical existence are shown to be more and more remarkable they bring us closer, believer and atheist alike, to join in a search. Part of what we are looking for is physical and part is metaphysical.

Consider a possible implication. If the physical universe is "pregnant with life," if purely physical chemical ingredients have the potentiality of life and of self-reflective human life, no one can ever truly die.

The dissolution of the body into the earth and into the atmosphere is the scattering of physical elements that by their basic nature are still potentially alive. Of course, life is spontaneous only in certain combinations of physical substance given certain circumstances, yet life is potential in what was alive, according to our way of thinking, and is no more, and yet is still alive. We consider this question, and the mystery that baffled us before becomes more mysterious.

Later Cech asks, "Does the fact that life arises more or less naturally from chemicals make such life any less valuable? ... Given the view that creation might have been a frequent occurrence, does this give us any less responsibility toward life on Earth today?"[210] His answer is no. "Life has what value it now has independent of its history, independent of what it might have been once a long time ago."[211]But, could we say that because life is nothing but a group of chemicals stimulated into life producing action it is therefore no longer a mystery?

Peacocke takes exception to the "nothing but" argument. [212]He calls it "nothing buttery" which implies that when something is reduced to something else its importance is reduced or even eliminated.

The Rapid Pace of Scientific Developments

These three instances: the interrelation of all things, intention versus accident and RNA as an enzyme are three only among many. The pace of scientific development has increased so greatly that those interested in the topic of science and religion must keep themselves continuously informed if they wish to deal constructively with the philosophical and theological issues involved. Within very recent years the possibility of cloning human beings (animals have been cloned) has raised several theological questions. "The unease about human cloning that I will express is widely shared," writes Gilbert Meilaender, who holds a chair in theological ethics at Valparaiso University. "...our theological tradition has addressed two questions that are both profound and mysterious in their simplicity: What is the meaning of a child? And what is good for a child?" A child he believes should be regarded as a gift, not a product, a gift from God.[213]

In Rochester, New York, where I live, a major ethical issue with religious implications is part of a recent debate about physician-assisted suicide. How does this affect our understanding of death? "On the one hand, life and its flourishing belong to the creative and redemptive cause of God... Acts which aim at death (physician assisted suicide perhaps)... do not fit this story, do not cohere with devotion to the cause of God, or with gratitude for the gifts of God."[214]

Since beginning this chapter a map of the human genome has been produced, the first complete sequence of the human genetic code. In *A Protestant Perspective in Ending Life* Allen Verhey writes, "Ultimately, this scientific breakthrough, like Darwin's bombshell, could challenge fixed social and theological ideas about humanity and its place in the universe."[215]

Can we now conclude that humans are 'nothing but their genes?' Or does this new advance in genetic science lead us in an opposite direction? Suzanne Holland, professor of religious and social ethics at the University of Puget Sound in Tacoma, Washington believes it does.

> This sort of combination of genes with the interplay of the environment is so magnificent and contains within it so much mystery that to my mind it's more reason for belief in God... We might come to see God as far more involved in the world than the Newtonian mechanistic view of a God that sets up everything and steps out of the way.[216]

Ursula Goodenough, professor of biology at Washington University, expresses a similarly positive though humanistic view.

> For me, the existence of all this complexity and awareness and intent and beauty, and my ability to apprehend it, serves as the ultimate meaning and the ultimate value. The continuation of life reaches around, grabs its own tail, and forms a sacred circle that requires no further justification, no creator, no superordinate meaning of meaning, no purpose other than that the continuation continue until the sun collapses or the final meteor collides.[217]

Now or Never

I am writing during the summer time. When I get tired of writing I go outside and work in the garden. There I look at my flowers, roses, sundrops, impatiens, several others, and a dahlia on its way. If I were a botanist I could explain them as "nothing but" a series of botanical causes and effects. That would not explain for me why they are beautiful, nor would it explain the existence of the science of horticulture, part of the complexity of the earth, which is part of the complexity of the interrelatedness of all things. By no means would I be satisfied by "nothing but", for the "but" has to be itself a source of wonder. I may not move from that to the assertion of the existence of a Creator. But I may. And I would feel it was not simply a leap in the dark, not blind faith, but an implication quite strongly suggested by the macro and the micro world around me.

Near the end of his life Charles Darwin wrote a letter to a Dutch student who had asked him for his views on religion.

> It is impossible to answer your question briefly; and I am not sure that I could do so, even if I wrote at some length. But I may say that the impossibility of conceiving that this grand and wondrous universe, with our conscious selves, arose through chance, seems to me the chief argument for the existence of God but whether this is an argument of real value, I have never been able to decide. I am aware that if we admit a first cause, the mind still craves to know whence it came and how it arose. Nor can I overlook the difficulty from the immense amount of suffering in the world. I am, also, induced to defer to a certain extent to the judgement of many able men who have fully believed in God; but here again I see how poor an argument this is. The safest conclusion seems to me that the whole subject is beyond the scope of man's intellect but man can do his duty.[218]

This moving passage illustrates the contradiction of thought and feeling which plays so great a part in the reflective life of persons who address this problem. It is beyond the scope of human intellect, but the intellect craves, rather wistfully at the end of life to bring it within its scope. The clock ticks away for all of us and we feel as the moments slip by, it's now or never to resolve these questions. Yet on the basis of a lifetime of unrewarded inquiry we doubt that it can be now, yet we shrink from the possibility that it might be never.

Chapter 9

Religion and Ethics

A Meeting in London

Last year I attended a meeting in London with a group of people interested in philosophy. We met in a pub. (I suppose beer is at least as conducive to discussion as wine in ancient Greece.) After the talk we had supper, and I found myself at a table with a lawyer, a physician, a graduate student in philosophy and a financial advisor. It interested them that I teach philosophy, especially philosophy of religion. Perhaps that is what led the financial advisor to tell me she had grown up a Roman Catholic but left the church, in fact her Christian faith, because of the manner in which Catholics, and Christians generally behaved. She shared with me a few not unfamiliar examples, the Inquisition being one, and declared she did not want to have anything to do with a "so called faith" that supported such cruelty. I agreed with her, but suggested that perhaps we can distinguish between the quality of a teaching and how people behave who claim to follow the teaching. We don't, for example in the United States, dismiss the presidency because of Watergate, or regard all doctors as corrupt because some break their Hippocratic Oath. To my surprise this had not occurred to her. It made sense; she would think about it she said. So we continued our discussion in the ambiance of the pub.

Making Distinctions

Reflecting on the incident since, I would say it illustrates two things.

1. Religion and behavior are strongly connected in peoples' thinking.
2. Quite simple distinctions can help resolve real problems.

Consider the second item first. It is scarcely a philosophical distinction, more a matter of common sense, almost obvious. Yet it was not obvious to the woman I met. Philosophers probably employ the distinction more often than others, but it can be used by anyone, though in matters of religion it frequently isn't. A painting I saw at a museum in Gdansk, Poland, of Teutonic Knights slaughtering a group of defenseless and terrified villagers was more distasteful to me because the knights were wearing white tunics emblazoned with a cross. In more recent history John Calvin denounced Michael Servetus for his anti-Trinitarian views. Servetus was condemned and then burnt to death, an actual loss to theological thinking and to medical science. Both incidents are contradictory to the Christian teaching of love. If Christianity is like that why bother?

One answer is to bring forward the distinction I made. Francis of Assisi founded the Franciscan Order only a few years after the founding of the Teutonic Knights in 1190, therefore the Knights do not represent all Christianity at that time. The historical argument is vulnerable, but vulnerable in both directions. Given two thousand years since Christianity began we can find instances to support either position: that Christianity is cruel, and that Christianity is loving. To be aware of this, and to recognize that the behavior of those who claim to be followers is not always an accurate guide to what they follow, may help avoid hasty judgments such as, perhaps, those of the woman in London whom I met.

A Further Complication

But there's a further complication. Much in the Old Testament, and not a little in the New, suggests that the God of love is not always loving. Nanak, the founder of Sikhism was a pacifist. He never used violence against his many enemies. Now the Sikhs are known and respected as warriors, although many of them try to maintain Nanak's pacifist tradition. We may have to make a distinction not only between teaching and behavior, but between various strands of the teaching itself, a more difficult distinction to make than the other. How do we make it? I believe we have to determine what are the basic premises of a faith, and what in the teaching is inconsistent with those premises. We then may say, this is what the teaching actually is, and we can judge the behavior of its followers according to it. Such an idea almost invites criticism and rebuttal; yet consider a comment by Rammohun Roy.

> ...a simple enumeration and statement of the receptive tenets of different sects may be a sufficient guide to direct their inquiries in ascertaining which of them is the most consistent with sacred traditions, and most acceptable to common sense...[219]

Reflecting on this, it does seem that if we examine a teaching closely we can determine with reasonable assurance what is most important to it, and we can make judgments that will help us to avoid unwarranted generalizations.

Religion and Behavior

With regard to the first item, that religion and behavior are strongly connected, it is a natural assumption, and a main reason for the connection made between religion and ethics, the title of this chapter. The business of ethics is behavior: what people do, why they do it and the standards and norms that apply to what they do or don't do.

Not much is more basic than behavior. We are born into families, we live in societies. Throughout our life we deal with other people. How we deal with them is a large part of our behavior. It follows that behavior is a large part of the subject of ethics.

Because we have to deal with others we have to take them into account when we behave. This may be for prudential reasons, as Thomas Hobbes argued or for generous reasons as in Zoroastrianism. According to that belief:

> This generosity is best: One who makes a present to a person from whom he has no hope of receiving anything in reward in this world, and he has not even this (hope) namely, that the recipient of his gift should hold him abundantly in gratitude and praise.[220]

"Behavior" as we use it here, will imply intention even though there can be aimless behavior and irrational behavior. Yet the fact that we qualify the term with such adjectives suggests that the normal understanding of behavior is that it is not aimless or irrational, but purposeful and rational.

The Value of Cooperation

Our ancestors must soon have learned that cooperation ensures a safer and more enjoyable life than antagonism, that, prudentially at least, such qualities as truthfulness, virtue, diligence, advocacy as well as generosity all listed in the Zoroastrian text, are in society's best interest to promote. Out of such understanding arose the legal and moral laws that govern our behavior, with penalties for those who ignore them.

Our Destination

A society which gives attention to these considerations only could function well, but an important element, perhaps a crucial element, would be missing. Some years ago the Russian novelist Alexander Solzhenitsyn gave a talk to a gathering of philosophers in Liechtenstein. He asked the question: What is your destination? We may indeed have a society governed by legal and moral laws, but we have to apply them in our dealings with one another. How we do that will be determined by what we regard as most important. What is the long-range goal of our society and the individuals in it or, in Solzhenitsyn's words: What is our destination?

We are familiar with short-term goals. We buy a plane ticket to go on a vacation; we turn up the thermostat to get more heat. Many people study to obtain qualifications to advance their career, or engage in exercise to improve their health. But there is a further objective or goal, as Aristotle put it in his Ethics, for the sake of which all else is done. Such a goal affects our total life.

It may be our children, or our job, or it maybe the nation itself. One would hope that our long-term goals would be constructive. Sometimes they are not. Parents who live for their children may cripple their children's development and be badly disappointed. Germany's long-term goals during the Second World War were vicious.

It is therefore important what kind of goals we choose to follow. The study of ethics gives attention to this. What kind of a life will a particular goal encourage us to lead, a constructive life or a useless life, a life that gives thought for others or a life lived for the self?

Sometimes our goal requires us to make hard choices. Socrates chose to die rather than bend his principles by escaping from prison.

The God that Failed

But as well as this we would expect that whatever it is we commit our life to is reliable, will not let us down. *The God that Failed*, the title of a book published in 1950, tells the story of six writers who became Communists. They were deeply committed to Communism, were disillusioned and left the party. Richard Wright tells a painful story of how, as he began to ask questions rather than simply accept the Communist line, he was blackballed by those he thought had been his friends, until during a May Day march he was physically attacked by two white Communists with black Communists looking on.

> I remembered the stories I had written, the stories in which I had assigned a role of honor and glory to the Communist Party, and I was glad that they were down in black and white, were finished. For, I knew in my heart that I should never be able to write that way again, should never be able to feel with that simple sharpness about life, should never again express such passionate hope, should never again make so total a commitment of faith.[221]

The title of the book is significant, *The God that Failed*. Commitment to Communism has often been likened to religious commitment, a total commitment with total obedience for the good of the cause, in Communist terms, for the good of the proletariat, the ordinary working people. The vision presented was that those who followed the ideology would be able to form a new and happy society; from each according to his ability to each according to his need. It was an ethical goal at the highest level - and it failed.

Not unconnected is that despite the most determined and prolonged effort in history to humiliate and destroy religion, after the fall of Communism the church arose like a Phoenix. It might have been an awareness that Communism failed not only because of a flawed ideology but because its leaders failed. It was a humanistic teaching to a large extent dependent on its leaders. When they failed it all failed.

The Religious Promise

The attractiveness of religion may be this. It offers a goal for people to achieve, a set of standards to live by if they can. It offers the help of spiritual guidance for those who are willing to take it, to help achieve those standards. It offers them out of concern and love for people in their most intimate lives.

As an ethic religion offers a goal it declares will not fail, because unlike a humanistic ethic it comes from the divine. It offers standards of behavior that it claims are true because they come from heaven. It offers spiritual strength and guidance, which we can be sure is always available because God promises them. Herein is the great strength and attractiveness of religious ethics.

Is Ethics Dependent Upon Religion?

The question is much debated. Is ethics dependent upon religion? The answer, "yes," would affirm a moral argument for the existence of God. Given the selfish and destructive nature of human beings who are restrained from injuring one another only by threat of punishment, from whence came our moral laws? Men and women themselves could not have devised them. (Although they do their best to follow them.) They are too faulty to have created such standards. Their origin must be found in some being of greater moral quality than humans, in other words God, or some divine and super moral source.

But despite its historical attractiveness this argument can easily be refuted. Aristotle, who wrote the first book on ethics, was not a religious man. His ethics is humanistic. Spinoza, two millennia later, wrote an ethic definitely not dependent on religion. Hobbes developed an egoistic ethic, also independent of religion. There may be a religious ethic, dependent on religion but ethics *as such* is not.

If we extract the ethical teaching from various religions we are left with prescriptions that humans could have devised. They are noble, but not beyond human endeavor. Theravada Buddhism which preserves what is claimed as the Buddha's teaching is not supernaturalistic. It is simply an ethic designed to address common human problems, in particular the problem of evil. The Four Noble Truths of Buddhism are that there is suffering, suffering is caused, suffering can be overcome, and the Eightfold Path overcomes it.

A later development of Buddhism, Mahayana, taught that some people who live life according to the Eightfold path and so could proceed to Nirvana, choose not to do so. Rather, they choose to return to help those who are still struggling along the path. These are Bodhisattvas. Buddhism therefore is an ethic, challenging but not humanly impossible. It is unlike Christianity which teaches that human effort is not sufficient to achieve salvation and communion with God. Yet despite this according to the Epistle of James, "Faith by itself, if it has not works, is dead." (James 2:17 RSV) Christians are expected to maintain a high level of ethical behavior even though, in Christian theology, people are born in sin. Consider the admonition in Ephesians, for example that,

> Fornication and indecency of any kind, or ruthless greed, must not be so much as mentioned among you, as befits the people of God. No coarse, stupid or flippant talk; these things are out of place... (Ephesians 5:3-4 NEB)

This is not so different from the teaching of the Stoic Epictetus, a contemporary of the Apostle Paul, who wrote, "Lay down for yourself from the first, a definite stamp and style of conduct, which you will maintain when you are alone and also in the society of men."[222]

Confucianism is primarily an ethic; a guide to behavior and its teachings are not unlike other religious ethical teachings.

In the Analects We Read:

> A man without virtue cannot long abide in adversity, nor can he long abide in happiness; but the virtuous man is at rest in virtue, and the wise man covets it.

The ultimate principle of Confucianism is Jen, translated as "virtue" "humanity" "benevolence" "true manhood" "moral character" "love" "human goodness" and "human-heartedness." It is a strongly humanistic ethic, yet in the Analects we find an admonition almost identical with the Second Commandment. "Do not do to others what you would not like yourself."[223]

One of the translations of Jen, "true manhood," is reflected in a passage from Chuang Tzu "The True Man."

> The true man of old
> knew no lust for life,
> no dread of death.
> Their entrance was without gladness,
> Their exit, yonder,
> Without resistance.
> Easy come, easy go.
> They did not forget where from,
> Nor ask where to,
> Nor drive grimly forward
> Fighting their way through life.
> They took life as it came, gladly;
> Took death as it came, without care;
> And went away, yonder,
> Yonder![224]

All these humanistic writers assume the ability of a human to live a rich, and enjoyable and constructive life in terms of this life only. The answer to the question is that by no means is ethics dependent upon religion.

Religion an Impediment to Ethics?

We might go further, as some critics do, as the woman I met in London did, and charge that religion is actually an impediment to ethics. Painful examples from the Christian church are well known. But they are not unique. For all its spiritual strength Islam is deeply unfair to women. Its concept of law, from the perspective of contemporary western jurisprudence, is appallingly backward. A friend of mine who taught recently in Saudi Arabia described the society there as "Eighth century with lap tops." Kemal Ataturk did his best in the 1920's to recreate Turkey as a secular society. Now, with the spread of what we call Islamic fundamentalism, pressures are mounting to redefine that secular society according to Islamic teaching.

The question is, if ethics can be independent of religion why does it bother with religion? Why introduce religion into our ethical life? What value-added factor does religion provide? To the believer, that may be an irrelevant question. Those who have religious faith will behave according to that faith without asking what it adds to life if they did not believe. They believe; that is how their behavior is determined.

An Answer

Perhaps the answer is not an answer, or perhaps the answer is a conviction drawn from the teachings of the faiths and the experiences of those who follow them, that contrary to a humanistic view, religion, however understood, is essential to the conduct of life.

Radhakrishnan writes,

> To know, possess and be the spirit in this physical frame, to convert an obscure plodding mentality into clear spiritual illumination, to build peace and self existent freedom in the stress of emotional satisfactions and sufferings, to discover and realize the life divine in a body subject to sickness and death has been the constant aim of the Hindu religious endeavor.[225]

At the end of his *Autobiography*, Mahatma Gandhi provides an account of his ethical- religious beliefs. For him, Truth is God, God is Truth.

> To see the universal and all pervading Spirit of Truth face to face one must be able to love the meanest of creation as oneself. And a man who aspires after that cannot afford to keep out of any field of life. That is why my devotion to Truth has drawn me into the field of politics; and I can say without the slightest hesitation, and yet in all humility, that those who say that religion has nothing to do with politics do not know what religion means.[226]

Rabinadrath Tagore, Indian poet and educator, believed that only by returning to the spiritual values which permeate all religions, could mankind save itself from destruction. On the last day of the nineteenth century he wrote a poem which described the Boer War, then taking place, and anticipated more than he realized the savagery and distress of the twentieth century.

> The last sun of the century sets amidst the blood-red clouds of the West and the whirlwind of hatred.

The naked passion of self love of Nations, in its drunken delirium of greed, is dancing with the clash of steel and the howling verses of vengeance.[227]

Speaking to his own people, who were still half a century away from independence, in his last stanza...

Be not ashamed, my brothers, to stand before the proud and the powerful
With your white robe of simpleness.
Let your crown be of humility, your freedom the freedom of the soul.
Build God's throne daily upon the ample bareness of your poverty
And know that what is huge is not great, and pride is not everlasting.[228]

These men believed that their religious faith was of practical value to them as they endeavored to live their lives.

Writing to the new Christians in Corinth the Apostle Paul opened his heart about the almost unbearable stress in his life. It was not completely unbearable because of the faith which sustained him. He described the danger of travel on land and sea, shipwreck, hunger, cold and exposure in freezing weather, dangers from robbers and his own people, flogging and imprisonment. As well as that the weight of responsibility for all the Christians in the various congregations he had gathered, solving their problems, trying to help in practical ways, only kept going by his perception of the closeness of Christ. (2 Corinthians 11:23 ff)

We could draw from other religious traditions but these examples show that not a few persons find in religious faith a strength which comes from no other source, a strength that helps them, as nothing else can, to deal with their lives. Life lived for this life alone, as Epicurus proposed, was not an option for them.

We must make our own judgment about this. On both sides sincere convictions, on both sides the belief that by those convictions, really, only by those convictions, are the people who have them able to live.

A Related Issue

A different though related issue has its origin in Plato's dialogue Euthyphro. The discussion there, at one point, is the relation between God and piety. The question: Is God pious because it is right to be pious, or is God pious because he/she determines that certain behavior is pious.

With regard to "good." If God is good because it is right to be good he/she is answerable to an external standard. If God is good because he determines what is good he could make what we call good – bad, and bad – good. He could behave in an arbitrary fashion

Christianity, Islam and Judaism reject that possibility. God is truly good; that is the character of his existence. In the biblical creation story at each stage of creation God saw that it was good. The problem is specific to monotheism. In polytheistic religion such as Hinduism the good and bad characteristics of divinity can be divided between the gods.

But a question remains. Is there an argument to support the claim that God is by nature good and would not act in an arbitrary fashion, calling what we say is good, bad, and what we call bad, good, switching moral values around much as the government in George Orwell's *Nineteen Eighty Four* decided that yesterday's enemy is today's friend? Is it simply a matter of faith? We believe that God is essentially good, and so we affirm?

A Possible Argument

I would propose that it is not only a matter of faith. Let me present an argument. The universe as a physical entity is neither good nor bad. It is, however, orderly. From its physical beginnings billions of years ago to the uttermost reach we can extend into the universe we find predictable order.

The universe is not rational in the way that human beings are rational, but it has given rise to rational human beings. When they observe the order of the universe it appeals to their rationality. Perhaps we could turn to a Stoic argument proposed by Cicero. "If flutes playing musical tones grew on an olive tree, would you doubt that some knowledge of flute playing existed in the olive tree... Why, therefore, is not the world (the universe) considered animate and intelligent, when it produces from itself animate and intelligent beings?"[229]

It is a more appealing argument now than it was then because we now know that whatever rationality humans have arose from the universe's physical elements. At least we can say for sure, the potential of rationality in the universe was there from the beginning, a potential actualized most eminently in humans. A.R. Peacocke writes...

Although the potentialities of our given universe may not be unlimited, their actualization nevertheless remains quite open from the vantage point of the twentieth-century scientific perspective... Only in a universe with this kind of ordered giveness is there the stable matrix within which freedom can be genuinely exercised and which makes perception and conceptualization possible. (He continues) A chaos in which no entity existed long enough to be stable and perceivable would be simply nothing at all in relation to conscious action or perception.[230]

Order is necessary to the existence of the universe. A disordered, chaotic universe, according to Peacocke, is "nothing at all." A disordered person can scarcely live. Order is therefore an essential quality both for the universe as a whole and individual lives.

Can we argue that order, given its necessity, is one way of describing what we mean by good? Disorder, which would make physical existence and human life impossible, is one way of describing what we mean by bad? Here I run the risk of trying to devise an ought from an is. Yet, incontrovertibly, an oughtness that does exist has proceeded from what is.

The "what is" is an ordered universe. Without that order the universe could not be, and without order humans could not be. We might call this a positive, the negative is nothing. We describe this as good. An ordered life is a good life, a disordered life, if it can be at all, can hardly be called good, but it may be called bad. Good, therefore, (and we may use perhaps the term 'moral') in humans is the reflection of the good of a universe characterized by order. This I propose is a tentative argument for the origin of what we call morality, concepts of good and bad, or order and disorder.

If we were to argue that the ultimate order – the order in the universe – has no reference to a divine creator we have a possible secular argument for the origin of moral values.

If we were to argue that the ultimate order was the result of divine creation we have a religious argument. The physical universe operates without conscious thought except for humans who are conscious and reflective. This enables them to make decisions that are contrary to the order which is in their best interest. Would this be the origin of what in theology is called sin?

The relationship between the necessary order of the universe and the necessary order of human life is physically close and intellectually self-reflective. That can be understood in religious terms, in which case the relationship between religion and ethics is very close. If not understood in religious terms the connection between religion and ethics does not exist. Which we choose is a matter of faith. But before we choose we may want to reflect further.

Suppose that the argument from the order of the universe to the order of human life succeeds. We are persuaded that order does provide a reasonable explanation of what we call good, and disorder, bad.

We would have reasoned empirically from the nature of the universe and the nature of humans to the existence of moral values.

In the case of the universe, it does operate in an orderly fashion. As we understand the order we understand the universe. Human beings also operate in an orderly fashion. Bodily activities, breathing and so on are necessarily ordered. When they become disordered we go to the doctor. It seems then that we have a reasonable argument, claiming that the order in human life, which is a reflection of the order in the universe, is the equivalent of positive moral value. This we say is good, to be preserved and maintained. To the extent we do so our lives are morally good.

Much of What Is Good In Life Is Not Orderly

But a great deal of what is of importance to humans is not ordered in that way. I have little choice about breathing, but I have a great deal of choice about many other things in my life. The doctor cures me, he restores physical, perhaps even mental order, for the sake of the other things in life I want to do. What are these other things? Consider some of them: we want to love, not just procreate, and not just have sex, but love. In Greek there are different words for love, describing different kinds of love. We may pass from one to the other levels of love, sometimes without intending to. Love is essential to a life, but it is often disordered, and it creates disorder in otherwise ordered people. Here is one quality of human beings which is essential, and is not orderly. We can turn to others: What about sport so important to humans, such as, for example mountain climbing, engaged in to enhance life, which actually can destroy life? There is so much of this we might argue that disorder not order characterizes humans, and that this is essential to their humanness. Imagination, creativity, spontaneity and generous, sometimes over generous concern for others are examples. Yet pushed to extremes the disordered person is a non-functional person. Some order is necessary to balance the disorder. What it is and how much, will vary from person to person. It will vary even within the life of one person. Yet unless a balance is maintained to some extent a person becomes disordered and hence non-functional. To be non-functional is to be disordered, and that as we said is bad.

A balance in a life is not usually maintained only by adjustments day to day. Such adjustments have to be made, but one adjusts usually to some standard. If we are running water in the bath we adjust it so that it is not too hot nor too cold. We make adjustments in our life generally – in the moral sense of good and bad – perhaps along the lines of Aristotle's mean. So although there are fluctuations in how we behave, there is a type of behavior that maintains a balance or mean.

The good in humans, we argued, is the reflection of the good of the universe characterized by order. This is the moral principle which provides an objective standard by which we live.

Yet the order of the universe is not simply replicated in human moral order. The order of the universe is impersonal and automatic.

The order of a human being is personal and not automatic. It is self-initiated. There has to be a personal recognition that this kind of order is important.

What inspires that recognition? What prompts it, what makes it possible? It may be the prudential consideration that without it life is the war of all against all, as described by Hobbes. So we consult our best selfish interests.

But that can't be quite all. The laws of nature to which the prudential interests of Hobbes turned are intrinsic to human reason. It is, going back to the Stoics, an indication of the essential rationality of humans, and in Hobbes, the mechanistic system of the universe.

We can say that rationality is just there without trying to explain why it is there. The religious explanation is that it is there because it reflects the divine rationality that caused it to be.

We do not *know* this, and we cannot prove it. Yet it is a belief held by people across the earth.

The rationality of humans is that which perceives the value of what we call morality – the consequence of order; according to this view not just physical order but psychological, emotional order.

Can we rule out that suggestion? Should we? As a hypothesis, equating human rationality with morality deserves our attention. It may be false, yet perhaps not entirely false.

If it is true it may be that those who claim allegiance to it behave in a manner unworthy of it, and thereby make possible the kind of disgusted criticism from the woman I met in London. But that, I would argue, does not make it less true, it indicates only that those who claim allegiance are less faithful.

Ethics for the New Millennium

Last May the Dalai Lama was in Britain, and was interviewed on the BBC. The interviewer questioned him about a statement in a book he had just written *Ethics for the New Millennium.*[231] In it he declared that religion itself was not important. What is important is being good. The actual quote from the book is this.

> I have come to the conclusion that whether or not a person is a religious believer does not matter much. For more important is that they be a good human being... we humans can live quite well without recourse to religious faith.[232]

All the world's major religions, he continued, are "directed toward helping human beings achieve lasting happiness. And each of them is, in my opinion, capable of facilitating this."[233] He explains that the concern of his book is "to reach beyond the formal boundaries of my faith"[234] He distinguishes between religion and spirituality. Religion is concerned with formal teaching of a faith "spirituality I take to be concerned with those qualities of the human spirit – such as love and compassion, patience, tolerance, forgiveness, contentment, a sense of responsibility, a sense of harmony – which bring happiness to both self and others."[235]

His definition of spirituality is a personal one. Spirituality as used by Christians, which is the most widespread faith in the United States, ordinarily implies sensitivity to the supernatural spirit of God as it relates to our spirit, which is the imperishable part of us. Spirituality, so understood, leads to "a closer walk with God" and a heightened awareness of God's continuous presence. The result will be a deeper prayer life, and it will inspire people to seek God's direction more earnestly both to honor the first commandment (to love God...) and, in practical ways, the second (to love your neighbor as yourself.)

For the Dalai Lama spirituality can be developed without reference to God or any divine power. It is a human endeavor, whose prime motivation is concern for others. That for him is the only way in which we can determine what is right and what is wrong, not by reference to a religious standard. He explains that the Tibetans speak of *shen pen kyi sem*, which means "the thought to be of help to others."[236] "We have no means of discriminating between right and wrong if we do not take into account others' feelings, others' suffering."[237] Hence, whereas spirituality in the Christian sense leads *to* concern for others, for the Dalai Lama spirituality *is* concern for others. This is consistent with the origins of Buddhism, to when the Buddha became aware of sickness, old age and death, and thereafter committed his life to teaching others how to deal with them. It is possible to do this, the Dalai Lama explains, as one develops *kun long*, that is, the overall state of one's heart and mind. This "drives or inspires ones actions"[238] a concept not unlike the Confucian Jen or "human heartedness."

Lying behind that and the Dalai Lama's teaching is the great importance of relationships. That is the basis of human order. The disordered life ignores or is unable to deal with relationships, the consequence is suffering. The recognition of suffering is the necessary condition for distinguishing between right and wrong. As Buddhist teaching is committed to overcoming suffering, it follows that suffering is bad, overcoming it by means of the eightfold path is good. Such a good life will be an ordered life, reflecting the order in the universe.

According to the Dalai Lama, humans have strength enough to achieve this. It is, however, the rare human who is able to do so, even with the help of friends. As the Christian hymn puts it, "Well our feeble frame he knows." The recourse that many have taken is to reach beyond the boundaries of this uncertain and contingent existence to what is believed to be a greater help to a certain and non-contingent "Other," that can meet human need with greater than human strength, and will never fail.

For the Dalai Lama spirituality is developing the positive qualities of the human spirit. Religion is the formalities of a faith. Spirituality can function without religion so religion is not really important. But in the finite world where spirituality is difficult to develop and sustain there has been and continues to be a felt need for the formalities of religion. They point the way to sources of more than human strength which provide a necessary basis, for many, for spirituality.

According to Nicolas Berdyaev, these religious formalities provide the necessary basis for everyone, "there cannot be a genuine society of persons unless this religious dimension is recognized, unless it is understood that the human being is more than a member of society."[239] In *Dream and Reality*, he writes, "the meaning of life lies in a return to the mystery of the spirit in which God is born in man and man is born in God."[240]

A good life is not dependent upon religion. Life without religion can be a satisfying and enjoyable, Epicurus is our model of that. But such a life requires courage and personal strength. For that reason, although the issues of religion and ethics could be resolved completely by rejecting religion, such a solution is seldom taken. The issues remain.

Chapter 10

Religion and Language

A Remarkable Contrivance

About four thousand years ago a young woman named Dabitum wrote a letter. She didn't have pen, pencil or paper. She wrote with a wedge shaped stylus on a damp clay tablet. That is why the letter survived until it was discovered some years ago and published.

Dabitum was pregnant, but the baby was dead inside her, so she believed. She wanted to see the absent father "once more before I die."[241] It is a tragic vignette, often repeated. It touches our heart. But it also makes a point which can be overlooked. We know nothing more of this poor woman, yet through that letter we enter as intimately into her life as if she were a living friend. The point we can overlook is the extraordinary nature of a human contrivance that enables us to reach across thousands of years, to cultures quite different from our own, and enter another person's life. The contrivance is language. It has enabled people to advance from the incoherence of prehominid existence to one in which expressions of love, of poetry, of philosophy are regarded as a normal part of human behavior.

That language exists is remarkable, yet not remarkable, because if it didn't we would not be able even to reflect upon the fact. About two hundred years ago the German philosopher Johann Herder wrote,

"Reason was incapable of action without a word symbol, and the first moment of rationality must also have been the first beginnings of language."[242]

Ideas and language inspire one another. An important part of Dr. Johnson's dictionary is his use of literary examples, which indicate how the words he defined are employed in living language. Language is determined by its use, but its use is determined by the inventiveness of those who use it. When the Beatles entitled their movie *A Hard Day's Night*, they were continuing that tradition.

Language Describes What is Not

Language does more than describes what is; it describes what is not, especially in poetry.

> The poet's eye, in a fine frenzy rolling, [heaven;
> Doth glance from heaven to earth, from earth to
> And, as imagination bodies forth
> The forms of things unknown, the poet's pen
> Turns them to shapes, and gives to airy nothing
> A local habitation and a name.

This is the nature of poetry, which Shakespeare was creating as he wrote, but in the following lines we wonder if he had in mind the genesis of religion.

> Such tricks hath strong imagination,
> That, if it would but apprehend some joy,
> It comprehends some bringer of that joy;
> Or in the night, imagining some fear,
> How easy is a bush supposed a bear![243]

One explanation of religion is that it is a product of wishful thinking – the thesis of Ludwig Feuerbach and Sigmund Freud.

Religion Is Dependent Upon Language

But even if religion is not a human invention it is dependent upon the invention of language, for without language, at least from the human side, there could be no religion. Religion must be conceptualized. While we may feel deeply, our feelings are always about something.

The feeling of the numinous, described by Rudolf Otto, is not simply undifferentiated emotion. Otherwise, why regard it as religious?

The Beginning of Language?

When such conceptualization began we don't know. Maybe language had no beginning, no point in time, no before and after, its genesis more like the manner in which a child learns to speak. The child, however, has something to learn, our ancient ancestors had to create language for themselves. Human intelligence inspired by curiosity may have led first to the means of communication, no doubt about simple necessities, but probably not only that. The relationship between a mother and her child is always an adventure in language. Was it the original adventure? One might guess that the emotions of love – surely not absent from the earliest humans – must have stretched their capacity to say more than was needed, and to invent terms for what they felt.

The Importance of Language in Religious Traditions

Language has a functional role, but language as such is important in several religious traditions apart from its practical function.

The Hebrew "word" (dabar) occurs in the Old Testament almost seven hundred times, its Greek counterpart (logos) in the New Testament more than two hundred times. Both dabar and logos mean more than simply "word." They include in their meaning reason, warning, judgement, and command. When the prophets announced "Thus saith the Lord" or "Hear the word of the Lord" they were speaking with the voice of God. What they said had tremendous authority. When Hosea declared to the recalcitrant Israelites, "I have torn you to shreds with my word." (Hosea 6.5 NEB) it was no mere metaphor. For the word of God was his entire teaching, spoken and written. It was powerful, to be treated with respect and caution. "For the word of God is quick and powerful, sharper than any two-edged sword." (Heb 4.12 KJV) warns the New Testament.

The divine word is of importance in various African traditions. The Dogon of Mali believe that Amma's creative word was given to mankind from an ark that descended to earth. The Bambara, also from Mali, have elaborate ceremonies to initiate boys into manhood. By learning the eternal Word of the Creator the initiates become immortal.[244]

In the Hindu *Rig Veda* a prayer is addressed to Vak, the god who personifies voice or speech. Enumerating his power the worshipper declares "I verily myself announce and utter the word that gods and men alike shall welcome."[245]

The Hebrew name for God, Yaweh, was (in fact, is) regarded as too sacred to be pronounced so the consonants were written in the text of the Old Testament with the vowels of Adoni (Lord) added to the consonants. The result is the term Jehovah introduced into the English language by William Tyndale.

The Adi Granth, the Sikhs holiest book, expresses similar respect for the holy name.

> If in this life I should live to eternity, nourished by nothing save air; if I should
> dwell in the darkest of dungeons, sense never resting in sleep; yet must your
> glory transcend all my striving; no words can encompass the Name...
>
> Listening to the Name bestows truth, divine wisdom, and contentment.
> To bathe in the joy of the Name is to bathe in the holy places.
> By hearing the Name and reading it one attains to honor;
> By listening, the mind may reach the highest blissful poise of meditation of God.
> Nanak says, the saints are always happy;
> By listening to the Name sorrow and sin are destroyed...
>
> Pilgrimages, penances, compassion and almsgiving bring a little merit, the
> size of a sesame seed.
> But one who hears and believes and loves the Name will bathe and
> be made clean in a place of pilgrimage within.[246]

All these illustrations indicate how powerful the role of language is in religion.

Text and Meaning

Every major religion has a text which contains the teachings of that religion; what to believe, how to behave. Obviously, it is very important that the believer should grasp the plain words of the teaching and also what they mean. The two are intertwined, yet they can be considered and dealt with separately. The Old Testament was written in ancient Hebrew (a few passages in Aramaic), the New Testament was written in Koine Greek, the colloquial Greek of the first century. Any who wish to study the Bible must either learn the two languages, (which many do,) or depend upon translations. Hundreds of translations now exist in almost every language and dialect.

The story of translating the Bible into English is long and interesting, beginning with King Alfred in the ninth century who translated part of the Bible. (His English however would not be understandable to English speakers now). In the fourteenth century John Wycliffe made, or caused to be made, a translation into English of the whole Bible from the Latin Vulgate, itself a translation. It was literal and stiff, but it was in English, so people could read it. Perhaps not surprisingly the church authorities objected. In 1524-26 William Tyndale published his translation of the New Testament in English from the original Greek. Later he translated parts of the Old Testament from Hebrew. Several translations were published in the sixteenth century until in 1611; the widely known Authorized Version was produced with the encouragement of James I. This became the standard translation in the English-speaking world for two hundred and seventy years. When in 1881 the Revised Standard Version of the New Testament was published there was great excitement. Three million copies were sold in England and the United States the first year of publication. *The Chicago Tribune* and the *Chicago Times* each printed the entire contents of the New Testament in succeeding issues, five days later. Now there are many contemporary translations: the Jerusalem Bible, the Ronald Knox Bible, the New English Bible, the Revised English Bible and a revision of the Revised Standard, the New Revised and so on. A person without Greek or Hebrew who speaks English can get closer to the original than at any time.

Translation Alone is Not Sufficient

The value of this is that if indeed these scriptures are the revealed word of God it is necessary that the believer understand them as exactly as possible. An accurate translation is essential. But a translation alone is not sufficient; texts differ and suffer from scribal errors and misreading. The earlier the text the closer it is likely to be to the autograph original. And this can affect not only the words, but also the meaning.

Consider this example. In the 1611 King James version (Mark 14.23) reads "And he took the cup, and when he had given thanks, he gave it to them: and they all drank of it." In the Revised Standard Version the verse reads "And he took a cup..." using an indefinite article instead of the definite article. Why the change? Because in the time between the one translation and the other, earlier versions had been discovered which strongly favored the different reading.

It was not, however, simply a difference in a word. The difference conveyed a theological nuance.

The reading "He took the cup..." suggests a special cup, a cup identified for that purpose, different from other cups. "He took a cup..." suggests that at this Passover meal ordinary tableware was used, and the specialness of the cup was not in itself but was conferred upon it by the use that Christ made of it. A different theological meaning is suggested by the different translation.

When I was in Ghana, several years ago, I traveled with a college friend who worked with the British and Foreign Bible Society as an advisor to translators in the northern part of the country. Two women missionaries were translating the gospel of Mark into Dagomba, a local dialect They translated (Mark14.23) as "He took a calabash..." because that was the ordinary drinking cup of the tribal people in that area. They would understand "calabash" better, the two women thought, than the western term "cup." But a neighboring Roman Catholic missionary, with whom they discussed this, objected. The original communion cup was too sacred an object to be down graded to a calabash! I don't know how that was resolved, but the point is, language can be significant in even small matters.

The Nicene Debate

Another example of the importance of one word (in this case one letter) to theological understanding comes from a conference held at Nicaea in 325. A notable heresy of that time, Arianism, named after its original proponent, Arius, denied that Christ was fully divine. The often raucous debate swirled about the question of whether Christ was of *like* substance with the Father, in Greek *homoiousios*, or of *one* substance with the Father, *homoousios*, a view which later prevailed and became Orthodox Christian teaching. A matter of great doctrinal importance therefore turned on what appeared to be a very small issue in religious language, the difference of one letter. It was not however, small, and it indicates the very important role that language plays in religion.

Textual Issues in Other Religious Traditions

Other traditions are not without their textual and interpretive difficulties. Discussing the text of the Vedas, Moore and Radhakrishnan write, "The relative clarity of most of the hymns quoted here should not minimize the fact that almost innumerable problems and theories of interpretation are involved throughout the Vedas."[247] And discussing the text of the Upanishads used in their book "Attention is called to the questionable and misleading translation of certain basic terms in the text used."[248]

The original teaching of Buddhism was spoken by the Buddha, as was the teaching of Christ. Later the Buddhist teaching the *Canon* was written in Pali with some commentaries first in Sinhala, which were then translated into Pali hundreds of years later.[249] There are similarities in the history of the Canon to the history of the New Testament text. In both cases the question is how close do these texts take the believer to the words of the founder?

Chuang-Tzu, the Taoist philosopher, who is believed to have lived in the fourth century before Christ, taught that the limitations of language are so great they cannot express truth. He parodies the confusions of language.

> There is a beginning. There is a not yet beginning to be a beginning. There is a not yet beginning to be a not yet beginning to be a beginning. There is being. There is non-being. There is a not yet beginning to be non-being. There is a not yet beginning to be a not yet

beginning to be non-being. Suddenly there is being and non-being. But between this being and non-being, I don't really know which is being and which is non-being. Now I have just said something. But I don't know whether what I have said has really said something or whether it hasn't said something. ...If Tao is made clear, it is not Tao. If discriminations are put into words, they do not suffice. [250]

Inclusive Language

A contemporary issue in religious language, developed since the Second World War, is concern with inclusive language. The introduction to *The New Testament and Psalms: An Inclusive Version*, explains, "This version has undertaken to replace or rephrase all gender-specific language not referring to particular historical individuals, all pejorative references to race, color, or religion, and all identification of persons by their physical disability alone, by means of paraphrase, alternative renderings, and other acceptable means of conforming the language of the work to an inclusive idea."[251]

The *Inclusive Version* speaks to the concern of many women in the church, that the New Testament is biased toward men. To offset that, some churches I know render the Lords Prayer as "Our Lord which art in heaven" rather than "Our Father which art in heaven" and John 3.16 is read "God so loved the world that God gave God's son..." (occasionally 'child' is substituted) which is awkward. But it is an attempt to indicate how the New Testament expresses a male point of view, consistent with the time, but not consistent with God's manifestly equal love for all people, both men and women. This has not been a prominent issue before because women have not had a voice. Mrs. Lucretia Mott's *Women's Bible* was not well received and not widely used. Now they do have a voice. In Carol Gilligan's phrase it is a different voice, different from men's, and women believe it should be listened to – as do children. The book, *Children's Letters to God*, includes this letter from a little girl.

Dear God, Are boys better than girls? I know you are one but try to be fair. Sylvia[252]

Inclusive language is an attempt by her older sisters to correct what they perceive as an unfairness in the texts and much of the activities of the Christian religion.

Language Problems Of a Different Kind

From the examples given we see that language is important to religion. It is important that texts represent accurately the teaching of a founder, and commentaries reflect the teaching as far as possible without bias. These may be impossible expectations when, as with the New Testament, considerable time elapsed between the writing and the revelation, and multiple copies now exist, each a little different. Over the years major guardians of the faith have disagreed.

For Muslims many of these difficulties are overcome because, as they believe, the Qur'an was written directly by God. Muhammad, it is claimed, was illiterate, and could not possibly have written these scriptures himself. The Qur'an therefore *is* the word of God. Mormons believe that golden plates were found by Joseph Smith who was then directed by God to translate them by means of translating spectacles discovered with the plates. Again, we have the very words. Moses came down from the Mount with the Ten Commandments engraved on stone in his hands. In various ways different faiths seek to affirm the authenticity of their sacred texts.

But problems of a different kind exist with religious language. Consider the Nicene debate over whether Christ was of one substance or of like substance with the Father. How do we know which is correct, how could we ever know? On both sides of the debate were sincere Christians who believed in their interpretation. Arius, a "heretic" was convinced that he was right. But who was right?

Beyond that, even with the orthodox consensus that Christ was of one substance, what does it mean? Substance is material. God is not material. If we combine two cups of water they become one cup. This will not satisfy Christian theology, for though of one substance with the Father, Christ is not identical with the Father. He retains his own identity.

The issue is this. We are mortal, finite, and our understanding limited. God, or whatever deity, is immortal, infinite, unrestricted by anything. What can we, with our finite nature, know about or say about the infinite nature of God?

We can know by faith through revelation. The Muslim knows because God's teaching was given directly to Mohammed. In a similar way the Mormon knows, and so does the Jew. Yet even so there is an almost unbridgeable gulf of understanding between God and his human creation. According to the Muslim mystic Shaikh Alí Hujwírí (eleventh century).

> God is not finite that the imagination should be able to define Him or that the intellect should comprehend His nature... contemplation is an attribute of the heart and cannot be expressed by the tongue except metaphorically.[253]

Two Issues

First, trying to ensure that what is presented as the teaching of a founder is indeed that teaching. Rammohun Roy, the eighteenth-nineteenth century Indian philosopher and British Civil servant, made a translation of the Vedant (Vendanta) to recover its teaching from the "dark curtain of the Sungscrit language" which only Brahmans were permitted to read,[254] and make them available to the public. This is what Wycliffe endeavored when he translated the Latin Vulgate into English, and what motivated Erasmus' Greek New Testament. "I totally disagree," Erasmus wrote in the preface to his Greek New Testament,

> ...with those who are unwilling that the Holy Scriptures, translated into the common tongue, should be read by the unlearned... I wish that the farm laborer might sing parts of them at the plough, that the weaver might hum them at his shuttle, and that the traveler might beguile the weariness of the way by reciting them.[255]

Second, trying to understand the teaching, seeing that the Founder is holy, infinite, and changeless and we are not holy, we are finite, always changing. The third issue is closely related. Typically in religion the worshipper desires to understand and communicate with the infinite Founder, but anything we say is likely to be inadequate, if not actually false. What can we do? Perhaps we can accept the fact there is little we can do, that we cannot truly understand teaching about God nor have any reliable concept of God, that we can never express any idea of God without distortion. According to this even the name "God" is a misrepresentation, because what word of finite language can represent an infinite being?

The Way Of Negation

If the answer is we can do nothing, that does not mean we are rendered speechless; while we cannot say anything positive about God we can at least say what he is not. For example: he does not weigh a thousand pounds; he is not wicked; he does not, we might say, play dice with the universe; he is not powerless. This is a method of indirection developed by the twelfth century Jewish philosopher Maimonides (Moses ben Maimon) in his *Guide for the Perplexed* which he wrote for those who, "trained to believe in the truth of our holy law," because of the many ambiguous expressions used in the holy writings are "lost in perplexity and anxiety."[256] Maimonides writes, "Know that the negative attributes of God, are the true attributes."[257] This method conducts the mind to God.

> When we say that it (the being of God) is not feeble, we mean that its existence is capable of producing the existence of many other things; by saying that it is not ignorant, we mean "it perceives" or "it lives"-- for everything that perceives is living.[258]

Yet it is difficult to avoid a positive inference even in negations. By saying that God is not powerless we are affirming it is appropriate to apply the concept of power and lack of power to him. We can claim that God does not weigh a thousand pounds because we know, or strongly suppose, that weight is not relevant to a non-material being. Our negations are therefore possible only because of what we assume that we know. As Aquinas put it "unless the human intellect knew something positively about God, it could not deny anything of Him."[259]

Analogy

Aquinas was critical of the way of negation; he wrote, "A mere addition of negations, would not lead to positive knowledge."[260] He believed, however, that we could have knowledge of God. He proposed the way of analogy.

A familiar analogy to those who read the Bible is that which likens the relation between God and those who trust him to the relation between a father and his child. (In one case a mother – Isaiah 66:13). As a father loves his child so does your heavenly father love you.

The relationship that we know, love between father and child, illustrates a relation we do not know, love between God and his creation. Analogy is a resolution between positive and negative statements. We have to work from our own experience. For example, we might wish to describe God that he is good. If we declare that God's love and human love are identical we would be claiming, in Aquinas' terminology, that they are univocal. That seems to be asserting too much. The maxim "Love is blind" indicates how faulty human love is. If, however, we claim that God's love and human love are quite different, equirocal, we would seem to overlook how pure and beautiful human love can be, and that it seems to be at least a faint image of God's love.

So we make the analogical claim. It is indirect. It does not press the positive or the negative. It asserts a qualified similarity. F.C. Copelston explains:

> When terms like 'wise' and 'good' are predicted of God they are predicted neither univocally nor equivocally but in an analogical sense... This is possible because creatures have a real relation to God; they depend on God and derive their perfection from him.[261]

Metaphor

In his *Guide for the Perplexed*, Maimonides discusses the use of metaphor as a means of understanding God, or religious truth. Metaphor is the use of a word to describe something quite different. It is used often in poetry. In Hilda Conkling's poem "I am"

> I am willowy boughs
> For coldness
> I am gold-finch wings
> For darkness

And Carl Sandbergs poem "Fog" which begins...

> The fog comes
> On little cat feet.

Obviously the writer of the first poem cannot be "willowy boughs" or "gold-finch wings" but she is trying to create an image for the reader.

Similarly, in Sandberg's poem, fog does not have feet, certainly not cat feet. What are the writers trying to do?

There are several explanations of metaphor. One, I believe, is especially helpful, what Max Black describes as an interaction view. Every word has a set of associated commonplaces. The associated commonplaces of tiger are fierce, swift, stealthy, intense, powerful, and dangerous. Some of the Asian countries were described as economic tigers. They are not actual tigers, but their growing economic strength marked them as fierce, powerful, maybe dangerous economic competitors, metaphorically tigers. What happens, according to this theory, is that the object of the metaphor, the Asian countries, is viewed through the screen of the associated commonplaces of the tiger. Some of the commonplaces don't apply, tigers are four-footed animals; they are predatory meat eaters. But in constructing the metaphor we choose those commonplaces that apply. We then get a vivid impression of those countries, more vivid than simply describing them as economically aggressive.

The poet is not a willowy bough, but perhaps the graceful curve of the bough as it bends over a river bank and over water, captures for her a feeling of cool and restful calm, as gold-finch wings express a flash of light in her own heart despite surrounding dark.

Fog does not have feet, but we do know that cat feet are small and often gray, in fact, just like fog. Understanding fog through the associated commonplace of cat feet creates an image in our minds of fog as it moves in quietly, gently, a gray presence which has arrived before we are aware of it.

The Bible uses many metaphors: "God is a consuming fire," "I am the door" "I am the bread of life" "God is love" In each case God and Christ are seen through a set of associated commonplaces. Like a fire, God will consume everything in our lives that is combustible, not solidly based on a firm foundation. As a door provides an entrance so Christ provides the way to a new life. As bread is a staple food, especially in poorer countries, Christ provides life-giving nourishment for the soul. As love is a wonderful experience in its pure form, caring, strengthening, energizing, so does God as love strengthen, energize and care for those who trust him. A metaphor does not provide new knowledge, it brings into focus those qualities of an idea which, within a particular context, we want to emphasize. A metaphor can do more than that. When it is new, the unfamiliar juxtaposition of terms; fog: cat feet, Christ: bread, provides an intellectual, imaginative jolt. The reader or the listener then has an experience of the metaphor itself, which illuminates the meaning with greater immediacy than could a straightforward description – obviously of importance when trying to understand a religious idea.

Language Issues Are Not An End in Themselves

But the philosophical issues of religious language are not an end in themselves. Not if they are to take account of the reference to religion. Religious language is an expression of the heart. It cannot be otherwise. How can I better illustrate this than by example?

Robert Southwell (1561-1595) was an English Jesuit, arrested because of alleged association with a conspiracy to assassinate Queen Elizabeth. He was cruelly tortured and then hanged at Tyburn. This poem "The Burning Babe" was written while he was in Tyburn awaiting execution.

> As I in hoary winter's night
>> Stood shivering in the snow,
> Surprised I was with sudden heat
>> Which made my heart to glow;
> And lifting up a fearful eye
>> To view what fire was near,
> A pretty babe all burning bright
>> Did in the air appear;
> Who, scorched with excessive heat,
>> Such floods of tears did shed,
> As though His floods should quench His flames,
>> Which with His tears were bred:
> "Alas!" quoth He, "but newly born
>> In fiery heats I fry,
> Yet none approach to warm their hearts
>> Or feel my fire but I!
> 'My faultless breast the furnace is;
>> The fuel, wounding thorns;
> Love is the fire, and sighs the smoke;
>> The ashes, shames and scorns;
> The fuel Justice layeth on,
>> And mercy blows the coals,
> The metal in this furnace wrought
>> Are men's defiled souls:
> For which, as now on fire I am

> To work them to their good,
> So will I melt into a bath,
>   To wash them in my blood."
> With this He vanish'd out of sight
>   And swiftly shrunk away,
> And straight I called unto mind
>   That it was Christmas Day.

The poet provides a series of bold metaphors: love is fire, sighs are smoke, ashes are shame and scorn, burning metal - defiled souls. Yes, they are metaphors, we can identify them and discuss them in a philosophical and literary fashion, but they arise out of utmost anguish, out of physical pain and the immediate prospect cruel death. It was these that gave rise to the metaphors. That we must recognize and ponder.

Wilfred Owen served in the First World War. He was wounded, hospitalized, returned to action, then killed seven days before the Armistice. His poem, "The Parable of the Old Man and the Young" is an analogy. We could describe it this way: as Abraham was to Isaac so was the First World War to those who fought in it. But he twists the analogy and turns it against itself, with powerful effect.

> So Abram rose, and clave the wood, and went,
> And took the fire with him, and a knife.
> And as they sojourned both of them together,
> Isaac the first-born spake and said, My Father,
> Behold the preparations, fire and iron,
> But where the lamb for his burnt-offering?
> Then Abram bound the youth with belts and straps,
> And builded parapets and trenches there,
> And stretched forth the knife to slay his son.
> When lo! An angel called him out of heaven,
> Saying, Lay not thy hand upon the lad,
> Neither do anything to him. Behold,
> A ram, caught in a thicket by its horns;
> Offer the Ram of Pride instead of him.
> But the old man would not so, but slew his son,
> And half the seed of Europe, one by one.[262]

Here is a literary device which we cannot really understand unless we are aware of the anger and the outrage of the man who wrote it.

Analogy and metaphor are the means by which powerful emotions can be directed toward the reader, but they are not an end in themselves. "Side by side with conceptual language," wrote Ernst Cassirer, "there is an emotional language; side by side with logical or scientific language there is a language of poetic imagination. Primarily language does not express thoughts or ideas, but feelings and affections."[263]

Symbols

These feelings and affections are expressed most characteristically through the use of symbols "Hence," according to Ernst Cassirer, "instead of defining man as an animal rationale, we should define him as an animal symbolicum."[264]

A symbol can be a word, or an object, or a story, or music or even a person, which, while representing whatever it is, represents something else. Paul Tillich uses the example of a flag. A flag essentially is a piece of cloth, but it may represent a nation, so that to honor the flag is to honor the nation, to desecrate the flag is to insult the nation. This became an issue in the United States during the Viet Nam War. Martin Luther King Jr. is one person, not free from ordinary human failings, but he has become a symbol of black people's struggle for equal rights. "Mother" means a woman who has a child, yet it is scarcely possible to use the world without calling to mind a wide range of associations: steadfastness, persisting love, personal sacrifice. The word "mother" symbolizes these in various ways to various people. A piece of music shared by a couple at some time, may be a private symbol that becomes poignant when one of them has died. A story can be a symbol. *The Diary of Anne Frank* is a moving symbol of Jewish suffering during the Second World War. Though her diary was not written to be a symbol, it illustrates a point that Tillich makes. Symbols are not artificially created, and they cannot be deliberately destroyed. But they do die, as for example, the symbols of an ancient religion no longer followed.

In the case of Anne Frank's diary it not only represented something, but it has influenced, even determined the understanding of those who read it, or saw the play. I found her diary more illuminating than all the news reports and documentaries I had seen and read. This is one of the functions of a symbol. It can affect not only our understanding of what is symbolized but also our understanding of ourselves in relation to it.

I was once told a story by a pastor who spent several years in a Japanese prisoner of war camp during the Second World War. The prisoners were forbidden to hold religious services. However, when they could, secretly, the men would gather in the corner of a field where they were working. The pastor had hidden a small container of wine. He would take a cup of water and pour one drop of wine into it and then conduct the communion service. Impossible to taste but impossible not to feel it's symbolic power.

We are symbolic animals because our lives are scarcely ever just what we do or say or see. At home in the afternoon, when I was small, I would say to my mother, "It's almost four o'clock." a straightforward report on the time. But four o'clock in England is tea time, so what my factual statement meant was "It's time for tea?" or "Are you getting tea ready?" or "Are you ready for the crumpet man?" who would walk down our street with a tray of crumpets on his head covered with a green beige cloth, ringing his bell just before four o'clock. In our ordinary communication, as Maimonides noted almost a thousand years ago, indirection is direction. This is pervasive in religion. Because of the nature of any faith we are always having to approach it, as it were sideways. For example, how can we explain what Christ has done for men and women? Consider Emily Dickinson's elusive poem.

> The Savior must have been
> A docile Gentleman - -
> To come so far so cold a Day
> For little Fellowmen - -
>
> The Road to Bethlehem
> Since He and I were Boys
> Was leveled, but for that 'twould be
> A rugged billion Miles - -[265]

It is almost a commentary upon the New Testament passage...

So now, my friends, the blood of Jesus makes us free to enter boldly into the sanctuary by the new, living way which he has opened for us through the curtain, the way of his flesh. (Hebrews 10. 19-20 NEB)

This approach to religious knowledge is found elsewhere than in Christianity and Judaism. In the Brihad-Āranyaka Upanishad we read...

It is – as, when a drum is being beaten, one would not be able to grasp the external sounds, but by grasping the drum or the beater of the drum the sound is grasped.[266]

And regarding the reality of God...

Incomprehensible is that supreme Self, (Ātman) unlimited, unborn, not to be reasoned about, unthinkable.[267]

What is the answer?

May he endow us with clear intellect!

Myth

A symbol may be a story as, I suggested, *The Diary of Anne Frank*. More typically a symbol is a single item: a word, an object, a person, even music, such as a national anthem. Often symbols are found in the larger context of what we call myth. Except for those who regard it as an historical event the biblical story of the Flood is a myth, most likely adapted from an earlier Babylonian version. It describes how God punished earth's inhabitants because of their disreputable behavior, and founded a new race in the family of Noah. After the water subsided Noah sent out a dove (for the second time) to discover whether there was any dry land. The dove returned at the end of the day with a newly plucked olive leaf in her beak. (Genesis 8.11) This incident is used with great effect by Benjamin Britten in his *Noah's Fludde*. Both the dove and olive branch are symbols of peace, and in the context of the Flood story, promise restoration, a new beginning, the kind of hope that people have after a great calamity. If we read on in the Old Testament we see that the hope was badly disappointed, just as in life such hopes frequently are. But the Flood myth as a whole conveys the message that humans are not free to behave as they wish. God sets restrictions

The strength and enduring quality of such a myth is that every generation of people everywhere must listen to it and act upon it. Geoffrey Parrinder, writing about African mythology, refers to Carl Jung who taught that myths provide clues to " the deepest hopes and fears of mankind, not to be despised as stories, but studied carefully for their revelation of the depths of human nature."[268] I wonder at times whether we can be too eloquent about the range and character of myths. If a myth is truly a part of a culture the people in it will treat it as an ordinary fact of life, not so much to be studied and reflected upon as to be accepted without much self-conscious thought. It affects how they think without their specifically thinking about it. The Bhagavad-Gita is an example. One could say that every Indian knows it but does not dwell on it. Yet the terrible quandary facing Arjuna touches human depths because animosity within families is socially destructive and personally tragic. The world has been full of this in recent years, including India.

The Gilgamesh Epic

The Babylonian flood story, which we have described, is part of a larger work known as the Gilgamesh Epic. Utnapishtim, the Babylonian Noah, was mortal but had gained immortality. Gilgamesh decided to search for the secret of immortality for himself. His friend, Enkidu, had died. He could not bear the thought of it.

> Day and night I have wept over him.
> I would not give him up for burial –
> In case my friend should rise at my plaint –
> Seven days and seven nights,
> Until a worm fell out of his nose.[269]

I once shared this with a class of students. Many of them laughed. It was like a Woody Allen joke, a worm coming out of a nose. But of course it is not a joke. It is poignant that Gilgamesh would imagine his depth of grief could bring his friend back to life. Indeed, the Gilgamesh Epic, the myth of Gilgamesh, does reveal "the deepest hopes and fears of mankind."

There is no deeper hope than that "the last enemy"[270] death could be overcome, and no deeper fear than of the loss of those we love and of our own death. Preoccupation with these matters on the part of almost all religions is a testimony.

Myth and Truth

The issue of truth needs to be addressed because many Christians and Jews would find my description of the biblical Flood story as a myth to be repugnant. "These are not myths," they would say, "They are true. They truly happened." Truth can be defined in different ways, but what these persons probably mean by truth is that the assertion or truth claim is matched by facts that support it. A correspondence exists between the truth claim and what the claim is about. "Noah built an ark," is the claim. It is true if it corresponds with a state of affairs such as: Noah did indeed build an ark. Calling this state of affairs a myth denies its reality, painful to those who believe in the inerrancy of scripture.

I think we should be sensitive to such belief, but also recognize what is important about the stories. If they were all true, that is, if all the stories in the Bible were true, their theological value would be not simply that the details took place as described, but in what they mean.

The importance of the narrative emerges only by a process of reflection and interpretation. This may be contrary to what I have just written that people don't reflect self consciously upon the myths that are part of their culture. But in this instance, when a quandary is felt about truth claims versus "this is not true in that sense, it is myth," there has to be a self-conscious grappling with the issue.

At the beginning of this chapter I described language as a remarkable contrivance. I regard it as the greatest human achievement. It makes communication possible, it makes society possible, for while there were families before there was language, as there is among animals, it was limited by the inability to develop relationships that require more than ostensive communication. The creative and intellectual potential, although implicit, is stirred into action by the opportunities presented by language. It would be largely denied expression before language exists. One of the beneficiaries of this is religion. If religion is our creation then it, as well as language, is a major human achievement. Religious language is the way that humans elaborate their religious story. But if religion is of divine origin, given to humans by intuition and revelation, language is the means of conveying what is interpreted to the finite mind. Analogy, metaphor, symbol and myth are some of the mechanisms we use. To study it from the outside, which we do for the most part as philosophers, puts us at a remove from the religious heart of it.

For the subject to come alive in a religious sense we must relate the mechanisms of religious language to the perpetual struggle of emotion and intellect, to belief. Then, in William Blake's words we may find it "Burning bright."

Language and Religious Devotion

Another matter to discuss as we consider religion and language is the relation between language and religious devotion. My own experience of this is with the liturgy of the Anglican church I attended when I was a boy. I'm not sure whether the repetition of prayers and readings impressed me most, or their devotional, religious, literary quality.

But something about the measure and solemnity of the language still creates for me a sense of worship. I have been intrigued that young couples wanting to get married occasionally ask that their marriage service use the traditional and now archaic language of thee, and thou, even though we are in the twenty-first century. Interestingly, at least in the Presbyterian Church, this "archaic" wedding service is no longer in print, which illustrates the gap that often exists between the thinking of church leaders, officials and others in those positions, and what the average churchgoer wants as a part of worship.

The eighteenth century hymn writers were especially gifted with devotional insight. Consider William Cowper's hymn...

> Ye fearful saints, fresh courage take;
> The clouds ye so much dread
> Are big with mercy, and shall break
> In blessings on your head
>
> Judge not the Lord by feeble sense,
> But trust him for his grace;
> Behind a frowning providence
> He hides a smiling face
>
> Blind unbelief is sure to err,
> And scan his work in vain;
> God is his own interpreter,
> And he will make it plain.

I find a wealth of implications here: the image of dark clouds unexpectedly providing a blessing, and what we might fear of God's judgment revealing in fact his love, and the promise that what we do not understand about our faith will be made plain. This is not philosophy or even theology but personal devotion which language both expresses and directs.

How many persons in times of stress have turned to the twenty-third psalm? Yet if we examine it critically, it is full of the kind of wishful thinking most adults regard as delusive: our cup does not run over, goodness and mercy don't follow us all the days of our life. But the words express something, despite frequent disappointments we still believe. It may not be true in our experience, but is true, we hope, of the world as a whole. Our experience is one thing, the character of existence is another, and that is what we trust.

Some of this is captured by what I regard as an especially beautiful prayer.

> Support us all the day long
> Until the shadows lengthen
> And the evening comes,
> And the busy world is hushed,
> And the fever of life is over,
> And our work is done.
> Then in thy infinite mercy
> > Grant us a safe haven,
> > And a holy rest,
> > And peace at last.

The quality of language is hugely important at critical moments in one's religious experience. Consider the consoling power of these words:

> O God, who healest the broken in heart, and bindest up their wounds: Look down in tender pity and compassion upon thy servants whose joy has been turned into mourning. Leave them not comfortless, but grant that they may be drawn closer to one another by their common sorrow. As thou hast given them this new tie to bind them to the world unseen, so grant unto them that where their treasure is, there may their hearts be also.

The deeply thoughtful expression of those who listen to this prayer at such a moment is a repeated example for me of the relation between language and religious devotion. Shakespeare's language has the ability to lift one out of one's self into the realm he is describing. That is one of the functions of religious language; as we use it or hear it we are moved closer to what it means.

The Sikhs have a sacred text, the Japji, reputedly written by Guru Nanak, the founder of their religion. It is regarded as the key to their teaching and they are expected to learn it by heart and repeat it everyday.

The Muslim community expresses its faith in the simplest way "There is no God, but God, and Muhammad is God's apostle." Cantwell Smith refers to the "liquid alliteration" of this statement in Arabic, which is how it is always repeated no matter what the country. The formula is used constantly. "…it is whispered in the ears of the new born baby, so that its affirmation may be the first words that a Muslim shall hear on entering this world. And between then and its use at his funeral he will hear it, and pronounce it, often and often and often."[271]

Evelyn Underhill writes,

> The response of a creature conditioned by time and space to a timeless and spaceless Reality will have characters which constantly break the bounds both of philosophy and of logic. The normal man, in his secret no less than in his corporate intercourse with God, must therefore be willing to use thought, feeling, and imagination as long and as much as he can; must worship under images that which is beyond image, and adapt the machinery and language of human emotion to his loving communion with the Unseen.[272]

Prayer

Prayer is a characteristically devotional use of language. We have referred to several prayers in this section. William James notes that "Prayer… is the very soul and essence of religion." He quotes a French theologian who writes "Religion… is an intercourse, a conscious and voluntary relation, entered into by a soul in distress with the mysterious power upon which it feels itself to depend, and upon which its fate is contingent. This intercourse with God is realized by prayer. Prayer is religion in act; that is, prayer is real religion."[273]

Prayers, however, may not be always expressions of distress. They can be questions, thanks, and expressions of joy. And prayers are not always solemn and literary.

The birth of a child is the occasion, generally though sadly not always, of happy thanks to God. Those who have worked with children and young people in religious settings know how much enthusiasm and often how little attention to the formalities of liturgy or the rules of language there can be. If they are excited they are just excited, and let the adults who are close to them know plainly. The term Hallelujah! sums up this characteristic of religious language.

But despite the importance of language, instances occur when emotion is so deep, words fail us. The value of spoken prayers at a service is that they express what a person attending may not be able to express. When an animal is sick it often goes away and hides. When we are hurt we will often do the same. William Cowper's poem "Mary," written about his long-time companion who did a great deal for him and then became ill and completely dependent upon him, comes as close as anything I know to expressing in words a depth of grief which is almost beyond them. Lord Tennyson wrote a long poem *In Memoriam* after the death of a friend. He touches upon the delicate balance of words and wordlessness in times of grief.

> I sometimes hold it half a sin
> To put in words the grief I feel;
> For words, like Nature, half reveal
> And half conceal the Soul within

Nevertheless, perhaps because he was a wordsmith or because what he wrote is true, he continued...

> But, for unquiet heart and brain,
> A use in measured language lies;
> The sad mechanic exercise,
> Like dull narcotics, numbing pain

Language may be more than a dull narcotic, as we have tried to show. It is the inseparable companion of religious emotion. It is that through which, in religious terms, we both give and receive.

Chapter 11

Religion and Education

As Little To Do With Religion As Possible

Writing about religion and education we can adopt a number of perspectives. One, currently popular among those in the United States who consider themselves guardians of educational independence, is that education should have as little to do with religion as possible unless the education is, as it would be in a seminary, intentionally religious. Otherwise, religion is to be treated with caution, even suspicion, rather like a computer virus. Samuel Miller observes wryly,

> Religion and education have been married, divorced, and remarried so often in their long history that it is easy to say that they cannot get along with each other any better than they can do without each other. There has always been a tendency for one party to dominate the situation, and then the inevitable split has occurred, forcing a temporary and uncomfortable separation. In time, however, separation proved painful, and the couple has always come to a hopeful reconciliation, yet never altogether satisfactorily, or for long.[274]

The current situation is an uneasy one, as Harvey Cox put it: "Today... when we talk about the relationship between religion and education it is almost unanimously agreed that there is a problem if not a crisis."[275]

The crisis, certainly the problem in recent years, goes back to the 1963 Supreme Court ruling that declared it unconstitutional to lead school children in a recitation of the Lords Prayer. This did not prohibit teaching religion in school. The Court noted specifically, "nothing we have said here indicates that... study of the Bible or of religion, when presented objectively as part of a secular program of education may not be effected consistently with the First Amendment."[276]

Nevertheless, many teachers are cautious. When the Pope was visiting the United States recently, and newspapers, radio and TV were full of it, the topic was not mentioned in a current-events discussion in a school on Long Island. The district superintendent who heard about this asked the teacher why. "Oh" she answered, "I would never mention the Pope in class!" [277] Her caution may seem excessive until we consider instances across the country when what was perceived, officially, as too much support of the Christian religion has led to a reprimand or even dismissal. People, ordinarily, do not take chances with their job.

An Objective Approach

The Supreme Court ruling itself suggests a less limited perspective. So long as religion is "presented objectively as part of a secular program of education," religion, understood in this way, is like history, or literature or sociology, something we should learn about as an object of study in its own right, and as an inescapable element of other subjects. Yet one can hardly study history in earlier centuries without studying religion, particularly sixteenth and seventeenth century Europe. What historical understanding can we have of Henry VIII's *Six Articles*, or the English Civil War, without a grasp of the theological motivations, which inspired them? As an undergraduate studying history at Cambridge I attended numerous lectures in the divinity school. This is to study religion as an adjunct of other subjects.

Religion can be studied for its own sake. A recent news item reports that a California high school teacher conducts two comparative religion courses in his school each semester. Our culture is "amazingly ignorant," he explains, about what Jews, Muslims, and Buddhists believe, even, in a still largely Christian country, what Christians believe.[278] Presumably these courses fall within allowable constitutional limits. But the limits are not always clear. "People for the American

Way Foundation" a Washington-based group that monitors church-state relations is objecting to a "Bible History" course taught in several Florida school districts because it does not teach in a "sufficiently objective and neutral fashion."[279]

Up to this point, and setting aside the charge against the Florida schools, even the most zealous advocate of separation between church and state should not be alarmed. To teach religion as one teaches history or sociology or (as the debasement of humanistic studies has it) 'social studies', is religiously innocuous because it is not teaching religion. It is teaching about religion.

Yet such teaching may not be as innocuous as we suppose. Human beings have an insatiable desire for assurance. We live in a world of more than six billion people, perhaps only a hundred may know us. The number of those who care for us is usually much smaller. It is a lonely existence, and rather frightening at times because we may discover that this world is not a comfortable or friendly place. The answer, as Tolstoy found, is to go beyond the boundaries of finite existence and explore the infinite, that is, turn to religious possibilities. There we may find the one who is closer than a brother, or the Ātman, self, who is the Brahman, all. In these ways the individual, nothing among billions, becomes something, a somebody, a being of importance. This belief is so wide spread, and so enduring it seems like a trivialization to explain it as egoism. Egoism may be psychological, built into the nature of a human, and unavoidable, or it may be the ethically unattractive characteristic of someone who just wants his own way.

Concern for self, whatever the motive, is that in the whole wide world my interests are important and deserve attention from the world. It is either enormous arrogance or the unself-conscious awareness of a truth which is half of the explanation of life. The other half is what responds to our "arrogance," which in various ways we describe as the divine. When we teach these things, however superficially, however ironically, we teach about something that cannot be only an item of information. Those who wish to defend the separation of church and state should be alert because the power of religious education may be greater than educational administration or teachers themselves can control. The nature of religion is to offer hope for the future and strength for the present. It is powerful medicine; hugely attractive to a world of the spiritually sick and under nourished. The nature of people is to want assurance and satisfaction, which often the world cannot give. Religion offers both. Despite its faults people turn to it and will continue to turn to it. For these reasons even teaching *about* religion may not be as innocuous as we might suppose.

Pushing Things Up to Their First Principles

The argument thus far is that even to teach religion objectively and academically, as surely the high school teacher whom we referred to does, may have consequences not intended by the teacher. But that can happen as the result of teaching any subject. Why give special attention to the consequences of teaching religion?

One answer is that "...religion has the habit," as John Henry Newman put it, "of pushing things up to their first principles." [280] Science, as is often noted, cannot explain itself. The scientist must simply deal with physical existence. Could we rest there? The data which science provides should be sufficient to satisfy our curiosity for a lifetime. But we do not rest, and perhaps we cannot; so we posit an unmoved mover, or an ultimate good, or a One, or a divine creator. We do this because the fact of existence presents a huge question mark, and we, as humans who are busy finding out what can be known, want also to find out what may never be known, namely the first principles which religious reflection is always calling upon. Religions, and the theology which explains them, are the result of that endeavor. Religious education is the attempt to understand those explanations. The potential problem is that one explanation will be stressed at the expense of others or in despite of the others. It is a problem because people's attachment to a religion is emotional, often held with passion without regard for reason. Perceived slights against religion, even serious criticism, create anger, even violence. Religion can be a disturbing element in education; good sense suggests, leave it alone.

The Individual as an Educational Center

Thus far, discussing the topic, religion and education, we have almost unconsciously dealt with it in its formal sense, beginning in grade school and continuing in University. This neglects the equally important education we receive from parents and other family members and friends, and the education we gain from our own experiences and deliberations. So much attention is attached to formal instruction we forget how important "social education" is both to receive as children and young people, and to give to persons younger then ourselves when we are older.

Much of it simply happens, we are not aware of it as education, namely, what our parents tell us, or how they behave in relation to what they believe. The mother of one of my students was raped, beaten and left for dead. She survived and told her daughter, then a child, "Get an education." The family lived in the worst of circumstances; the chances of getting an education were low. But the daughter, my student, took what her mother said to heart, and fifteen years later repeated it to me with great earnestness. She had learned something from the example of her mother, and that was as much a part of her education as anything I could teach. Similarly, a belief in God professed and acted upon can make a difference in what a child believes and continues to believe in later life.

We could think of an individual as an educational center, or his /her own web page, receiving a continuous flow of data. This data is our life's experience which we transmute into knowledge and pass on to others. Yet we may not transmute it well. We may not take the trouble or give it sufficient thought, so that what we pass on is not wise and not helpful. But whatever in the data we receive that concerns itself with religion is part of our religious education, and whatever we pass along, deliberately or not, concerned with religion, is also religious education. We are responsible as a recipient to pay attention, and we are responsible as a provider to be aware of what data we provide. Thus every one of us is an educator; good or bad, independent of formal schooling, and part of what we teach is religion.

The Point of View of This Believer

Something should be said about the importance of religious education from the point of view of the believer. In 1944, during the Second World War, the British Government passed an education act that required school children in all grades to receive religious instruction every week. A number of Teacher' Guides were printed. One was entitled *Christianity Goes into Action*, its sub-title *Lessons on Great Deeds in Christ's Name*. The book contained forty-five biographies of prominent Christian men and women. The Preface states its position clearly,

The aim of this book is to show how the principles of Christianity, as laid down by its Founder, have transformed the life of the world, when they have been worked out in practice, or applied to contemporary conditions of life. It has always been difficult to *explain* Christianity to children, and to make its relevance to daily life clear to the adolescent; these difficulties face the teacher today with greater force and reality than ever before. Experience suggests that the most successful way of teaching Christianity is to *show it at work* in the lives of individual Christians. This, in essence, is the purpose of this volume, and explains both its contents and their arrangement.[281]

The emphasis is on teaching by example rather than teaching doctrine, but the writer, expressing the position of the British government, considered it of great importance that children in the country should receive such education. It's worth remembering that 1944, when the Act was passed, was during the Second World War. By then the conflict was turning in favor of the allies, but the debates which led to the passing of the Act began when it was by no means certain that Britain would survive. It was felt, however, that a nation fighting against a manifest evil should know what principles it stood for. The strongly Christian principles of those days would be out of favor now when Britain has a large and growing Muslim minority as well as many Hindus. But the principle is valid, as it was then, that to a great number of persons religious beliefs are the foundation of life. In a recent issue of *Hinduism Today* the writer of an article "Hinduism, the Greatest Religion in the World" expresses this thought.

No other faith boasts such a deep and enduring comprehension of the mysteries of existence, or possesses so vast a metaphysical system. The storehouse of religious revelations in Hinduism cannot be reckoned. I know of its equal nowhere.[282]

The writer is critical of the Pope who had visited India a short time before and called upon Christians to pour more energy in converting the 'lost souls' of India. Obviously the Pope believes that Christianity is the world's greatest religion. But both would agree that education in their faiths is important.

A Christmas letter I received this year from long time friends discusses their concern about the education of their five-year-old son. They have decided to send him to a private school. "It seems," they write "that public schools today go out of their way to exclude God and morality from the classroom, and then people wonder why students do immoral and sometimes tragic things." What they appreciate most about this school is that their young son "is taught and shown Biblical principles and morals. This kind of teaching is priceless as it has lifelong and even eternal value. So, to us, it is well worth the cost of tuition." Were my friends to meet the writer of the article on Hinduism, despite their differences they would have much in common, that what they believe about God be taught fairly and fully to their children.

John Milton writes plainly in his letter addressed to Master Samuel Hartlib. "The end then of learning is to repair the ruins of our first parents by regaining to know God aright and out of that knowledge to love Him, to imitate Him to be like Him." [283] Milton provides a justification of an education rooted in religious teaching. If we interpret "the ruins of our first parents" as the pride, willfulness and ignorance of our forebears then what we do to repair that is of value. And if what we do is to give serious thought to the most profound issues of existence which are the first concern of religion, religious education is certainly desirable. Some might object that this is not different from the study of philosophy. In the Indian tradition there is no difference. In the West we perceive a difference, yet perhaps not so much difference. A religious explanation is a metaphysics which posits certain explanatory hypotheses such as, there is one being, God. The difference is not between philosophy and religion but between philosophers and theologians, between those whose views are always open-ended and those who at a point make a commitment "Here we stand."

Non-Western Points of View

A non-western reader might object to the discussion thus far as biased. The quote from Samuel Miller at the beginning of this chapter in which he refers to religion and education having been married, divorced and remarried, makes sense when the two are regarded as separate entitles. But in Islam, for example, there is no such clear distinction. The Qur'an, which is God's revealed word, is regarded by Muslims as the source of all knowledge, therefore all knowledge depends upon it. According to this, religious education is education, and education is religious education, even if the immediate subject of study seems remote, such as contemporary physics. Upon reflection it will be seen from a Muslim view that, while not directly stated, what we claim as modern knowledge is implied in that ancient text.

In Hinduism and Buddhism the nature of the teaching is that it flows through the whole of life. It would be difficult to separate instruction about the eightfold path from whatever else a Buddhist student might learn, or to ignore the role of self, Ātman, and its relation to the universal Brahman in Hinduism. They are integrally a part of the knowing and learning subject. Religion in these traditions is not a separate item of life's experience; it is part of that experience.

My earlier argument, that to teach about religion may have consequences not intended, perhaps not even wanted by the teacher, seems to be irrelevant when life is understood in terms of religious culture. The closest that the western world comes to this is in what is known as civil religion.

Civil Religion

In recent years much has been written about America's civil religion. It has no creed or sacred text, no liturgy, no place of worship, yet it is widespread in American society, influential and important, "a central source of coherence in American public culture." [284] In one respect America would seem to be a thoroughly secular and materialistic society, strict public controls over expressions of religion, many churches empty which once were full, staggering crime rates, an almost manic preoccupation with material possessions. This is the picture which often repels people in other parts of the world. Yet there is another side, an extremely high rate of church attendance despite the empty churches, (usually the older mainline churches), a high level of personal religious belief, (if we accept the Gallup polls), and a strong commitment to the general religious and ethical principles of the Bible. The polls may be exaggerated; churchgoing not so great as people claim, yet there is a wide respect for religion. "One of the strongest identifiers of America as a religious society is the way its religion is publicly invoked and symbolically brandished." [285]

Prayer in schools is restricted, but most sessions of Congress begin with prayer. Coins bear the legend "In God We Trust." The current presidential candidates have gone out of their way to assure potential voters how religious they are. It's quite unlikely that a candidate who declared frankly that he did not believe in God could be elected. Numerous public functions are opened with prayer, including presidential inaugurations, and in crises, such as the bombing in Oklahoma City, a whole community turns to prayer.

The paradox in this chapter should be obvious; all this, yet the utmost awkwardness when it comes to religion and education. N.J. Demerath offers an explanation.

> Actually, these two seemingly inconsistent syndromes are strangely symbiotic. Each is a guard against the others' excesses, and each provides a countervailing assurance as a boost to the others' legitimacy. That is, we can indulge a symbolic civil religion precisely because there is a substantive separation of church and state in important matters of government policy; at the same time, our separation is never a total rupture because of the presence of overarching civil religious ceremonials.[286]

This may be accurate, or it may be providing too much of an explanation for a normal feature of society. Demerath writes further about American civil religion as a "binding cultural force." That is true of other societies; Islam in Bosnia for example, Catholicism in Croatia, Orthodox Christianity in Bulgaria. Watching teenagers in Blagoevgrad, Bulgaria, carrying lighted candles through the streets of their town at midnight after an Easter service, it was obvious that although these young people were not especially religious, giggling, laughing, running back and forth, having fun, their Orthodox faith was important to them.

Simply put, religion is part of education because it is part of life. We need to know about it, not only as believers in a particular religious faith but as members of a society where we live among people, many of whom are believers, with whom we do business. I believe that it is part of the responsibility of society, as well as a home, to provide it. And I believe that it is part of our responsibility to make sure we receive it.

Religious Education in the Academy

Important to this discussion is the place of religion in University education, specifically the American University. An issue of *Academe*, the Bulletin of the American Association of University Professors, devoted one of its issues to the topic. "The Academy: Freedom of Religion or Freedom from Religion?" Martin Marty, who wrote the lead article, warns that he is going to preach the gospel. He explains, "Preaching the gospel... here will mean commending the teaching and study of religion as an enjoyable endeavor, a potentially exuberant adventure, a privilege which comes with the enterprise of educating in a pluralistic environment." [287]

Why is it necessary to preach such an obvious truth? University education in this country was nurtured in a religious context, and a great many religion courses continue to be taught. At Cornell, for example, there are so many it would require, so it is said, more than eight years to take them all! The complaint however, is that "virtually all these courses are taught from a perspective that considers religion as a cultural artifact... it is dissected in ways that are indifferent to truth claims." [288] One cannot be indifferent to truth claims when studying religion. The core of a religion is its truth claims. Nevertheless, the academy does not want to get any closer to a subject it regards widely with suspicion, if not disdain. As one article put it, "Religion has not been able to find a way fully to participate in the intellectual conversation of the contemporary American university. For the academy, religion is not a kind of difference that matters." [289]

I found myself surprised but pleased that the articles in this issue are critical of the prevailing skeptical academic view. "We do our students no educational service by pretending that religion isn't out there and doesn't matter. We cannot promote the tolerance of something we trivialize or ignore." [290] The writers argue strongly against the negative attitudes they perceive in the universities toward religion." To bar the campus gates against religion therefore deprives students of a vital opportunity to discover who they are through thoughtful and self critical engagement with competing accounts of the nature of the world and the ground of value." [291]

In my own institution almost every course offered that is or appears to be about religion quickly fills, with other students sometimes pleading with the instructor to be added to the class as an overload. Often students misunderstand the objective of a course (Philosophy of religion is not a course in world religions) and they may resent having to study seriously a topic they consider they already know. But interest is considerable. Students actually have little knowledge of the Bible or any religious text. Their primary and secondary schools were not helpful, and often their churches and synagogues and other places of worship were not much help either. The students come to university largely ignorant of religious knowledge, other than a scattering of doctrine. Many are not satisfied with that. They want to find out. They want to learn about something they believe is important and yet have missed.

I speak for one campus only, but the articles in this issue of Academe suggest there may be a shift - at least the beginnings of one - toward the place of religion on the college and university campus. Understandably, these articles are written from the point of view of the professor. But student attitudes are plain, and in the tradition of universities which, despite their academic independence, are still led by what their clientele want, religious instruction will play a continuingly larger role.

What will be needed are teachers able to take up that larger role who can be sensitive to the many sides of religious debate, and respectful of different opinions. The traditional ideal of the university professor (no doubt, a parody) is that he/she teaches all subjects objectively and without emotion. The mind must be at work, but not the heart. In teaching religion, however, and not only that, the mind must be at work, and the heart. A university reflects and explains the society which creates it. Society includes the whole range of human interest. It is made up of persons. Hence the university, reflecting and explicating society, is reflecting and explicating the persons who constitute it. Could we claim that a university is an individual writ large? If so, if even partly so, as a person is both mind and heart, a university must attend to both, particularly when teaching religion. If it does it may be able to enter into the spirit of Martin Marty's claim that the teaching and study of religion is an "enjoyable endeavor, a potentially exuberant adventure, a privilege which comes with the enterprise of educating in a pluralistic environment."

Chapter 12

Many Religions

It is almost inevitable that our religious journey begins from within our own tradition. It is what we are born into, what becomes dear to us. It is the truth, because our parents and our family tell us true things. We trust them, we believe them. We believe what they believe. So begins the process of constructing our convictions on the scaffold of the faith bequeathed to us, the invisible hand of countless moments putting in place the initial artifacts of what becomes our life.

When we refer to religious faith, our own or any other, we are referring to deeply rooted experiences of great importance to those who have them, and because of that, usually resistant to change. Only by recognizing this can we understand and respect what other people in their different traditions claim to believe.

That awareness should be a prerequisite, uppermost in out minds as we approach the subject, called by various names: "Christian faith and other faiths," "The challenge of world religions," "A religiously pluralistic world." The first takes the point of view of a Christian, surveying other beliefs compared with the teachings of Christ. The second, a term used by Hans Kühn, again from a Christian point of view, identifies the difference as potentially dangerous. The third recognizes the existence of many religions and studies them impersonally or objectively to try to reach an unbiased understanding.

But these three approaches among many that can be taken are not quite satisfactory. To study the deeply rooted experiences of religion impersonally is to stand outside it and so be separated from it. It is a problem when we attempt to understand religions other than our own. Yet it is a problem which has to be faced and as far as possible overcome. It is unavoidable, because while we grow up with our own traditions we have to "learn about" others. It is like growing up with a language or learning a language later. If we haven't grown up with a language, yet want to speak it, we have to learn it. The same is true when studying religions, but in doing so we may regard them simply as "other." We lump them together, perhaps not deliberately, in the way we lump together other countries: we give foreign aid to "third world" or "underdeveloped" countries. It's handy, but misleading. Yet for the most part we are not dismissive, we just don't know, or we are not that much interested unless other religions affect our lives.

The study of religions is often described in college catalogues as "World Religions" and "Comparative Religions." We study them to find out about their teachings, the nature of their worship, and their role in society. After a while we learn how they differ from one another. To attempt that is a large undertaking; to do it thoroughly is a lifetime task.

The philosopher will have to cover much of that ground. As the philosopher of science requires an understanding of science to function adequately as a philosopher in that field, so the philosopher of religion requires an understanding of religion, and in these days, I would say, an understanding of religions other than the one he or she grew up in. This is entirely consistent with a philosophic approach, and distinguishes the philosopher from the theologian. Traditionally, the theologian is concerned with understanding one religion, generally believed to be a true metaphysical account of reality as a whole. The philosopher will not deny this but will ask questions about it. Truth is more complex than most believers are inclined to admit. The one genuinely philosophical question in the New Testament is Pilate's response to Christ's claim that he came to bear witness to the truth. Pilate's answer, "What is truth?" (John 18:37-38) suggests he was familiar with philosophical thinking, but theologically, indicates his ignorance of who Christ was. The philosopher now is better able to understand whom Christ claimed to be, having available John's Gospel and the rest of the New Testament, and so is better able to question the Christian faith. But the philosopher questions every faith, because philosophy gives no credence to one above the other except, as John Hick argues, on account of qualitative differences, not hard to recognize as between Buddhism and the murderous extremes of the cult in Uganda.[292]

The philosopher, therefore, may not be welcome in god-fearing circles where truth is relied on and accepted by faith. In the Introduction we touched briefly on the differences between philosophy and religion. Some thinkers, such as William Temple and Geddes MacGregor, were of the view that there could be no interrelationship. "The primary assurances of religion," wrote Temple, "are the ultimate questions of philosophy." MacGregor warned that philosophy has a tendency to kill religion. It would follow from this that here are two different approaches to life, mutually incompatible.[293]

Non-Western Religious Traditions

But throughout the book we have referred to non-Western religion, in particular to the religions of India, primarily Hinduism and Buddhism. There the distinction we take for granted between philosophy and religion does not exist. As one writer explained, the chief mark of Indian philosophy "is its concentration on the spiritual," a characteristic usually ruled out of Western philosophical thinking.[294] Intuition, generally treated with suspicion by western philosophy, is regarded as "the only method through which the ultimate can be known."[295]

It is a different thought world, and we are intellectually and religiously insular if we do not try to understand it.

The Indian religious philosophical tradition is the most ancient that we know, going back fifteen centuries before the time of Christ, to the mid-second millennium. When Abraham and his family were traveling southwest to Canaan at the command of God, (taking a broad chronological view) some unknown authors were composing the Vedas, the oldest known Indian scriptures, and the earliest examples of metaphysical speculation. Geographically the distance between Canaan, now Israel, and the Indus valley, where Indian religion developed, is a few hours flight. But conceptually, the distance is enormous.

Consider two texts which illustrate this: one is the familiar opening passage in the Old Testament "In the beginning God created the heavens and the earth." The other is the Vedic *Hymn of Creation*.

The biblical passage (Genesis 1:1) is a plain assertion of the creative supremacy of God echoed throughout the Old Testament and in the

New. It affirms unambiguously who is the Creator, what he did, and what we are to believe. The Vedic *Hymn of Creation* is quite different:

> Non-being then existed not nor being:
> There was no air, nor sky that is beyond it.
> What was concealed? Wherein? In whose protection?
> And was there deep unfathomable water?...
> Who knows for certain? Who shall here declare it?...
> None knoweth whence creation has arisen;
> And whether he has or has not produced it:
> He who surveys it in the highest heaven,
> He only knows, or haply he may know not.[296]

The Old Testament states that the Spirit of God moved over the face of the deep. The Vedic *Hymn of Creation*, written many years before, appears to be searching behind that moment before anything existed. "What was concealed?" the writers ask. "Wherein? In whose protection? And was there deep unfathomable water?" These are philosophical questions of a kind that could destroy faith. Yet they do not. They rather represent faith as inquiry, not something achieved but a process of searching for what might be achieved. The fact that it might instead of will be for sure is not a failure. It is part of its nature. To have questions in the face of imponderable mystery is neither pessimism nor optimism. The Kena Upanishad, as its name indicates, asks "By whom?"

> By whom impelled soars forth the mind projected?
> By whom enjoined goes forth the earliest breathing?
> By whom impelled this speech do people utter?
> The eye, the ear—what god, pray, them enjoineth?"

The questions are not answered. We cannot answer them.

> There the eye goes not;
> Speech goes not, nor the mind.
> We know not, we understand not
> How one would teach It, ...[297]

> It is not understood by those who [say they] understand it
> It is understood by those who [say they] understand it not.[298]

There can be a way of understanding as the Mundaka Upanishad explains.

> Taking as a bow the great weapon of the Upanishad,
> One should put upon it an arrow sharpened by meditation.
> Stretching it with a thought directed to the essence of That,
> Penetrate that Imperishable as a mark, my friend.
> The mystic syllable *Om* (pranava) is the bow.
> The arrow is the self (*ātman*)
> *Brahman* is said to be the mark. (laksya)[299]

Ātman and Brahman are like the Yin Yang in Chinese thought, distinct yet inseparable, understood only in terms of the other. Our rationality, our divinity, our status are derived from our unity with the whole. The Indian concept is captured in the phrase "Tat Tvam asi", That thou art. We are Ātman and we are Brahman. We are ourselves, yet we are God.

It is a strange concept to those nurtured on the Christian faith. The final blasphemy, which led to Christ's execution, was his claim to be God. What does it mean, to be God? The monotheistic view is more graspable: we are here, God is there. The infinite is greater than our finitude. But in Hindu religion to be God is to be one with all things.

As we probe these ideas we are as much in the realm of philosophy as religion. The ideas are not entirely separate from the Judaeo Christian tradition. Indeed, God is spirit, and his/her creation is physical. All that exists proceeds from God and bears his mark, and Christians can be one with God. (1. John 2:24; John 14:20) The interaction is extremely close. What this suggests is that teachings other than our own may have a way of illuminating our own, although on the face of it they are very different.

Sri Aurabindo wrote, "Philosophy is the intellectual search for the fundamental truth of things, religion is the attempt to make the truth dynamic in the soul of man."[300] All religions are engaged in that quest, and consequently all religions should be able to learn from one another.

Buddhism

Buddhism has a strong presence in the United States with its own magazines, such as *Tricycle*, and *Shambhala Sun* and it has developed a great deal of confidence in its importance as a world religion. The exiled Dalai Lama attracts much sympathy from people who are repelled by the situation of a peaceable country occupied and victimized by a foreign power. The Dalai Lama himself is a symbol of the freedom that the Tibetans want and probably everyone wants, as they understand it, in their own way. The Chinese see political freedom and too much social freedom as a threat. By limiting freedom they hope to enhance the influence and the well being of their country. But that is a mistake. In a recent book an economist from India, a poor country and a free country, writes "The success of a society is to be evaluated, in this view, primarily by the substantive freedoms that the members of that society enjoy."[301]

But beyond what the Dalai Lama represents politically he has drawn attention to Buddhism as a religion and way of life. The oldest form of Buddhism is known as Theravada, and is non-theistic. Individuals must seek enlightenment for themselves without reference to gods or any supernatural agency. An individual is responsible for his or her own life. It is a type of humanism, which appeals primarily to disciplined persons. As one writer comments "Had Buddhism remained as it was at the beginning, it is doubtful that more than a handful of people would have been interested in it."[302] But after the Buddha's death his teaching underwent a change. It was declared, and became a tenet of faith, that the Buddha's known teaching was not all that he had taught. The story is told that once when the Buddha was teaching in a forest he picked up some leaves. These, he explained, were only a few of all the leaves that there were in the forest, so his teaching included much more than had been given openly.

From this tradition developed Mahayana Buddhism, according to which the Buddha was more than a man. He came to earth to help humankind, and he was not the only Buddha. There were many Buddhas, divine beings to whom people could pray for help and understanding. Mahayana Buddhism created the concept of the Bodhisattvas; humans who, by the pure quality of their lives, could have achieved Nirvana, but chose to return to earth to help their fellow humans. This is reflective of Christian teaching, of the one who came to save and give his life as a ransom for many. Some Christians do not find it difficult to relate to Buddhism. It appears to offer the best qualities of Christian teaching without the harshness of its doctrinal condemnation of unbelievers.

Dorothy Donath is an American who became Buddhist. In the Foreword to her book *Buddhism for the West*, she provides an illuminating explanation of what led her to make her decision.

> *Why I became a Buddhist* is one of the questions I am most often asked. Here is my answer: I became a Buddhist because Buddhism (the Buddha-Dharma) is a religion of reason: it is pragmatic but at the same time preeminently of the Spirit – and so a deeply satisfying way of life; because it imposes no creeds or dogmas and demands no submission to or blind faith in any separate deity, person, or thing, and thus is devoid of every dualistic belief and concept; because it teaches unity with all life everywhere, and compassion for every living being, man and animal alike; because it accords to man the beauty and dignity of original perfection, not original sin, and shows him the way by means of his own efforts, intuitive insights, and growing realization to uncover this perfection – his real and intrinsic Buddha-nature – which is enlightenment itself; and finally, I became a Buddhist because Buddhism affirms that the Cosmos, with all its evolving worlds in all their relative reality, is not a "creation" in specific time by any personal God or Being, however transcendent, but is a manifestation, an outpouring, of universal Infinite Intelligence, Mind.[303]

A Christian might claim that Christianity also is a religion of reason. There are depths of truth in Christian teaching which most Christians don't explore, which perhaps this writer, if she had been a Christian, did not explore. Of course there are depths in Buddhist teaching, as Donath explains, and in all serious attempts to try to understand the nature of reality from a greater perspective than is provided by our own environment. As we study these teachings we become acquainted with their depths. But it is not as if they were entirely new to us even before we study them, because, without reflecting specifically upon other religions than our own, we may range in our private thoughts through many kinds of religious understanding that could, if we were to do so, compare surprisingly with the teachings of various religions. And there may be, as a consequence and without intention, an intuitive recognition of their spiritual value. It is as if the outer casing of our faith remained the same, and to those who deal with us, familiar, but within the casing a gyration of belief which, if it could be visualized, would resemble lapsed time pictures of clouds in motion.

Several years ago, during the Vietnam disturbances, it became almost a cliché for young people to confront the National Guard with what they called "flower power," by placing flowers in the muzzles of the rifles that the guardsmen were holding. It seemed eccentric, certainly naïve. Yet it had a basis in Buddhist teaching. The young people were trying to make a statement. In the Dhammapada, reputedly the actual words of Buddha, we read, "...like a beautiful flower full of colour and full of scent are the well spoken and fruitful words of him who acts."[304] So it seemed to those protesters that a flower, in its simple beauty and fragility, represented a force equally powerful to that represented by the also young and often bewildered National Guardsmen.

Gentleness and Force

The teaching of non-violence is not unique to Buddhism, we can think of the Quakers, and of Gandhi and Martin Luther King, Jr., none of whom was Buddhist. But Buddhism, as a growing and important religion, may be more in keeping with the needs of the world now than the more structured teachings of Judaism, Christianity and Islam, whose emphasis it could be argued is on being right rather than doing good, and the much more diffuse teachings of Hinduism. The Dalai Lama's book *Ethics for a New Millennium*[305] is an argument for the values of absolute compassion, and the need to control anger. In a BBC interview the interviewer asked the Dalai Lama "shouldn't we be angry when we see what, for example, Mr. Milosevic has done to those poor Albanians in Kosovo. Isn't that a just cause to be angry?" We might add to that, since the interview, the terrible behavior of the Indonesians towards the East Timorese. The Dalai Lama did not agree that some circumstances justify, or require anger According to him "compassion, love, forgiveness, tolerance" are a stronger force against evil. [306] But the pragmatic view is that compassion got nowhere with Milosevic, he backed down only after eighty days of bombing. Similarly, the Indonesian army withdrew from East Timor only when actually confronted by heavily armed United Nations peacekeeping forces. Perhaps one can say that neither NATO bombing nor the United Nation force were deployed in anger, and in fact both took place only after considerable discussion, which diffused the anger even as it led to a decision. But it was force not gentleness that carried the day.

While Buddhism can provide spiritual consolation, its greater appeal philosophically would seem to be in its original non-supernaturalistic (Theravada) form, which presents an ideal of reason and grace, but requires the individual in his/her own strength to apply that ideal to the practical concerns of life without forfeiting the ideal.

The value of any teaching other than our own, (because we get used to our own, take it for granted, overlook in it what is important and what should be criticized) is that we are made aware of how essential ideals are, religious and secular, and how weak and unreliable is the link between theory and practice. Marxism failed here, and so has Christianity on many occasions. This does not thereby prove an ideal wrong, but shows that work must be done to strengthen that link.

The prevalence of religions across the world indicates a deep need which religion alone can satisfy. That should be honored, supported, enhanced by all religious and social means. But the weakness of the relationship between theory and practice is a political failure, due to a lack of appropriate structure. When ideals are needed, but the business of life subverts them, political means must be found to make a better connection. The political means, however, must be guided and disciplined by a sense of right and wrong, not right and wrong here and for now, but right and wrong, period, in the sense represented in the UN Declaration of Human Rights.

This is related to the core of every religion (excluding of course some negative and destructive variants) because while religion teaches about infinite objectives it does so for those who are rooted in the finite and need to be helped along their way by moral teaching on how to live. Those religions such as Theravada Buddhism, which reject infinitude, are nevertheless concerned with human behavior. Our awareness of the plurality of religions, which is now a feature of contemporary life, is therefore of the greatest practical value to that life.

Islam

We have referred to Hinduism and Buddhism, but what about Islam? In a recent interview Kenneth Cragg, for many years assistant bishop in the Anglican Archdiocese of Jerusalem was asked how a Christian might counter the view "that Islam is a great threat to Western civilization."[307] The western world has been repelled by callous violations of human rights in Islamic countries: cutting off the hands of thieves, disregard of the rights of women, the public call to murder the writer Salman Rashdie because his book *Satanic Verses* was deemed offensive to Islamic teaching. All this is so contrary to internationally accepted norms of behavior that Islamic society is regarded by many as irrational, vindictive, and chauvinistic, whose moral development stopped at the middle ages.

Cragg's response was that with what measure you mete it shall be meted out to you. How we treat others, in this case Muslims, will influence how they treat us. With 600,000 Muslims in Britain and with 1250 Mosques and Islamic centers in the United States, the matter is a pressing one. We have to deal with them internationally; they are our global neighbors. We have to deal with them socially in our own societies. Yet we know little about them in the West and are generally biased against them. The Palestinians rightly complain that in Arab-Israeli issues the American Press favors the Jews. There is no one in the Muslim world comparable to the Dalai Lama in the Buddhist world. Many non-Buddhists are drawn to him and want to learn more about Buddhism because of his personality. We are not drawn to Yasir Arafat although he is the person with whom we have to do business. Nor are we drawn to other Arab leaders. We do business with them largely because they control important oil fields, or their mutual animosities, and animosity towards us, threaten to disturb the peace. So the question about Islam as "a great threat to Western civilization" is relevant to how Islamic peoples do behave. They appear as an ominous anachronism. These are reasons for giving serious attention to what Muslims believe.

Islam received notoriety in the United States through the Black Muslim movement. Many blacks concluded that a primarily white Christian society, responsible for slavery which it gave up so reluctantly that it fought a civil war, did not provide a spiritual home for black people. Islam, they felt, does not distinguish between people to their disadvantage, as does Christianity. It is a universal religion. It embraces everyone. It is also simple compared with Christian theology. A person becomes Muslim just by repeating the creed sincerely "There is no God but Allah and Muhammad is his prophet." A Muslim satisfies the requirements of the faith by obedience to the five pillars, five obligations: repeating the creed as often as possible, daily prayer, almsgiving, fasting during the month of Ramadan, and pilgrimage to Mecca.

The Black Muslim's embrace of Islam was an often bitter turning away from their white society. In *The Fire Next Time* James Baldwin writes,

God is black. All black men belong to Islam; they have been chosen. And Islam shall rule the world. The dream, the sentiment is old; only the color is new. And it is this dream, this sweet possibility, that thousands of oppressed black men and women in this country now carry with them after the Muslim minister has spoken, through the dark, noisome ghetto streets, into the hovels where so many have perished. The white God has not delivered them; perhaps the Black God will.[308]

This book, published now over thirty years ago, was yet another reason why Islam appeared as a threat. Yet there were small counter examples which provided hopeful signs, a little book *Christian and Islamic Spirituality: Sharing a journey,* expressing the view that, "at the center of both Islamic and Christian contemplative experience: at the heart of Jesus' and Mohammed's message is a similar truth and transformative path."[309]

Yet it is possible that Islam is more remote, puzzling, even unattractive to the average person in North America, apart from those few who have had direct contact with it, than any other major religion represented on this continent. The sacred teaching of Islam is the Qur'an revealed to Muhammad during the last twenty-three years of his life. Tradition has it that he was illiterate and did not know what he was writing. It was consequently pure revelation, and therefore to be treated with the utmost reverence. Even to repeat it incorrectly is a grave error. To the extent that one takes a philosophic approach, one should not neglect or be misinformed about a religion with now over a billion followers worldwide. Islam is important enough religiously, politically and intellectually that we should become acquainted with its teaching and not be dissuaded by the behavior of Islamic fundamentalists.

Yet those teachings, namely the Qur'an, however certain Muslims are of their truth, and however unwilling they are to hear any critical questions about them, are not immune from criticism. As we mentioned in the chapter on language, Muslims believe that the Qur'an is God's final revelation superseding all that went before. But that is what the Mormons believe about the golden plates discovered by Joseph Smith and published in 1830 in Palmyra, New York. Is the Mormon claim false? The Mormons don't believe that. In the first chapter of the Book of Mormon we read "And I know that the record which I make is true, and I make it with mine own hand; and I make it according to my Knowledge."[310] Muslims claim that Muhammad was illiterate. Without divine control he could not have written the Qur'an. Joseph Smith, too, was not a literary person; to all appearances he was a quite ordinary resident of Palmyra, New York. Reportedly he could read but not write. How was it that he found and translated the golden plates, which are accepted as scripture by Mormons across the world?

If the Mormon claim is true what do we make of the Muslim claim that the Qur'an is a final revelation. Is it more preposterous to question these claims than to describe the gospel of John, for long believed to contain the very words of Christ, as a reverent but imaginary reconstruction of Christ's teaching?[311]

How much religious authority should we allow for Mary Baker Eddy's book *Science and Health with Key to the Scriptures*, who regarded her work as a revelation of the truth about human sickness.[312] Or are such considerations meaningless because faith cannot be compared. Should we say that all three teachings are valid revelations given to different people at different times, each representing some part of the divine wisdom which, if we were to follow it to its source, would be seen to contain all these teachings? Hindu eclecticism could serve as a model. As Hinduism absorbed Buddhism in India so perhaps in a post denominational age, when boundaries are falling, a new understanding of religious truth is that it has absorbed the truths that came before without denying them and not destroying them.

Chinese Religion

Like Islam, Chinese religion is not well known in North America, but unlike Islam the reason is not the result of animus against it. There are many Chinese in the United States, but little attention given to their religious beliefs. Partly because Confucianism, one of the traditional religions of China, scarcely qualifies as a religion. It is more a way of life whose primary purpose is quality of behavior. There are no gods to placate, no future reward to strive for. It is concerned with living life now, and so is more of a humanistic ethic than a religion.

The preferred way is the middle way, an idea familiar in the west from Aristotle, and yet a matter of simple good sense. Seldom can we get just what we want. Our life is in a continual tension between desire and what can be achieved. In theistic beliefs we can refer difficult tensions to God or to some other divine agent. With Confucianism we must take the responsibility ourselves. For that, the teaching of Taoism can help us by strengthening the quality of our inner life. Perhaps we could say that the two faiths provide an individual with order and inspiration.

What undergirds Confucianism and Taoism is a strong moral sense. Regarding both as philosophies as well as religions, one writer comments that "the assessment of philosophers in China depends, in the last analysis, upon their moral character."[313] This is achieved by maintaining the middle way, symbolized by the Yin Yang whose opposite principles are eternally interacting, a complementariness which, rather than excluding one of the opposites as typically is done in western thought, includes both: not A or B, but A and B.[314]

It is actually not difficult to take a skeptical view of religion. We might imagine the often invoked visitor from another planet. In this case it is a planet without religious belief, concerned only with this life, an individual's own behavior, and with friends. He visits the earth with its multiplicity of religions, some of them contradictory, others mutually antagonistic, and he might reflect with amused tolerance upon the absurdities of these humans who exercise themselves about things they cannot see, and believe and call true what is founded on nothing more than apprehension and wishful thinking. Upon his return he might entertain his colleagues with tales of the absurdity. He might do that, and he might be witty, perceptive, intelligent, good natured, any or all, but he would not be a philosopher. In the area of religion the responsibility of philosophy is not simply to be critical or dismissive, but to respect opinions when they are sincerely held, no matter how strange, to try to understand them, to try to stand on their side and *then* to be critical. That approach requires patience, care, intelligence and also a certain amount of intellectual modesty, even humility, a term not often used.

Let us imagine that our visitor has a companion who regards the multiplicity of faiths he finds on earth in a different way, and sees in them not the absurdity of contradictory presumptions, but the consequence of worldwide human yearning. As he studies the history of the planet, examining some of its earliest stages, he finds that as far back as he can go there is evidence of this religious sense, from the grave sites of the earliest hominids, in villages, cities, states, from then until now. He might discover as he reads that one of the most thoroughgoing and sustained attempts in history to destroy religious beliefs, carried out by an ideologically driven group called communists, failed. As soon as restrictions were lifted people began to express openly what repression had not been able to eliminate privately. He might wonder about this phenomenon so ancient, so persistent, so widespread; he might wonder whether it was only a human invention, whether commitments obviously profound could be explained simply as the result, for example, of fear, or the influence of society. He might decide that that was too simplistic, that he was dealing with something quite mysterious. He might find it extremely puzzling that a race of beings which—as contemporary biology informs us—has entirely physical origins, reaches a point in its evolution at which it reflects upon non-physical reality and characterizes its answers as religions. These it believes to be true explanations; none of them may be accurate, yet surely, together, they are not only delusive.

The two visitors would return and give their accounts of what they observed and what they think it means. The one dwelling on what he regarded as absurdities would reaffirm the good sense of his atheistic society. The other, as a result of his observations, might question whether life lived totally within the compass of its physical boundaries is a full life. In this chapter we have considered some of those who asked that question, and whose answer is "no."

Chapter 13

A Feeling Intellect and a Thinking Heart

Thought and Feeling

Having spent much of my life trying to balance rational examination of religious belief with attempts to deal with the religious and spiritual problems of people's lives, I find that rationality, arid as it often is, is indispensable. Yet my emotional interaction with people in pain, or scoured by questions they cannot answer, is necessarily suffused with the warmth of life because without it we cannot function as humans.

My concern for people is affected by my training, experience and commitment to critical thinking, yet that commitment is ever in danger of being submerged, if I am not on guard, by feeling.

The sometimes contradictory gifts of thought and feeling have blessed us in extraordinary ways. If given by God, they are a sign of our spiritual origins. Yet they can tear us apart like Lucifer, tempt us into foolish behavior like Adam, or drive us into near despair like the Apostle Paul. However, they also lifted Paul to the third heaven. So might they lift us?

Is It How We Regard Them?

Perhaps thought and feeling are contradictory only when we consider them so. Horace Bushnell, the nineteenth century American theologian wrote, "I am glad I have a heart as well as a head." For him faith was validated by the inward testimony of the heart, [315] that is, by the experience of faith. About sixty years earlier, Friedrich Schleiermacher had defined religion as a "feeling of absolute dependence." The experience of such feeling is the person's religious assurance and entrance to theological understanding. As one writer put it, for Schleiermacher, "the condition of the heart…is religion."[316] That is what influenced Bushnell.

Perhaps Not

But Paul Tillich questions this. "Experience," he writes, referring to the experience described by Schleiermacher, "is not the source from which the contents of systematic theology are taken but the medium through which they are existentially received."[317] Yet, although systematic theology is a product of thought – to the believer based on revelation –should it become only that, one could argue, it ceases to be the logos of Theos. Similarly, philosophy is a product of thought, but one could also argue, should it become only that it ceases to be the philos of sophos. They become pretentious. Theology is not, should not be, an end in itself. Its purpose is to draw men and women to God. That one can hardly dispute. Neither is philosophy an end in itself. Its purpose is to lead to understanding. My view is that understanding is rarely complete with intellectual grasp only.

Thought and Feeling in Hinduism

Hindu teaching recognizes this. With regard to Brahman, the ultimate religious principle, the Kena Upanishad declares…

> It is not understood by those who [say they] understand It.
> It is understood by those who [say they] understand It not.[318]

And with regard to Ātman, self

> This soul (Ātman) is not be obtained by instruction,
> Nor by intellect, nor by much learning.[319]

Then, commenting upon the close relation between feeling and understanding in search of the self:

Not he who has not ceased from bad conduct,
Not he who is not tranquil,
Not he who is not composed.
Not he who is not of peaceful mind
Can obtain him by intelligence (*prajna*).[320]

Like life and death, in Walt Whitman's poem of that name:

The two old, simple problems ever intertwined,
Close home, elusive, present, baffled, grappled.
By each successive age insoluble, pass'd on.
To ours today – and we pass on the same.[321]

Perhaps We Can Laugh At The Problem

How we receive the two old problems, how we deal with them when
we have them, how we pass them on is different for each of us. It's best
I think not to be too serious about what we only partly understand, and
what we may feel when we may not always able to control our feelings.
Most of us who are not philosophers and theologians are pragmatic
about it, quizzical, sometimes amused when we can't cry. But that can
be misunderstood.

A Taoist disciple was rebuked for frivolous behavior at the funeral
of a friend Sung Hu. He was heard singing:

Hey, Sung Hu!
Where'd you go?
Hey, Sung Hu!
Where'd you go?
You have gone
Where you really were.
And we are here –
Damn it! We are here![322]

Sustaining Ourselves

In the face of Whitman's "old, simple problems," and the confusing
relation between thought and feeling, skepticism and amusement are a
way of sustaining oneself through life. For most people sustaining is
what counts, which may be the ultimate philosophical doctrine, not the

"primary concern" as with Tillich but basic sustenance. That is why theodicies fall to the ground and arguments about death and the afterlife evaporate. They become irrelevant, even annoying. Turning to Chuang Tzu again,

> Pleasure and rage
> Sadness and joy
> Hopes and regrets
> Change and stability
> Weakness and decision
> Impatience and sloth;
> All are sounds from the same flute,
> All mushrooms from the same wet mould [323]

Do We Understand Ourselves?

The previous chapter discussed several religions; put simply, they are the many ways people try to understand what is beyond their ability to understand. Does that make sense? What people want to understand is the meaning of their own lives. Not to understand would be quixotic; not to understand the one thing that should be at the base of all our knowledge.

We know when we are hungry, we know when we are afraid, we know when we are in love, and we know when life strikes us in tragic ways. Why shouldn't we know ourselves? The fact is we do, but generally don't believe it because to analyze ourselves is to be self-conscious, and that sets us stumbling.

Yet the ability to analyze self or anything else is part of our God-given nature, if we believe in God. And if we do believe in God our God-given nature compels us to analyze the nature, the activities, and the claims of God, and even whether God exists.

Opting Out

If you have read this book and thought about it you are in the camp of those who consider the enterprise worthwhile. Many don't. I have students who, a third of the way through my philosophy of religion course, have literally cried out in class against the process of reflecting upon religious topics. The course seemed interesting to begin with, even enjoyable, like working in a candy factory, "Eat all you want," but gradually the spiritual system is satiated as the bodily system is satiated. "I can't stand it," wrote one student to me, "Constantly questioning, constantly talking, going over and over. It never stops." Then with polite compliments about how good a course it is, "I have to leave."

Yet from my biased view as a philosopher can such students leave? Can anyone leave? Are we not committed to the process of thinking? Humans like to be comfortable, bodily and mentally, bodily and spiritually. Television can achieve that as we sit in a comfortable chair and cast our minds on the drift of entertainment. But no one of us is far from Whitman's two old simple problems.

Last night I was at a Bob Dylan concert. A large crowd of mainly young people, smoking a lot – I doubt it was only tobacco – drinking wine, dancing, and laughing. They were having a good time. Who among them I wondered, also drinking wine, is thinking philosophically, or religiously? Chuang Tzu could have made merry with that possibility. Yet none of us is far from Whitman's two old simple problems Far perhaps from the second, death, completely involved with the first, life. If I could have leapt the protective wall of any of those who were there and spoken directly to them, I would have found both problems expressed inarticulately to the barely comprehending self. They are the quandary of being human, which can be sublimated into conviction or anesthetized into disbelief, and so contained. Then it would not do the damage that people fear. But then it also could not provide what is the greatest value for faith. If we imagine that at any point in our faith understanding we have reached the horizon, we are wrong. We may rest there for a while, but it must be rest not residence.

The fears that spring from our feelings are often as misleading as the pride that springs from our intellect. Both are needed to correct, balance and enrich the other with different emphases at different times in constant interaction. Our mind creates Pygmalion; our feelings bring her to life. We need both, something I have tried to indicate in the title of this chapter and of my book: *A Feeling Intellect and A Thinking Heart.*

[1] *The New York Times Magazine.* (7 Dec. 1997)

[2] Miles, Jack. *God: A Biography.* New York: Knopf, 1995.

[3] *The New York Times Magazine.* (17 Oct. 1999) cover.

[4] Russo, Richard. "How 'I' Moved Heaven and Earth." *The New York Times Magazine.* (17 Oct. 1999): 86.

[5] *Ibid.*, p. 87.

[6] *Ibid.*, p. 85.

[7] Paley, William. *Natural Theology or Evidence of the Existence and Attributes of the Deity from the Appearances of Nature.* 1802. Weybridge: South Hamilton, 1809. p. 198.

[8] Hume, David. *Dialogues Concerning Natural Religion.* Parts II and V, Indianapolis: Bobbs-Merrill, 1779. p. 198.

[9] Wildman, Wesley J. "Teleology without Divine Action." and "Evaluating the Teleological Argument for Divine Action" in *Evolutionary and Molecular Biology: Scientific Perspectives on Divine Action.* Robert John Russell et alia, Vatican City State: Vatican Observatory, 1998.

[10] Glanz, James. "Science vs. the Bible: Debate Moves to the Cosmos." *The New York Times Magazine.* (10 Oct. 1999): 1.

[11] Cowen, Robert C. "Hubble's Keen Eye Puts Age of Universe In Astronomers' Sights." *The Christian Science Monitor.* (26 May 1999): 3.3.

[12] Johnson, George. "Ideas & Trends; Building a Cosmic Tape Measure." *The New York Times Magazine.* Week in Review. (6 June 1999): 6.1.

[13] Swinburne, Richard. *The Existence of God.* Oxford and New York: Oxford UP, 1979. p. 142.

[14] Aquinas, Thomas. "Summa Theologica." *The Basic Writings of St. Thomas Aquinas.* Vol. I, Ed. Anton C. Pegis. New York: Random House, 1945. Part 1. Q 2. Art 3. pp. 22-33.

[15] Polkinghorne, John. *Science and Creation The Search for Understanding.* London: SPCK, 1988. pp. 25-26.

[16] Swinburne, Richard. *The Existence of God.* p. 142

[17] Gingerich, Owen. "The Universe as Theatre for God's Action." *Theology Today.* (October 1998): 311

[18] *Ibid.*

[19] Hebblethwaite, Brian. *The Ocean of Truth: A Defense of Objective Theism.* Cambridge and New York: Cambridge UP, 1988. p. 90.

[20] Aquinas, Thomas. *The Basic Writings of St. Thomas Aquinas.* pp. 22-23.

[21] Misner, C. W. "Cosmology and Theology." *Cosmology, History and Theology.* Ed. W. Yourgrau and A.D. Breck. New York and London: Plenum, 1977. p. 90. Also printed in A. R. Peacocke. *Creation and the World of Science.* Oxford and New York: Clarendon, 1979. p. 63.

[22] Taylor, Richard. *Metaphysics*, 3rd ed. Englewood Cliffs: Prentice-Hall, 1983. p. 112.

[23] Malcolm, Norman. "Anselm's Ontological Arguments." *The Ontological Argument.* Ed. Alvin Plantinga with an Introduction by Richard Taylor. New York: Doubleday, 1965. p. 158.

[24] *Ibid.*

[25] Radhakrishnan, Sarvepalli and Charles A. Moore, eds. *A Source Book in Indian Philosophy.* Princeton: Princeton UP, 1957. p. 4.

[26] *Ibid.*, pp. 23-24.

[27] *Ibid.*, p. 24.

[28] *Ibid.* p. 18.

[29] Maynell, Alice. "Christ in the Universe." *The Faber Book of Religious Verse.* Ed. Helen Gardner, London and Boston: Faber, 1972. p. 292.

[30] Hume, Robert Ernest. *The Thirteen Principal Upanishads Translated from the Sanscrit,* Oxford, Oxford UP, 2nd ed. rev., 1931, pp. 114, 116-117.

[31] Parrinder, Geoffrey. *Religion in Africa.* Penguin African Library. Baltimore: Penguin Books, 1969. pp. 39-40.

[32] Parrinder, Geoffrey. *African Mythology.* London: Hamlyn, 1967. p. 20.

[33] Parrinder, Geoffrey. *Religion in Africa.* p. 46.

[34] Radhakrishnan, Sarvepalli and Charles A. Moore, eds. *A Source Book in Indian Philosophy.* p. 613.

[35] Capra, Fritjof. *The Tao of Physics.* Boston: Shambala, 1975, 1983, 1991. pp. 90-91, 147-149. Text by Douglas E. Barrett and Basil Gray. *Painting of India: Treasures of Asia Series.* Paris: d'art Albert Skira. Distributed by the World Publishing Company, Cleveland, 1963. pp. 25-26, 31.

[36] Clooney, Francis X. "When Religions Become Context." *Theology Today*. XLVII, 1. (April 1990): pp. 14, 30-38.

[37] Licht, Hans. *Sexual Life in Ancient Greece*. London: Routledge, 1932. p. 180.

[38] Kiefer, Otto. *Sexual Life in Ancient Rome*. London: Routledge, 1934. p. 108.

[39] Grant, Michael. *From Alexander to Cleopatra: The Hellenistic World*. New York: Macmillan, Collier Books, 1982. p. 228.

[40] Lewis, Clive Staples. *The Problem of Pain*. New York: Macmillan, 1962. p. 26.

[41] Wierenga, Edward R. *The Nature of God: An Inquiry into Divine Attributes*. Ithaca and London: Cornell UP, 1989. p. 17.

[42] Lewis, Clive Staples. *The Problem of Pain*. p. 28.

[43] *Ibid.*

[44] Wierenga, Edward R. *The Nature of God: An Inquiry into Divine Attributes*. p. 13.

[45] *Ibid.*, p. 32ff.

[46] Boethius. *The Consolation of Philosophy*. Trans. with an Introduction and explanatory notes by P. G. Walsh. Oxford: Clarendon, 1999. p. 13.

[47] Rowe, William L. *Philosophy of Religion*. Encino and Belmont: Dickenson, 1978. p. 166.

[48] Boethius. pp. 111-112.

[49] Galloway, George. *The Philosophy of Religion*. Edinburgh: Clark, 1914, 1951. p. 486.

[50] *Ibid.*

[51] Burtt, E. A. *The Teachings of the Compassionate Buddha*. 1955. New York: A Mentor Book, 1982. p. 12.

[52] Underhill, Evelyn. *Mysticism*. New American Library, New York: A Meridian Book, 1974. p. 4.

[53] Plotinus. *The Enneads*. Trans. Stephen Mackenna. Burdett and New York: Larson, 1992. Ennead I. Sixth Tractate. 9. p. 71.

[54] Coles, Robert. *The Spiritual Life of Children*. Boston: Houghton Mifflin, 1990. p. 65.

[55] Broad, C. D. *Religion, Philosophy and Psychical Research*. New York: Humanities, 1969. p. 190.

[56] Plotinus. *The Enneads*. p. 233.

[57] Underhill, Evelyn. *Mysticism*. p. 453.

[58] McGiffert, Arthur Cushman. *A History of Christian Thought*. Vol. II. New York and London: Scribner, 1954. p. 375.

[59] Radhakrishnan, Sarvepalli and Charles A. Moore, eds. *A Source Book in Indian Philosophy*. Princeton: Princeton UP, 1957. p. 38.

[60] *Ibid.*, p. 43.

[61] *Ibid.*, p. 47.

[62] McGiffert, Arthur Cushman. *A History of Christian Thought*. Vol. II. p. 360.

[63] *Ibid.*, p. 362-363.

[64] Plotinus, *The Enneads*. Fifth Ennead Tractate I. p. 249.

[65] Saunders, Jason L. *Greek and Roman Philosophy After Aristotle*. New York: The Free Press, 1966. p. 94.

[66] *Ibid.*

[67] *Ibid.*, p. 127.

[68] Thouless, Robert H. *An Introduction to the Psychology of Religion*. Cambridge: Cambridge UP, 1950. pp. 240-241.

[69] Hume, Robert Ernest. *The Thirteen Principal Upanishads Translated from the Sanscrit*, Oxford, Oxford UP, 2nd ed. rev., 1931. p. 435.

[70] Hebblethwaite, Brian. *Preaching Through the Christian Year*. London and Oxford: Mobray, 1985. p. 83.

[71] Underhill, Evelyn. *Mysticism*. p. 450.

[72] Bloom, Harold. *Omens of Millennium: The Gnosis of Angels, Dreams, and Resurrection*. New York: Riverhead, 1996. p. 5.

[73] *Ibid.*, p. 234.

[74] *Ibid.*, pp. 1-2.

[75] Lash, Nicholas. *Easter in Ordinary: Reflections on Human Experience and the Knowledge of God*. London: SCM, 1988. pp. 144-145.

[76] Matson, Wallace. *The Existence of God*. Ithaca and London: Cornell UP, 1965. p. 28.

[77] Forman, Robert. *Mysticism, Mind, and Consciousness*. Albany: State University of New York, 1999. p. 1.

[78] Proudfoot, Wayne. *Religious Experience*. Berkeley, Los Angeles, London: The University of California, 1985. p. 107.

[79] Forman, Robert. *Mysticism, Mind, and Consciousness*. p. 3.

[80] *Ibid.*, p. 51.

[81] *Ibid.*, p. 172.

82 Carter, Stephen. *The Culture of Disbelief: How American Law and Politics Trivialize Religious Devotion.* New York, London, Toronto: Anchor, Doubleday, 1994. pp. XIII-XIV.

83 Bloom, Harold. *Omens of Millennium: The Gnosis of Angels, Dreams, and Resurrection.* p. 20.

84 Stace, W. T. *Religion and the Modern Mind.* Philadelphia: Lippincott, 1952. pp. 257-258.

85 O'Brien, George Dennis. *God and the New Haven Railway And Why Neither One is Doing Very Well.* Boston: Beacon, 1988. p. 138.

86 Hebblethwaite, Brian. *Preaching Through the Christian Year.* p. 81.

87 Cashman, John. *The LSD Story.* Quoting Huston Smith and William James. Greenwich: Fawcett Gold Medal, 1966. pp. 72-78.

88 Hopfe, Lewis M. and Mark R. Woodward. *Religions of the World.* 7th ed. Upper Saddle River: Prentice Hall, 1998. pp. 43-45.

89 Cox, Harvey. *The Feast of Fools: A Theological Essay on Festivity and Fantasy.* Cambridge: Harvard University, 1969. p. 107.

90 Roof, Wade Clark. "Modernity, the Religious, and the Spiritual" in *The Annals of the American Academy of Political and Social Sciences.* July, 1998. p. 214.

91 Mill, John Stuart. *Three Essays on Religion.* New York: Henry Holt, 1874. pp. 176-177.

92 Whitehead, Alfred North. *Process and Reality: An Essay in Cosmology.* 1929. New York: Harper, 1957. p. 527.

93 *Ibid.,* p. 532.

94 Koller, John M. *Oriental Philosophies.* 2nd ed. New York: Scribner, 1985. p. 157.

95 Lewis, Clive Staples. *A Grief Observed.* London: Faber, 1961, 1990. pp. 7-8.

96 Eddy, Mary Baker. *Science and Health with Key to the Scripture.* Boston: Trustees under the Will of Mary Baker Eddy, 1934. pp. 353, 480.

97 Ray, Benjamin C. *African Religions: Symbol, Ritual, and Community.* Englewood Cliffs: Prentice-Hall, 1976. p. 34.

98 Hick, John. *Evil and the God of Love.* 1966. San Francisco: Harper and Row, 1978. p. 256.

99 *Ibid.,* p. 259.

100 Delahaye, Luc. *Mémo.* Paris: Editions Hazan, 1997.

101 Thomas, D. Winton. ed. *Documents from Old Testament Times.* New York: Harper, 1961. p. 164.

[102] Mackie, John Leslie. *The Miracle of Theism Arguments for and Against the Existence of God.* Oxford: Claredon, 1982. pp. 165-166.

[103] Copleston, Frederick. *Auquinas.* Harmondsworth and Middlesex: Pelican, 1957. p. 149.

[104] Kushner, Harold S. *When Bad Things Happen to Good People.* New York: Schocken, 1981. p. 30.

[105] *Ibid.*, p. 135.

[106] Epictetus. "Manual, or Enchiridion." *Greek and Roman Philosophy after Aristotle.* Jason Saunders, ed. New York and London: The Free Press, 1966. p. 34.

[107] Hick, John. ed. *Classical and Contemporary Readings in the Philosophy of Religion.* Englewood Cliffs: Prentice-Hall, 1964. p. 477.

[108] Hick, John. *Evil and the God of Love.* 1966. San Francisco: Harper and Row, rev. ed. 1978. p. vii.

[109] Stewart, David. ed. *Exploring the Philosophy of Religion.* 2nd ed. Englewood Cliffs: Prentice-Hall, 1988. p. 254.

[110] Peterson, Michael L. *God and Evil An Introduction to the Issues.* Boulder: Westview, 1998. p. 8.

[111] Henneberger, Melinda. "A Shaken City, Ever Devout, Turns to God." *The New York Times.* (30 April 1995): 1.1.

[112] Kierkegaard, Soren. *Concluding Unscientific Postscript.* Trans. David F. Swenson and Walter Lowrie. Princeton: Princeton UP, 1941. p. 539.

[113] Radhakrishnan, Sarvepalli and Charles A. Moore, eds. *A Source Book in Indian Philosophy.* Princeton: Princeton UP, 1957. p. 618.

[114] *Ibid.*, p. 153.

[115] Whitman, Walt. "Specimen Days and Collect." 1882. *Complete Poems and Prose of Walt Whitman.* Philadelphia: Ferguson, 1888. pp. 71-72.

[116] MacKinnon, D. M. "Death." *New Essays in Philosophical Theology.* 1953. Ed. Antony Flew and Alasdair MacIntyre. New York: Macmillan, 1983. pp. 261 ff.

[117] Atkins, Peter. "Purposeless People." *Persons and Personality.* Ed. Arthur Peacocke and Grant Gillett. Oxford and New York: Basil Blackwell, 1987. p. 13.

[118] Ayer, Alfred Jules. *Language, Truth and Logic.* New York: Dover, 1936. p. 116.

[119] *Ibid.*, p. 118.

120 MacKinnon, D. M. "Death." in *New Essays in Philosophical Theology*. p. 265.

121 *Ibid.*, p. 263.

122 Swinburne, Richard. "The Structure of the Soul." in *Persons and Personality*. p. 33.

123 MacKinnon, D. M. "Death." *New Essays in Philosophical Theology*. p. 262.

124 Rahner, Karl. *On the Theology of Death*. New York: Herder, 1961. p. 35.

125 Aurobindo, Sri. Printed in *A Source Book in Indian Philosophy*. eds. Sarvepalli Radhakrishnan and Charles A. Moore. Princeton: Princeton UP, 1957. p. 578.

126 Biko, Steve. "Some African Cultural Concepts." Printed in *The African Philosophy Reader*. P. H. Coetzee and A. P. Roux, Eds. London and New York: Routledge, 1998. p. 29.

127 Ray, Benjamin C. *African Religions: Symbol, Ritual and Community*. Englewood Cliffs: Prentice-Hall, 1976. p. 140.

128 *Ibid.*, p. 141.

129 Mbiti, John S. *African Religions and Philosophy*. New York: Praeger, 1969. p. 150.

130 *Ibid.*, p. 84.

131 A.M.T. Moore, G. C. Hillman, A. J. Legge. *Village on the Euphuates*. Oxford, New York, Oxford University Press, 2000, p. 292.

132 *Ibid.*, p. 86.

133 *Ibid.*, p. 87.

134 Flew, Antony. *A New Approach to Psychical Research*. London: Watts, 1993. pp. 127-129. See also John Beloff "Is There Anything Beyond Death? A Parapsychologist's Report." and Paul and Linda Badham "The Evidence from Psychical Research." *Immortality*. Ed. Paul Edwards. London: Watts, 1953. pp. 250ff and 259ff.

135 Johnson, Thomas H. ed. *The Poems of Emily Dickinson*. 1951. Cambridge: Harvard UP, 1955, 1979, 1983.

136 Rahner, Karl. *On the Theology of Death*. p. 37.

137 Radhakrishnan, Sarvepalli and Charles A. Moore, eds. *A Source Book in Indian Philosophy*. Princeton: Princeton UP, 1957. p. 634.

138 Bolle, Kees W., *The Bahagavadgītā A New Translation*, Berkeley, Los Angeles, London, University of California Press, 1979. p. 21, 23.

[139] Edwards, Paul, ed. *Immortality*. Introduction. New York, Toronto, Oxford: Macmillan, p. 1.

[140] Taylor, Richard. *Metaphysics*, 2nd ed. Englewood Cliffs: Prentice-Hall, 1963. p. 19.

[141] Norris, Kathleen. Introduction. 1995. *My Ántonia*. 1918. By Willla Cather. Boston and New York: Houghton Mifflin, 1954. p. 14.

[142] Grant, Michael. *From Alexander to Cleopatra: The Hellenistic World*. New York: Macmillan, 1982. p. 230.

[143] Fernandez, Elizabeth. "Priest's Healing Hands Credited With Miracles." *San Francisco Examiner*. (20 Feb. 2000): C 1:1.

[144] Hume, David. *An Inquiry Concerning Human Understanding*. First published as *Philosophical Essays Concerning Human Understanding*. 1748. New York: The Liberal Arts Press, 1955. Sec. X, 'Of Miracles.' p. 122.

[145] Mackie, John Leslie. *The Miracle of Theism*. Oxford: Clarendon, 1982. p. 25.

[146] *Ibid.*, p. 26.

[147] Hume, David. *An Inquiry Concerning Human Understanding*. p. 118.

[148] Moore, E. Caldwell. *The History of Christian Thought Since Kant*. 1912. London: Duckworth, 1947. p. 180. Also see, Kenneth L. Woodward. *The Book of Miracles: The Meaning of Miracle Stories in Christianity, Judaism, Buddhism, Islam*. New York: Simon and Schuster, 2000.

[149] St. Augustine, *The City of God.* XXI 4-5 and *On the Trinity*. III 5.11-6.11. Printed in *The Essential Augustine*. Ed. Vernon J. Bourke, Indianapolis: Hackett, 1964-1974. pp. 110-119.

[150] Aquinas, Thomas. *Summa Contra Gentiles*. 3.99.9 *On the Truth of the Catholic Faith*. Trans. Vernon J. Bourke. New York: Doubleday, 1956.

[151] Letter to the Editor. "Science and Belief in Miracles." *The London Times*. (13 July 1984): 15, col. 7

[152] Hume, David. *An Inquiry Concerning Human Understanding*. p. 126.

[153] Polkinghorne, John. *Science and Creation: The Search for Understanding*. London: SPCK, 1988. p. 82.

[154] *Ibid.*, Introduction. pp. xii-xiii.

[155] Hoyle, Fred. Quoted in "The Universe as Theatre for God's Action." by Owen Gingerich in *Theology Today*. Ed. Patrick D. Miller. Vol. 55. (3 Oct. 1998): 311.

[156] Polkinghorne, John. *Science and Creation: The Search for Understanding*. p. 80.

[157] Temple, William. *Nature, Man and God*. London: Macmillan, 1964. pp. 266-267.

[158] Macquarrie, John. *Principles of Christian Theology*. 2nd ed. New York: Scribner, 1977. p. 248.

[159] *Ibid.*, pp. 251-252.

[160] Mackie, John Leslie. *The Miracle of Theism*. pp. 27-28.

[161] Holland. R. F. "The Miraculous." *Miracles*. Ed. Richard Swinburne. New York and London: Macmillan and Collier Macmillan, 1989. pp. 53-55.

[162] Fieser, James and John Powers. eds. From the "Nihonshoki (Nihongi) Chronicles of Japan." *Scriptures of the World's Religions*. Boston: McGraw Hill, 1998. pp. 220-221.

[163] Farmer, Herbert Henry. *The World and God*. 2nd ed. London: Nisbet and New York: Harper and Row, 1936. Chap. 7. pp. 107-108.

[164] Palmer, E. H. Trans. *The Koran (Qur'an)*. Introduction R. A. Nicholson, London, New York, Toronto: Oxford UP, 1928. Rpt. 1947. Chap. xxii, p. 284.

[165] Fieser, James and John Powers. eds. *Scriptures of the World's Religions*. pp. 245-247.

[166] *Ibid.*, pp. 220-221.

[167] Grant, Michael. *From Alexander to Cleopatra*. pp. 230-231.

[168] Mbiti, John S. *African Religions and Philosophy*. London, Ibadan, Nairobi, Heinemann, 1969. pp. 194-195.

[169] Phillips, Dewi Zephaniah. *The Concept of Prayer*. London, Routledge: Kegan Paul, 1965, p. 146.

[170] *Ibid*, p. 145.

[171] *Ibid*, p. 147.

[172] Zip, Yvonne. "Christianity: All the Rage At the Movies." *The Christian Science Monitor*. (7 Dec. 1999): 1.1.

[173] White, Andrew. *A History of the Warfare of Science with Theology in Christendom*. Two Volumes. New York: Appleton, 1896.

[174] Peacock, Arthur. "Biological Evolution – A Positive Theological Appraisal." in *Evolutionary and Molecular Biology: Scientific Perspectives on Divine Action*. Robert John Russell et alia eds.

Berkeley and Vatican City State: Center for Theology and the Natural Sciences and Vatican Observatory Publications, 1998. p. 357.

[175] Polkinghorne, John. *Science and Creation: The Search for Understanding*. London: SPCK, 1988. p. xii. Also see, Ian G. Barbour. *When Science Meets Religion*. New York, San Francisco: Harper, 2000. p. xiv.

[176] Van Till, Howard J. "The Creation: Intelligently Designed or Optimally Equipped?" *Theology Today*. (October 1998) p. 351.

[177] Gordon, Dane R. *Thinking and Reading in the Philosophy of Religion: the Religious Sensibility: Coming to Grips With What We Believe*. New York: Haven, 1994. pp. 287-288.

[178] Scroggs, Robin. "Tradition, Freedom and the Abyss." in *New Theology* No. 8. Eds. Martin Marty and Dean G. Peerman. New York and London: Macmillan and Collier Macmillan, 1971. p. 100.

[179] Küng, Hans. *On Being a Christian*. New York: Doubleday, 1976. New York: Pocket Books, Gulf and Western Corp., 1978. p. 89.

[180] Raman, Varadaraja V. "Science and Religion: Connections and Contradictions." *Choice*. (July/August 1996): 1755.

[181] Peacocke, Arthur Robert. *Creation and the World of Science*. Oxford and New York: Oxford UP and Clarendon, 1979. p. 64.

[182] Hawkin, Stephen. "In Defense of 'A Brief History." *The Cambridge Review*. Vol. 113. No. 2316. (March 1992) p. 16.

[183] Capra, Fritjof. *The Tau of Physics*. Boston: Shambala, 1991. p. 131.

[184] Zukar, Gary. *The Dancing Wu Li Masters An Overview of the New Physics*. New York, Toronto, London: Bantam, 1980. p. 72.

[185] Capra, Fritjof. *The Tau of Physics*. p. 87.

[186] Hume, Robert Ernest. *The Thirteen Principal Upanishads Translated from the Sanscrit*. Oxford, Oxford UP, 2nd ed. rev., 1931. p. 209-210.

[187] Teffo, Lesiba J. and Abraham P. J. Roux. "Metaphysical Thinking in Africa" printed in The African Philosophy Reader. P. H. Coetzee and A. P. J. Roux, Eds. London and New York: Routledge, 1988. pp. 140, 146. In the same volume see references to a similar belief among the Akan of Ghana, Kwasi Wiredu "On Decolonizing African Religions." p. 187.

[188] Gingerich, Owen. "The Universe as the Theatre of God's Action." *Theology Today*. (October 1998): 305.

[189] *Ibid.*

190 Peacocke, Arthur. *Evolutionary and Molecular Biology: Scientific Perspectives on Divine Action.* p. 358.

191 *Ibid.*, p. 363.

192 Gingerich, Owen. "The Universe as the Theatre of God's Action." *Theology Today.* p. 315.

193 *Ibid.*, p. 306.

194 Van Till, Howard. "The Creation: Intelligently Designed or Optimally Equipped?" *Theology Today.* p. 355. See also *Science and Creation.* p. 22.

195 Rolston III, Holmes. "Evolutionary History and Divine Presence" *Theology Today.* (October 1998) p. 434.

196 Rolston III, Holmes. ed. *Biology, Ethics and the Origins of Life.* Boston and London: Jones and Bartlett, 1995. p. 2.

197 *Ibid.*

198 *Ibid.*, p. 3.

199 Cech, Thomas R. "The Origins of Life and the Value of Life." in *Biology, Ethics and the Origins of Life.* Ed. Holmes Rolston III. p. 24. Also see, Thomas R. Cech, "RNA as an Enzyme." *Scientific American.* 255, 1986. pp. 64-75,

200 Cech, Thomas R. "The Origins of Life and the Value of Life." in *Biology, Ethics and the Origins of Life.* p. 25.

201 *Ibid.*, p. 26.

202 *Ibid.*, p. 31.

203 *Ibid.*, p. 33.

204 *Ibid.*, p. 31.

205 de Dure, Christian. "Vital Dust: The Origin and Evolution of Life on Earth." Quoted in *Theology Today.* (October 1998) pp. 423-424.

206 Wald, George, "Fitness in the Universe: Choice and Necessity." Quoted in *Theology Today.* (October 1998) p. 424.

207 Calvin, Melvin. "Chemical Evolution." Quoted in *Theology Today.* (October 1998) p. 424.

208 Eigen, Manfred. "Self Organization of Matter and the Evolution of Macro-molecules." Quoted in *Theology Today.* (October 1998) p. 424.

209 Hawkins, Stephen W. *Stephen Hawking's A Brief History of Time: A Reader's Companion.* New York: Bantam, 1992. p. 175.

210 Cech, Thomas R. "The Origins of Life and the Value of Life." in *Biology, Ethics and the Origins of Life.* p. 32.

211 *Ibid.*, p. 34.

[212] Peacocke, Arthur Robert. *Creation and the World of Science*. 1979. Oxford: Claredon, 1998. p. 112.

[213] Meilaender, Gilbert. "Begetting and Cloning." *Flesh of my Flesh: The Ethics of Cloning Humans. A Reader*. Ed. Gregory E. Pence. Lanham, Boulder, New York, Oxford: Rowman and Littlefield, 1998. pp. 39-40.

[214] Verhey, Allen. "A Protestant Perspective on Ending Life." *Physician Assisted Suicide*. Eds. Margaret P. Battin, Rosamond Rhodes, and Anita Silvers. New York and London: Routledge, 1998. p. 352.

[215] Belsie, Laurent. "As Gene Map Nears, Big Questions." *The Christian Science Monitor*. (7 June 2000): 1.2.

[216] *Ibid.*, p. 4.6.

[217] Goodenough, Ursula. *The Sacred Depths of Nature*. Oxford and New York: Oxford UP, 1998. p. 171.

[218] Darwin, Charles. *Life and Letters of Charles Darwin including an Autobiographical Chapter*. Ed. Francis Darwin, Two Volumes. New York: Basic, 1959. Vol. I pp. 276-277. Also see, *The Origin of Species and the Desent of Man*. Charles Darwin. New York: Modern Library, 1936. Also see, *Darwin's Lost Theory of Love: A Healing Vision for the Twenty First Century*. David Loye. San Jose: Excel, 2000.

[219] Roy, Rammohun. "The Precepts of Jesus, the Guide to Peace and Happiness." Printed in *Sources of Indian Tradition*. Eds. William Theodore de Bary et alia. New York: Columbia UP, 1958. p. 577.

[220] Fieser, James and John Powers, eds. *Denkard*. 6-23, 24, C82. *Scriptures of the World's Religions*. Boston and New York: McGraw Hill, 1998. p. 248.

[221] Crossman, Richard. ed. *The God That Failed*. New York: Bantam, 1950. p. 146.

[222] Epictetus. *The Manual*. Printed in *Greek and Roman Philosophy After Aristotle*. Ed. Jason Saunders. New York and London: The Free Press, 1966. p. 142.

[223] Confucius. *The Analects*. Trans. William Edward Soothill. London, New York, Toronto: Oxford UP, 1937. Book IV chap. II. p. 29. Book XV chap. XXIII. p. 169.

[224] Merton, Thomas. *The Way of Chuang Tzu*. New York: New Directions, 1969. p. 61.

[225] Radhakrishnan, Sarvepalli. *An Idealist View of Life*. chap. III. Printed in *A Source Book in Indian Philosophy*. Eds. Sarvepalli

Radhakrishnan and Charles Moore. Princeton: Princeton UP, 1957. pp. 615.

226 Gandhi, Mohandas Karamchand. *An Autobiography, or the Story of my Experiments with Truth*. Trans. Mahader Desas, Ahmedabad: Navajivan, 1927. p. 615.

227 de Bary, William Theodore. et alia, eds. *Sources of Indian Tradition*. New York: Columbia UP, 1958. p. 786.

228 *Ibid.*, p. 787.

229 Saunders, Jason L. ed. *Greek and Roman Philosophy After Aristotle*. New York: The Free Press and London: Collier Macmillan, 1966. p. 94.

230 Peacocke, Arthur Robert. *Creation and the World of Science The Bampton Lectures 1978*. Oxford: Clarendon, 1979. p. 71.

231 Paxman, Jeremy. BBC Radio 4 Interview. "Start the Week" Printed in *Philosophy Now*. (Summer 1999) p. 8.

232 Lama, His Holiness the Dalai. *Ethics for the New Millennium*. New York: Riverhead, 1999. p. 20.

233 *Ibid.*

234 *Ibid.*, p. 22.

235 *Ibid.*

236 *Ibid.*

237 *Ibid.*, p. 28.

238 *Ibid.*, pp. 30-31.

239 Copleston, Frederick C. *Philosophy in Russia, From Herzen to Lenin and Berdyaev*. Notre Dame, U of Notre Dame: Search Press, 1986. p. 381.

240 *Ibid.*, p. 372.

241 Oppenheim, A. Leo. *Letters From Mesopotamia*. Chicago: University of Chicago, 1967. p. 85.

242 Herder, Johann. *The Origin of Language*. 1772. Quoted in *The Miraculous Birth of Language*. Richard Albert Wilson. London: British Publishers Guild, 1937, 1946. p. 152.

243 Shakespeare, William. *A Midsummer Nights Dream*. Act V. Scene I.

244 Ray, Benjamin C. *African Religions*. Englewood Cliffs: Prentice-Hall, 1976. pp. 25, 111

245 Radhakrishnan, Sarvepalli and Charles A. Moore, eds. *A Source Book in Indian Philosophy*. Princeton: Princeton UP, 1957. p. 16.

[246] Fieser, James and John Powers. *Scriptures of the World's Religions.* Boston and New York: McGraw Hill, 1998. pp. 135-136.

[247] Radhakrishnan, Sarvepalli and Charles A. Moore, eds. *A Source Book in Indian Philosophy.* p. 5.

[248] *Ibid.*, p. 39.

[249] Fieser, James and John Powers. *Scriptures of the World's Religions.* p. 79.

[250] *Ibid.*, p. 193.

[251] Gold, Victor Roland, et alia, eds. *The New Testament and Psalms: An Inclusive Version.* New York and Oxford: Oxford UP, 1995. pp. viii – ix. Also see, Gail R. O'Day. "Probing an Inclusive Scripture." Review of *The New Testament and Psalms: An Inclusive Version.* *Christian Century.* (3 July 1996) pp. 692-693

[252] Crystal, David. *The Cambridge Encyclopedia of Language.* Cambridge and New York: Cambridge UP, 1987. p. 47. Quotation from *Children's Letters to God.* Eric Marshall. New York: Pocket Books, 1966.

[253] de Bary, William Theodore, et alia, *Sources of Indian Tradition.* New York: Columbia UP, 1958. p. 429.

[254] *Ibid.*, p. 574.

[255] Bruce, F. F. *The English Bible: A History of Translations.* London, Methuen: University Paperbacks, 1961. p. 29.

[256] Maimonides, Moses. *The Guide for the Perplexed.* 2nd ed. Revised throughout. Trans. Michael Frieländer. New York: Dover, 1956. p. 2.

[257] *Ibid.*, p. 81.

[258] *Ibid.*, p. 82.

[259] Aquinas, Thomas. (DePotentia 7.5) Quoted in *Aquinas.* Fredrick Charles Copleston. Harmondsworth, Baltimore: Penguin, 1955. p. 132.

[260] Copleston, Frederick Charles. *Aquinas.* Harmondsworth, Baltimore: Penguin, 1955. p. 129.

[261] *Ibid.*, p. 130.

[262] Lewis, Cecil Day. ed. *The Collected Poems of Wilfred Owen.* London: Chatto and Windus, 1968. p. 42.

[263] Cassirer, Ernst. *An Essay on Man: An Introduction to a Philosophy of Human Culture.* New Haven and London: Yale UP, 1944. p. 25.

[264] *Ibid.*, p. 26.

[265] Johnson, Thomas Herbert ed. *The Complete Poems of Emily Dickinson*. 1960. Boston and Toronto: Little, Brown, 1987. p. 627.

[266] Hume, Robert Ernest. *The Thirteen Principal Upanishads Translated from the Sanscrit*. Oxford, Oxford UP, 2nd ed. rev., 1931. p. 100.

[267] *Ibid.*, p. 95.

[268] Parrinder, Geoffrey, *African Mythology*. London: Hamlyn, 1968. p. 16.

[269] Prichard, James B. *Ancient and Near Eastern Texts Relating to the Old Testament*. Princeton: Princeton UP, 1969. pp. 89-90.

[270] I Corinthians. 15.26.

[271] Smith, William Cantwell. *The Faith of Other Men*. Toronto: Canadian Broadcasting Co. 1962. pp. 28-29.

[272] Underhill, Evelyn. *Worship: Man's Response to the Eternal*. New York: Harper and Brothers, Harper Torchbook, 1957. pp. 173-174.

[273] James, William. *The Varieties of Religious Experience*. London, New York, Toronto: Longmans Green, 1944. p. 454.

[274] Miller, Samuel H. "Oppositions Between Religion and Education." *Religion and Public Education*. Ed. Theodore R. Sizer. Boston and New York: Houghton Mifflin, 1967. p. 112.

[275] Cox, Harvey G. "The Relationship Between Religion and Education." in *Religion and Public Education*. Ed. Theodore R. Sizer. Boston and New York: Houghton Mifflin, 1967, p. 99.

[276] Eastland, Terry. ed. *Religious Liberty in the Supreme Court: The Cases that Define the Debate over Church and State*. Washington, DC: Ethics and Public Policy Center, 1993. pp. 152, 162.

[277] Coeyman, Marjorie. "Talking Religion in the Classroom." *The Christian Science Monitor*. (14 Dec. 1999): 16.3.

[278] *Ibid.*, p. 15.

[279] Coeyman, Marjorie. "New Study Calls Florida "Bible History" Courses Unconstitutional." *The Christian Science Monitor*. (18 Jan. 1999) p. 12.

[280] Pelikan, Jaroslav. *The Idea of the University: A Re-examination*. New Haven and London: Yale UP, 1992. p. 22.

[281] Hays, Ernest H. *Christianity goes Into Action: Lessons on Great Deeds in Christ's Name*. Wallington, Survey: The Religious Education Press, 1946. p. 11.

[282] Subramuniyaswami, Satguru Sivaya. "Hinduism, the Greatest Religion in the World." *Hinduism Today*. (February 2000) p. 11.

[283] Milton, John. *Aereopagitica and of Education.* Ed. George H. Sabine. New York: Appleton Century Crofts, 1951, p. 59.

[284] Hirsch, Eric Donald. *Cultural Literacy: What Every American Needs to Know.* Boston: Houghton Mifflin, 1987. p. 99.

[285] Demerath III, Nicholas Jay. "Excepting Exceptionalism American Religion in Comparative Belief." *The Annals of the American Academy of Political and Social Science: Americans and Religions in the Twenty-First Century.* Ed. Wade Clark Roof. (July 1998) p. 28.

[286] *Ibid*, p. 30. Also see, Robert N. Bellah. "Civil Religion in America." *Daedalus.* Vol. 96 (Winter 1967) pp. 1-21

[287] Martin, E. Marty. "You Get to Teach and Study Religion." *Academe.* Vol. 82. No. 6. (Nov – Dec 1996) p. 14.

[288] Kramnick, Isaac and R. Laurence Moore. "The Godless University." *Academe.* Vol. 82 No. 6. (Nov – Dec 1996) p. 21.

[289] Green, William Scott. "Religion within the limits." *Academe.* Vol. 82 No. 6. (Nov – Dec 1996) p. 26.

[290] *Ibid*, p. 28.

[291] Hoekema, David A. "Politics, Religion, and Other Crimes Against Civility." *Academe.* Vol. 82 No. 6. (Nov – Dec 1996) p. 35.

[292] Hick, John. *God has Many Names.* 1980. Philadelphia: Westminster, 1982. p. 115.

[293] MacGregor, Geddes. *Philosophical Issues in Religious Thought.* Boston: Houghton Mifflin, 1973. p. 38. Also see, William Temple. *Nature, Man and God.* New York and London: St. Martins and Macmillan, 1960. p. 35.

[294] Radhakrishnan, Sarvepalli and Charles A. Moore, eds. *A Source Book in Indian Philosophy.* Princeton: Princeton UP, 1957. p. xxii.

[295] *Ibid.*, p. xxv.

[296] *Ibid.*, pp. 23-24.

[297] Hume, Robert Ernest. *The Thirteen Principal Upanishads Translated from the Sanscrit.* Oxford, Oxford UP, 2nd ed. rev., 1931. p. 335.

[298] *A Source Book in Indian Philosophy.* p. 42.

[299] Hume, Robert Ernest. *The Thirteen Principal Upanishads Translated from the Sanscrit.* Oxford, Oxford UP, 2nd ed. rev., 1931. p. 372.

300 Aurobindo, Sri. *Araya*. (15 Aug. 1915): 2-9. Printed in *A Source Book in Indian Philosophy*. Eds. Sarvepalli Radhakrishnan, and Charles A. Moore. p. 578.

301 Sen, Amartya. *Development as Freedom*. New York: Knopf, 1999. p. 18.

302 Hopfe, Lewis M. and Mark R. Woodward. *Religions of the World*, 7th ed. Upper Saddle River: Prentice Hall, 1998. p. 143.

303 Donath, Dorothy C. Forward. *Buddhism for the West Theravada, Mahayana, Vajrayana*. New York, et alia: McGraw-Hill, 1971. p. vii.

304 Babbit, Irving, trans. *The Dhammapada*. New York: New Directions Paperbook, 1965. p. 11.

305 Lama, His Holiness The Dalai. *Ethics for the New Millennium*. New York: Riverhead, 1999.

306 Paxman, Jeremy. BBC Radio 4 Interview with His Holiness The Dalai Lama. "Start the Week." 10 May 1999. Printed in *Philosophy Now*. Issue 24. (Summer 1999) p. 8.

307 Cragg, Kenneth. Interview. "Cross Meets Crescent." 17 February 1999. Printed in *The Christian Century*. p. 180.

308 Baldwin, James. *The Fire Next Time*. New York: Dial, 1963. p. 71.

309 Jaoudi, Maria. *Christian and Islamic Spirituality Sharing a Journey*. New York, Mahwah, New Jersey: Paulist, 1993. p. 86.

310 Smith, Joseph. trans. *The Book of Mormon*. Chapter 1 Verse 3. Salt Lake City: The Church of Latter-Day Saints, 1981. Also see, Douglas J. Davies. *The Mormon Culture of Salvation*. Brookfield: Ashgate, 2000.

311 Harris, Stephen L. *The New Testament: A Students Introduction.* 2nd ed. Mountian View: Mayfield, 1995, p. 172.

312 Eddy, Mary Baker. *Science and Health with Key to the Scriptures*. Boston: Trustees under the Will of Mary Baker Eddy. 1906.

313 Kollar, John M. *Oriental Philosophies*. 2nd ed. New York: Scribner, 1985. p. 246.

314 *Ibid.*, p. 247.

315 Hudson, Winthrop Still. *Religion in America* 4th ed. New York: Macmillan and London: Collier Macmillan, 1987. p. 254.

316 Moore, E. Caldwell. *The History of Christian Thought Since Kant*. 1912. London: Duckworth, 1947. p. 81.

317 Tillich, Paul. *Systematic Theology*. Vol. 1. Chicago: University of Chicago, 1951. p. 42.

[318] Radhakrishnan, Sarvepalli and Charles A. Moore, eds. *A Source Book in Indian Philosophy*. Princeton: Princeton UP, 1957. p. 42.

[319] Hume, Robert Ernest. *The Thirteen Principal Upanishads Translated from the Sanscrit*. Oxford, Oxford UP, 2nd ed. rev., 1931. p. 350.

[320] *Ibid.*

[321] Whitman, Walt. "November Boughs." *Complete Poems and Prose of Walt Whitman*. Philadelphia: Ferguson, 1881. p. 32.

[322] Merton, Thomas. *The Way of Chuang Tzu*. New York: New Directions, 1965. p. 55.

[323] *Ibid.*, pp. 40-41.

Bibliography

Aquinas, Thomas. (De Potentia 7.5) Quoted in *Aquinas*. Frederick Charles Copleston. Harmondsworth, Baltimore: Penguin, 1955.

Aquinas, Thomas. "Summa Theologica." *The Basic Writings of St. Thomas Aquinas*. Vol. I, Ed. Anton C. Pegis. New York: Random House, 1945.

Aquinas, Thomas. *Summa Contra Gentiles*. 3.99.9 *On the Truth of the Catholic Faith*. Trans. Vernon J. Bourke. New York: Doubleday, 1956.

Atkins, Peter. "Purposeless People." *Persons and Personality*. Ed. Arthur Peacocke and Grant Gillett. Oxford and New York: Basil Blackwell, 1987.

Aurobindo, Sri. Printed in *A Source Book in Indian Philosophy*. eds. Sarvepalli Radhakrishnan and Charles A. Moore. Princeton: Princeton UP, 1957.

Ayer, Alfred Jules. *Language, Truth and Logic*. New York: Dover, 1936.

Babbit, Irving, trans. *The Dhammapada*. New York: New Directions Paperbook, 1965.

Badham, Linda and Paul "The Evidence from Psychical Research." *Immortality*. Ed. Paul Edwards. London: Watts, 1953.

Baldwin, James. *The Fire Next Time*. New York: Dial, 1963.

Barbour, Ian G. *When Science Meets Religion*. New York, San Francisco: Harper, 2000.

Barrett, Douglas E. and Basil Gray. *Painting of India: Treasures of Asia Series*. Paris: d'art Albert Skira. Distributed by the World Publishing Company, Cleveland, 1963.

Beloff, John "Is There Anything Beyond Death? A Parapsychologist's Report." *Immortality*. Ed. Paul Edwards. London: Watts, 1953.

Biko, Steve. "Some African Cultural Concepts" *The African Philosophy Reader*. Eds. P. H. Coetzee, A. P. Roux. London and New York: Routledge, 1998.

Bloom, Harold. *Omens of Millennium: The Gnosis of Angels, Dreams, and Resurrection*. New York: Riverhead, 1996.

Boethius. *The Consolation of Philosophy*. Trans. with an Introduction and explanatory notes by P. G. Walsh. Oxford: Clarendon, 1999.

Broad, C. D. *Religion, Philosophy and Psychical Research*. New York: Humanities, 1969.

Bruce, F. F. *The English Bible: A History of Translations*. London, Methuen: University Paperbacks, 1961.

Burtt, E. A. *The Teachings of the Compassionate Buddha*. 1955. New York: A Mentor Book, 1982.

Capra, Fritjof. *The Tau of Physics.* Boston: Shambala, 1991.

Carter, Stephen. *The Culture of Disbelief: How American Law and Politics Trivialize Religious Devotion.* New York, London, and Toronto: Anchor, Doubleday, 1994.

Cashman, John. *The LSD Story.* Greenwich: Fawcett Gold Medal, 1966.

Cassirer, Ernst. *An Essay on Man: An Introduction to a Philosophy of Human Culture.* New Haven and London: Yale UP, 1944.

Cech, Thomas R. "The Origins of Life and the Value of Life." in *Biology, Ethics and the Origins of Life.* Ed. Holmes Rolston III. p. 24. Also see, "RNA as an Enzyme." *Scientific American.* [255:64-75] Thomas R. Cech. 1986.

Coles, Robert. *The Spiritual Life of Children.* Boston: Houghton Mifflin, 1990.

Confucius. *The Analects.* Trans. William Edward Soothill. London, New York, Toronto: Oxford UP, 1937.

Copleston, Fredrick Charles. *Aquinas.* Harmondsworth, Baltimore: Penguin, 1957.

Cox, Harvey G. "The Relationship Between Religion and Education." in *Religion and Public Education.* Ed. Theodore R. Sizer. Boston and New York: Houghton Mifflin, 1967

Cox, Harvey. *The Feast of Fools: A Theological Essay on Festivity and Fantasy.* Cambridge: Harvard University, 1969.

Crossman, Richard. ed. *The God That Failed.* New York: Bantam, 1950.

Crystal, David. *The Cambridge Encyclopedia of Language.* Cambridge and New York: Cambridge UP, 1987.

Darwin, Charles. *Life and Letters of Charles Darwin including an Autobiographical Chapter.* Ed. Francis Darwin, Two Volumes. New York: Basic, 1959.

Darwin, Charles. *The Origin of Species and the Descent of Man.* New York: Modern Library, 1936.

Davies, Douglas J. *The Mormon Culture of Salvation.* Brookfield: Ashgate, 2000.

de Bary, William Theodore, et alia, *Sources of Indian Tradition.* New York: Columbia UP, 1958.

Delahaye, Luc. *Mémo.* Paris: Editions Hazan, 1997.

Demerath III, Nicholas Jay. "Excepting Exceptionlism: American Religion in Comparative Belief." *The Annals of the American Academy of Political and Social Science.* July, 1998.

Dickinson, Emily. *The Complete Poems of Emily Dickinson.* Ed. Thomas H. Johnson. Boston, Toronto: Little Brown, 1960.

Donath, Dorothy C. Forward. *Buddhism for the West Theravada, Mahayana, Vajrayana*. New York, et alia: McGraw-Hill, 1971.

Eastland, Terry. ed. *Religious Liberty in the Supreme Court: The Cases that Define the Debate over Church and State*. Washington, DC: Ethics and Public Policy Center, 1993.

Eddy, Mary Baker. *Science and Health with Key to the Scripture*. Boston: Trustees under the Will of Mary Baker Eddy, 1934.

Edwards, Paul, ed. *Immortality*. Introduction. New York, Toronto, and Oxford: Macmillan.

Epictetus. *The Manual*. Printed in_*Greek and Roman Philosophy After Aristotle*. Ed. Jason Saunders. New York and London: The Free Press, 1966.

Farmer, Herbert Henry. *The World and God*. 2nd ed. London: Nisbet and New York: Harper and Row, 1936.

Fieser, James and John Powers, eds. *Scriptures of the World's Religions*. Boston and New York: McGraw Hill, 1998.

Flew, Antony. *A New Approach to Psychical Research*. London: Watts, 1993.

Forman, Robert. *Mysticism, Mind, and Consciousness*. Albany: State University of New York, 1999.

Galloway, George. *The Philosophy of Religion*. Edinburgh: Clark, 1914, 1951.

Gandhi, Mohandas Karamchand. *An Autobiography, or the Story of my Experiments with Truth*. Trans. Mahader Desas, Ahmedabad: Navajivan, 1927.

Gbadegesin, Segun "Eniyan: The Yoruba Concept of Person." In P. H. Coetzee and A. P. H. Roux, Eds. *The African Philosophy Reader*. London, New York, Routledge, 1988.

Gingerich, Owen "The Universe as Theatre for God's Action." *Theology Today*. Ed. Patrick D. Miller. Oct. 1998.

Gold, Victor Roland, et alia, eds. *The New Testament and Psalms: An Inclusive Version*. New York and Oxford: Oxford UP, 1995.

Goodenough, Ursula. *The Sacred Depths of Nature*. Oxford and New York: Oxford UP, 1998.

Gordon, Dane R. *Thinking and Reading in the Philosophy of Religion: the Religious Sensibility: Coming to Grips With What We Believe*. New York: Haven, 1994.

Grant, Michael. *From Alexander to Cleopatra: The Hellenistic World*. New York: Macmillan, Collier Books, 1982.

Harris, Stephen L. *The New Testament: A Students Introduction*. 2nd ed. Mountain View: Mayfield, 1995.

Hawkins, Stephen W. *Stephen Hawkins' A Brief History of Time: A Reader's Companion*. New York: Bantam, 1992.

220   *A Feeling Intellect and a Thinking Heart*

Hays, Ernest H. *Christianity goes Into Action: Lessons on Great Deeds in Christ's Name*. Wallington, Survey: The Religious Education Press, 1946.
Hebblethwaite, Brian. *Preaching Through the Christian Year*. London and Oxford: Mobray, 1985.
Hebblethwaite, Brian. *The Ocean of Truth: A Defense of Objective Theism*. Cambridge and New York: Cambridge UP, 1988.
Herder, Johann. *The Origin of Language*. 1772. Quoted in *The Miraculous Birth of Language*. Richard Albert Wilson. London: British Publishers Guild, 1937, 1946.
Hick, John. ed. *Classical and Contemporary Readings in the Philosophy of Religion*. Englewood Cliffs: Prentice-Hall, 1964.
Hick, John. *Evil and the God of Love*. 1966. San Francisco: Harper and Row, rev. ed. 1978.
Hick, John. *God has Many Names*. Philadelphia: Westminster, 1982.
Hirsch, Eric Donald. *Cultural Literacy: What Every American Needs to Know*. Boston: Houghton Mifflin, 1987.
Hoekema, David A. "Politics, Religion and Other Crimes Against Civility." *Academe*, Vol. 82.6 Nov-Dec. 1996.
Holland. R. F. "The Miraculous." *Miracles*. Ed. Richard Swinburne. New York and London: Macmillan and Collier Macmillan, 1989.
Hopfe, Lewis M. and Mark R. Woodward. *Religions of the World*, 7th ed. Upper Saddle River: Prentice Hall, 1998.
Hudson, Winthrop Still. *Religion in America* 4th ed. New York: Macmillan and London: Collier Macmillan, 1987.
Hume, David. *An Inquiry Concerning Human Understanding*. First published as *Philosophical Essays Concerning Human Understanding*. 1748. New York: The Liberal Arts Press, 1955. Sec. X, 'Of Miracles.'
Hume, David. *Dialogues Concerning Natural Religion*. Parts II and V, Indianopolis: Bobbs-Merrill, 1779.
James, William. *The Varieties of Religious Experience*. London, New York, Toronto: Longmans Green, 1944.
Jaoudi, Maria. *Christian and Islamic Spirituality Sharing a Journey*. New York, Mahwah, New Jersey: Paulist, 1993.
Johnson, Thomas Herbert ed. *The Complete Poems of Emily Dickinson*. 1960. Boston and Toronto: Little, Brown, 1987.
Kiefer, Otto. *Sexual Life in Ancient Rome*. London: Routledge, 1934.
Kierkegaard, Soren. *Concluding Unscientific Postscript*. Trans. David F. Swenson and Walter Lowrie. Princeton: Princeton UP, 1941.
Koller, John M. *Oriental Philosophies*. 2nd ed. New York: Scribner, 1985.

Kramnick, Isaac, and R. Laurence Moore. "The Godless University." *Academe*, Vol. 82.6. Nov.-Dec. 1996.

Küng, Hans. *On Being a Christian*. New York: Doubleday, 1976. New York: Pocket Books, Gulf and Western Corp., 1978.

Kushner, Harold S. *When Bad Things Happen to Good People*. New York: Schocken, 1981.

Lama, His Holiness The Dalai. *Ethics for the New Millennium*. New York: Riverhead, 1999.

Lash, Nicholas. *Easter in Ordinary: Reflections on Human Experience and the Knowledge of God.* London: SCM, 1988.

Lewis, Cecil Day. ed. *The Collected Poems of Wilfred Owen*. London: Chatto and Windus, 1968.

Lewis, Clive Staples. *A Grief Observed*. London: Faber, 1990.

Lewis, Clive Staples. *The Problem of Pain*. New York: Macmillan, 1962.

Licht, Hans. *Sexual Life in Ancient Greece*. London: Routledge, 1932.

Loye, David. *Darwins Lost Theory of Love: A Healing Vision for the Twenty First Century.* San Jose: Excel, 2000.

MacGregor, Geddes. *Philosophical Issues in Religious Thought.* Boston: Houghton Mifflin, 1973.

Mackie, John Leslie. *The Miracle of Theism Arguments for and Against the Existence of God.* Oxford: Clarendon, 1982.

MacKinnon, D. M. "Death." *New Essays in Philosophical Theology.* 1953. Ed. Antony Flew and Alasdair MacIntyre. New York: Macmillan, 1983.

Macquarrie, John. *Principles of Christian Theology*. 2nd ed. New York: Scribner, 1977.

Maimonides, Moses. *The Guide for the Perplexed*. 2nd ed. Revised throughout. Trans. Michael Frieländer. New York: Dover, 1956.

Malcolm, Norman. "Anselm's Ontological Arguments." *The Ontological Argument*. Ed. Alvin Plantinga with an Introduction by Richard Taylor. New York: Doubleday, 1965.

Marty, Martin E. "You Get to Teach and Study Religion." *Academe*. Nov.-Dec., 1996.

Matson, Wallace. *The Existence of God*. Ithaca and London: Cornell UP, 1965.

Maynell, Alice. "Christ in the Universe." *The Faber Book of Religious Verse*. Ed. Helen Gardner, London and Boston: Faber, 1972.

Mbiti, John S. *African Religions and Philosophy*. London, Ibadan, Nairobi, Heinemann, 1969.

McGiffert, Arthur Cushman. *A History of Christian Thought*. Two Volumes. New York and London: Scribner, 1954.

Meilaender, Gilbert. "Begetting and Cloning." *Flesh of my Flesh: The Ethics of Cloning Humans. A Reader*. Ed. Gregory E. Pence. Lanham, Boulder, New York, Oxford: Rowman and Littlefield, 1998.

Merton, Thomas. *The Way of Chuang Tzu*. New York: New Directions, 1969.

Miles, Jack. *God: A Biography*. New York: Knopf, 1995.

Mill, John Stuart. *Three Essays on Religion*. New York: Henry Holt, 1874.

Miller, Samuel H. "Oppositions Between Religion and Education." *Religion and Public Education*. Ed. Theodore R. Sizer. Boston and New York: Houghton Mifflin, 1967.

Milton, John. *Aereopagitica and of Education*. Ed. George H. Sabine. New York: Appleton Century Crofts, 1951.

Misner, C. W. "Cosmology and Theology." *Cosmology, History and Theology*. Ed. W. Yourgrau and A.D. Breck. New York and London: Plenum, 1977.

Moore, E. Caldwell. *The History of Christian Thought Since Kant*. 1912. London: Duckworth, 1947.

Norris, Kathleen. Introduction. 1995. *My Ántonia*. 1918. By Willla Cather. Boston and New York: Houghton Mifflin, 1954.

O'Brien, George Dennis. *God and the New Haven Railway And Why Neither One is Doing Very Well*. Boston: Beacon, 1988.

Oppenheim, A. Leo. *Letters From Mesopotamia*. Chicago: University of Chicago, 1967.

Paley, William. *Natural Theology or Evidence of the Existence and Attributes of the Deity from the Appearances of Nature*. 1802. Weybridge: South Hamilton, 1809.

Palmer, E. H. Trans. *The Koran (Qur'an)*. Introduction R. A. Nicholson, London, New York, Toronto: Oxford UP, 1928. Rpt. 1947.

Parrinder, Geoffrey, *African Mythology*. London: Hamlyn, 1968.

Parrinder, Geoffrey. *Religion in Africa*. Penguin African Library. Baltimore: Penguin Books, 1969.

John Russell et alia eds. Berkeley and Vatican City State: Center for Theology and the Natural Sciences and Vatican Observatory Publications, 1998.

Peacocke, A. R. *Creation and the World of Science*. Oxford and New York: Clarendon, 1979.

Peacocke, Arthur Robert. *Creation and the World of Science The Bampton Lectures 1978*. Oxford: Clarendon, 1979.

Pelikan, Jaroslav. *The Idea of the University: A Re-examination*. New Haven and London: Yale UP, 1992.

Peterson, Michael L. *God and Evil An Introduction to the Issues.* Boulder: Westview, 1998.

Phillips, Dewi Zephaniah. *The Concept of Prayer.* London, Routledge: Kegan Paul, 1965.

Plantinga, Alvin A. *The Ontological Argument.* New York, Anchor Books, Doubleday and Co., 1965.

Plotinus. *The Enneads.* Trans. Stephen Mackenna. Burdett and New York: Larson, 1992.

Polkinghorne, John. *Science and Creation The Search for Understanding.* London: SPCK, 1988.

Prichard, James B. *Ancient and Near Eastern Texts Relating to the Old Testament.* Princeton: Princeton UP, 1969.

Proudfoot, Wayne. *Religious Experience.* Berkeley, Los Angeles, London: The University of California, 1985.

Radhakrishnan, Sarvepalli and Charles A. Moore, eds. *A Source Book in Indian Philosophy.* Princeton: Princeton UP, 1957.

Radhakrishnan, Sarvepalli. *An Idealist View of Life.* chap. III. Printed in *A Source Book in Indian Philosophy.* Eds. Sarvepalli Radhakrishnan and Charles Moore. Princeton: Princeton UP, 1957.

Rahner, Karl. *On the Theology of Death.* New York: Herder, 1961.

Ray, Benjamin C. *African Religions.* Englewood Cliffs: Prentice-Hall, 1976.

Rolston III, Holmes. ed. *Biology, Ethics and the Origins of Life.* Boston and London: Jones and Bartlett, 1995.

Roof, Wade Clark "Modernity, the Religious and the Spiritual." in *American Annals of Political and Social Sciences.* July, 1998.

Rowe, William L. *Philosophy of Religion.* Encino and Belmont: Dickenson, 1978.

Roy, Rammohun. "The Precepts of Jesus, the Guide to Peace and Happiness." Printed in *Sources of Indian Tradition.* Eds. William Theodore de Bary et alia. New York: Columbia UP, 1958.

Saunders, Jason L. ed. *Greek and Roman Philosophy After Aristotle.* New York: The Free Press and London: Collier Macmillan, 1966.

Scroggs, Robin. "Tradition, Freedom and the Abyss." in *New Theology* No. 8. Eds. Martin Marty and Dean G. Peerman. New York and London: Macmillan and Collier Macmillan, 1971.

Sen, Amartya. *Development as Freedom.* New York: Knopf, 1999.

Smith, Joseph. trans. *The Book of Mormon.* Salt Lake City: The Church of Latter-Day Saints, 1981.

Smith, Wilfred Cantwell. *The Faith of Other Men.* Toronto: Canadian Broadcasting Co. 1962.

St. Augustine, *The City of God.* and *On the Trinity.* Printed in *The Essential Augustine.* Ed. Vernon J. Bourke, Indianapolis: Hackett, 1964-1974.

Stace, W. T. *Religion and the Modern Mind.* Philadelphia: Lippincott, 1952.

Stewart, David. ed. *Exploring the Philosophy of Religion.* 2nd ed. Englewood Cliffs: Prentice-Hall, 1988.

Swinburne, Richard. "The Structure of the Soul." in *Persons and Personality.*Ed. Arthur Peacocke, Grant Gillett. Oxford: Basil Blackwell, 1987.

Swinburne, Richard. *The Existence of God.* Oxford and New York: Oxford UP, 1979.

Taylor, Richard. *Metaphysics,* 3rd ed. Englewood Cliffs: Prentice-Hall, 1983.

Teffo, Lesiba, Abraham A.P.J. Roux. "Metaphysical Thinking in Africa." *African Philosophy Reader.* P. H. Coetzee and A. P. J. Roux. London, New York: Routledge, 1988.

Temple, William. *Nature, Man and God.* London: Macmillan, 1964.

Thomas, D. Winton. ed. *Documents from Old Testament Times.* New York: Harper, 1961.

Thouless, Robert H. *An Introduction to the Psychology of Religion.* Cambridge: Cambridge UP, 1950.

Tillich, Paul. *Systematic Theology.* Vol. 1. Chicago: University of Chicago, 1951.

Underhill, Evelyn. *Mysticism.* New American Library, New York: A Meridian Book, 1974.

Underhill, Evelyn. *Worship: Man's Response to the Eternal.* New York: Harper and Brothers, Harper Torchbook, 1957.

Verhey, Allen. "A Protestant Perspective on Ending Life." *Physician Assisted Suicide.* Eds. Margaret P. Battin, Rosamond Rhodes, and Anita Silvers. New York and London: Routledge, 1998.

White, Andrew. *A History of the Warfare of Science with Theology in Christendom.* Two Volumes. New York: Appleton, 1896.

Whitehead, Alfred North. *Process and Reality: An Essay in Cosmology.* 1929. New York: Harper, 1957.

Whitman, Walt. "Specimen Days and Collect." *Complete Poems and Prose of Walt Whitman.* Philadelphia: Ferguson, 1888.

Wierenga, Edward R. *The Nature of God: An Inquiry into Divine Attributes.* Ithaca and London: Cornell UP, 1989.

Wildman, Wesley J. "Teleology without Divine Action." and "Evaluating the Teleological Argument for Divine Action" in *Evolutionary and Molecular Biology: Scientific Perspectives on*

Divine Action. Robert John Russell et alia, Vatican City State: Vatican Observatory, 1998.

Wilson, Richard Albert. *The Miraculous Birth of Language.* London: British Publishers Guild, 1937 and 1946.

Winton, Thomas D. *Documents from Old Testament Times.* New York: Harper, 1961.

Woodward, Kenneth L. *The Book of Miracles: The Meaning of Miracle Stories in Christianity, Judaism, Buddhism, Islam.* New York: Simon and Schuster, 2000.

Woodward, Kenneth L. The Book of Miracles: *The Meaning of Miracle Stories in Christianity, Judaism, Buddhism, Islam.* New York, Simon & Schuster, 2000.

Zukar, Gary. *The Dancing Wu Li Masters An Overview of the New Physics.* New York, Toronto, London: Bantam, 1980.

Index

Schleiermacher, Friedrich, 196
Scroggs, Robin, 114
Seneca, 40
Serbia, 60
Servetus, Michael, 128
Settle, T.W., 65
Sex, 26
Sextus-Emipiricus, 40
Shakespeare, William, 26, 146, 166
Sikhs, 128, 148, 167
Singh, Sadhu Sundar, 41
Sinhala, 151
Smith, Cantwell, 167
Smith, Huston, 47
Smith, Joseph, 191
Socrates, 29, 63, 131
Solzhenitsyn, Alexander, 130
South America, 75
Southwell, Robert, 158
Spencer, Stanley, 87
Spinoza, Benedict, 55, 57, 132
Sri Lanka, 75
Stace, W.T., 45
Stapp, Henry, 116
Stoics, 40, 140
Sujin, emperor, 105
Strauss, David, 113
Swinburne, Richard, 7, 77

Tagore, Rabinadrath, 135
Taoism, 192, 193
Teresa, St., 2
Temple, William, 101, 183
Tennyson, Lord, 168
Thouless, Robert H., 41
Tillich, Paul, 160, 196, 198
Titanic, 5, 104
Tolstoy, 74, 171
Troeltsch, Ernest, 49

Teleological Argument, 6, 7, 9, 11, 16, 59
Tutsi cattle herders, 58
Tyndale, William, 148, 149
Tzu, Chuang, 134, 151, 198, 199

Underhill, Evelyn, 35, 42, 167
United States, 7, 96, 108, 127, 141, 149, 160, 169, 170, 185, 190, 192
Upanishad, 38, 41, 116, 151, 184, 185
Upanishad, Brhādaranyaka, 22
Upanishad, Katha, 39
Upanishad, Kena, 196
Upanishad, Mundaka, 185

Vak, 148
Van Till, Howard J., 113
Vedanta, 154
Verhey, Allen, 125
Viet Nam War, 160
Virgin Mary, 28
Viśvakarman, 18
Voltaire, 57
Vulgate, 149, 154

Washington, DC, 68
Western Europe, 17, 75, 94
Whistler, James McNeill, 76
White, Andrew, 112
Whitehead A.N., 53, 54, 55
Whitman, Walt, 72, 87, 197
Wierenga, Edward, 29
Wordsworth, William, 46
World Trade Center, 68
Wright, Richard, 131
Wycliffe, John, 154, 149

Yin Yang, 185, 193